FRENCH PHRASEBOOK

Marie-Hélène Girard
Anny Monet

French phrasebook
1st edition – October 1997

Published by
Lonely Planet Publications Pty Ltd ABN 36 005 607 983
90 Maribyrnong St, Footscray, Victoria 3011, Australia

Lonely Planet Offices
Australia Locked Bag 1, Footscray, Victoria 3011
USA 150 Linden St, Oakland CA 94607
UK 10a Spring Place, London NW5 3BH
France 1 rue du Dahomey, 75011 Paris

Cover illustration
Le Café au coin de la rue by Penelope Richardson

ISBN 0 86442 450 7

Printed through Colorcraft Ltd, Hong Kong
Printed in China

CONTENTS

INTRODUCTION

French is one of the great languages of the world; a language of society, culture and diplomacy. Being able to speak some French will broaden your travel experience and ensure that you are treated with great appreciation. Like Italian, Spanish, Romanian and Portuguese, French is one of the Romance languages, which means that it is descended from Latin. In France itself there are over 50 million French speakers. It is one of the official languages in Belgium, Switzerland and Luxembourg, which have around four million, 1.2 million and 300,000 Francophones respectively. French is also spoken by about 150,000 inhabitants of the Val d'Aosta in north-western Italy, and it has a million speakers in Monaco. Major areas outside Europe where you'll find French spoken are Africa, South-East Asia, the Pacific, Canada (Quebec), the USA (especially Maine and Louisiana) and Haiti and the French Caribbean. It is the mother tongue of about 75 million people around the world. The total number of French speakers, including those who use it as a second language, is more than 200 million.

French began to emerge as a distinct language in the 9th century AD. The earliest surviving text in French is that of the Strasbourg Oaths (842 AD), an agreement uniting two of Charlemagne's grandsons against the third in a quarrel over the division of the empire. It was not until the 11th century, however, that a vernacular literature really established itself in France. When Paris became the capital of France in the 12th century the dialect of the Parisian region *(Francien)* spread, to the detriment of the Provençal language in the south and other regional dialects.

The edict of Villers-Cotterets, issued by François I in 1539, made the use of French compulsory for official documents. During the French Rennaissance, in the 16th century, efforts were made to enrich and dignify the national tongue, to make it a worthy vehicle for serious literature. This involved coining words from Greek and Latin roots, and the adoption of etymological spellings, which later reformers have not been able to rationalise. During the 17th century there was a reaction to this trend. The poet Malherbe and the grammarian Vaugelas, a founding member of the French Academy *(l'Académie française),* were influential in a movement to 'purify' the language and codify its usage, establishing norms which have, to a large extent, remained in force.

The Academy, established in 1635, has preserved its purist stand by opposing the introduction of English words such as 'sandwich', 'weekend', 'shopping' and 'record'. But you will hear much of this 'franglais' on your travels. From the 17th to the 19th century, French was the foremost international language, though it has now been overshadowed by English. It remains one of the official languages at the United Nations and UNESCO.

ARTHUR OR MARTHA?

In this book the masculine form of a word appears first. The feminine ending is separated by a slash. For example un/e ami/e ('a friend') indicates that the masculine form is un ami and the feminine form is une amie (see Grammar, page 19, for how to make nouns feminine). In cases where the feminine is more complicated than adding an e to the masculine form, both forms of the word appear in full, masculine first, eg le serveur/la serveuse. In some cases we have used the abbreviations (m) and (f) to indicate masculine and feminine.

ABBREVIATIONS USED IN THIS BOOK

adj	adjective
f	feminine
inf	informal
m	masculine
n	noun
pl	plural
pol	polite
sg	singular
v	verb

HOW TO USE THIS PHRASEBOOK

You *Can* Speak Another Language

It's true – anyone can speak another language. Don't worry if you haven't studied languages before, or that you studied a language at school for years and can't remember any of it. It doesn't even matter if you failed English grammar. After all, that's never affected your ability to speak English! And this is the key to picking up a language in another country. You don't need to sit down and memorise endless grammatical details and you don't need to memorise long lists of vocabulary. You just need to start speaking. Once you start, you'll be amazed how many prompts you'll get to help you build on those first words. You'll hear people speaking, pick up sounds from TV, catch a word or two that you think you know from the local radio, see something on a billboard – all these things help to build your understanding.

Plunge In

There's just one thing you need to start speaking another language – courage. Your biggest hurdle is overcoming the fear of saying aloud what may seem to you to be just a bunch of sounds. There are a number of ways to do this.

Firstly, think of some French words or phrases you are familiar with, such as rendezvous, en route and fait accompli. These are phrases you are already able to say fluently. From these basic beginnings you can start making sentences. You might know that quand means 'when' in French (cuando is Spanish, quando is Italian and Portuguese – they all sound much the same). So, let's imagine you've arranged to meet someone but don't know the time. You could ask Rendezvous quand? Don't worry that you're not getting a whole sentence right first time. People will understand if you stick to the key words of the sentence. And you'll find that once you're in the country it won't take long to remember the complete sentence.

The best way to start overcoming your fear is to memorise a few key words. These are the words you know you'll be saying again and again, like 'hello', 'thank you' and 'how much?'. Here's an important hint though: right from the beginning, learn at least one phrase that will be useful but not essential. Such as 'good morning' or 'good afternoon', 'see you later' or even a conversational piece like 'lovely day, isn't it?' or 'it's cold today' (people everywhere love to talk about the weather). Having this extra phrase (just start with one, if you like, and learn to say it really well) will enable you to move away from the basics, and when you get a reply and a smile, it'll also boost your confidence. You'll find that people you speak to will like it too, as they'll understand that at least you've tried to learn more of the language than just the usual essential words.

Ways to Remember

There are several ways to learn a language. Most people find they learn from a variety of these, although people usually have a preferred way to remember. Some like to see the written word and remember the sound from what they see. Some like to just hear it spoken in context (if this is you, try talking to yourself in French). Others, especially the more mathematically inclined, like to analyse the grammar of a language, and piece together words according to the rules of grammar. The very visually inclined like to associate the written word and even sounds with some visual stimulus, such as from illustrations, TV and general things they see in the street. As you learn, you'll discover what works best for you – be aware of what made you really remember a particular word, and if it sticks in your mind, keep using that method.

Kicking Off

Chances are you'll want to learn some of the language before you go. So you won't be hearing it around you. The first thing to do is to memorise those essential phrases and words. Check out the basics (page 47) ... and don't forget that extra phrase (see Plunge In!). Try the sections on making conversation or greeting people for a phrase you'd like to use. Write some of these words and phrases down on a piece of paper and stick them up around the place: on the fridge, by the bed, on your computer, as a bookmark – somewhere where you'll see them often. Try putting some words in context – the 'How much is it?' note, for instance, could go in your wallet.

Building the Picture

We include a chapter on grammar in our books for two main reasons.

Firstly, some people have an aptitiude for grammar and find understanding it a key tool to their learning. If you're such a person, then the grammar chapter in a phrasebook will help you build a picture of the language, as it works through all the basics.

The second reason for the grammar chapter is that it gives answers to questions you might raise as you hear or memorise some key phrases. You may find a particular word is always used when there is a question – check out the grammar heading on questions and it should explain why. This way you don't have to read the grammar chapter from start to finish, nor do you need to memorise a grammatical point. It will simply present itself to you in the course of your learning. Key grammatical points are repeated through the book.

Any Questions?

Try to learn the main question words (see page 42). As you read through different situations, you'll see these words used in the example sentences, and this will help you remember them. So if you want to hire a bicycle, turn to the Bicycles section in Getting Around (use the Contents or Index pages to find it quickly). You've already tried to memorise the word for 'where' and you'll see the word for 'bicycle'. When you come across the sentence 'Where can I hire a bicycle?', you'll recognise the key words and this will help you remember the whole phrase. If there's no category for your need, try the dictionary (the question words are repeated there too, with examples), and memorise the phrase 'How do you say ...?' (page 52).

I've Got a Flat Tyre

Doesn't seem like the phrase you're going to need? Well, in fact it could be very useful. As are all the phrases in this book, provided you have the courage to mix and match them. We have given specific examples within each section. But the key words remain the same even when the situation changes. So while you may not be planning on any cycling during your trip, the first part of the phrase 'I've got ...' could refer to anything else, and there are plenty of words in the dictionary that, we hope, will fit your needs. So whether it's 'a ticket', 'a visa' or 'a condom', you'll be able to put the words together to convey your meaning.

Finally

Don't be concerned if you feel you can't memorise words. On the inside front and back covers are the most essential words and phrases you'll need. You could also try tagging a few pages for other key phrases, or use the notes pages to write your own reminders.

PRONUNCIATION

French pronunciation can be difficult for an English speaker but if you remember a few basic rules you won't have any trouble making yourself understood.

VOWELS

a as the 'u' in cup
e sometimes barely pronounced, as the 'e' in 'open', and sometimes as the 'e' in 'merry' but slightly longer
é as the 'ay' in 'may'
è as the 'e' in 'merry', but slightly longer
i as the 'ee' in 'sweet'
o as in the 'lot' but sometimes as in 'spoke'
u to make this sound, purse your lips as if you were saying 'oo' but make the sound 'ee'

Diphthongs (Vowel Combinations)

ai as the 'e' in 'bet' but a bit longer
eu as the 'er' in the British 'berth' but shorter
oi sounds like 'wa'
ui sounds like 'wee'
au as the 'o' in 'or'
eau as the 'ow' in 'show'
ou as the 'oo' in 'book'

DID YOU KNOW ...

A circumflex over a vowel tells you that it was once spelt with an 's'. This can help you to guess the meaning of some French words: **tâche** ('task'), **île** ('isle'), **côte** ('coast'), **forêt** ('forest').

Nasal Vowels

During the production of nasal vowels the breath escapes partly through the nose and partly through the mouth. There are no nasal vowels in English; in French there are three. They occur where a syllable ends in a single n, m or nt: the last consonants are not pronounced, but indicate the nasalisation of the preceding vowel. They sound approximately like this:

on	nasal 'o' as in 'long'	bon ('good')
in	nasal 'a' as in 'bang'	vin ('wine')
an or en	nasal 'a' as in 'varnish'	blanc ('white'), lent ('slow')

In words ending in 'ien', for example bien ('well'), the 'en' is not pronounced in the way shown here but in the same way as 'in'.

PRONUNCIATION HINTS

- In some cases, for ease of pronunciation, t is inserted between a word ending with a vowel and a word beginning with a vowel. For example, A-t-il un chien? ('Does he have a dog?').
- The -ent ending of verbs in the third person plural is not pronounced at all. For example finissent ('they finish/are finishing') is pronounced 'fin-ees'. See Grammar, page 31, for discussion of verbs.
- In most cases e is not pronounced at all the end of words when there is a preceding syllable. This happens most often with the feminine of adjectives, for example bonne (from bon 'good') or fatiguée (from fatigué 'tired')

CONSONANTS

These are generally pronounced as in English but there are some you should note. Consonants at the end of a word are not pronounced, unless they run on to the following word (see Liaison, page 18)

c	hard, like 'k' before a, o and u soft, like 's', before e, i and y
ç	always soft, like 's'

g hard, as in 'get', before a, o and u
soft, as in 'germ', before e and i

h silent

j as the 's' in 'measure'

q as 'k'

s between two vowels it is pronounced as 'z'; elsewhere, as the 's' in 'sit'

l always pronounced with the tip of the tongue touching the back of the upper incisors, and the surface of the tongue higher than for an English 'l'. Be especially careful to maintain this tongue position for 'l's at the ends of words, as in il.

r the standard r of Parisian French is produced by moving the bulk of the tongue backwards to constrict the air flow in the pharynx, while the tip of the tongue rests behind the lower front teeth. It is quite similar to the noise made by some people before spitting, but with much less friction. For those who know Spanish, it is similar to the *jota*, except that it is 'softer' and voiced (involves vibration of the vocal cords).

DID YOU KNOW ...

As French does not have any strong word stress, it is easy to make puns on phrases that sound exactly the same but mean something quite different.

Tu vois, scélérat!
('You see, little rascal!')

Tu vois, c'est les rats!
('You see, it's the rats!')

LIAISON

French consonants at the end of a word are only pronounced when the following word begins with a vowel or a silent h. This 'running-on' of a sound is called liaison. When spoken, the sentence Il est artiste ('He is an artist') sounds like 'eelay tarteest'.

s or x sounds like 'z'	vous avez ('you have') is pronounced 'voozavay'
	les yeux ('the eyes') is pronounced 'layzyer'
d sounds like 't'	grand animal ('big animal') is pronounced 'grontaneemull'

WORD STRESS

Stress in French is much weaker than in English. All it really does is lengthen the final syllable of the word, so it is important to make an effort to pronounce each syllable with approximately equal stress.

This chapter is designed to give you an idea of how French phrases are put together, providing you with the basic rules to help you to construct your own sentences.

WORD ORDER

The word order in French is subject-verb-object:

I eat the cake — **Je mange le gâteau.** (lit. 'I eat the cake')

When the object (eg **le gâteau**) is turned into a pronoun, however, the word order becomes subject-object-verb:

I eat it — **Je *le* mange** (lit. 'I it eat')

(See page 28 for discussion of pronouns.)

ARTICLES

French has a definite article ('the' in English) and an indefinite article ('a/an' in English). There are three definite articles and three indefinite articles in French. Which of the three you use depends upon whether the noun after it is masculine, feminine or plural (see Nouns, page 20).

	Masculine	Feminine	Plural
Definite	**le** garçon the boy	**la** fille the girl	**les** enfants the children
Indefinite	**un** pays a country	**une** région a region	**des** arbres some trees

The definite articles le and la change to l' before a noun beginning with a vowel or silent h:

the ear	l'oreille	the hotel	l'hôtel

NOUNS

Gender

All French nouns are either masculine or feminine. The gender of a noun is often indicated by the article before it, and sometimes by its spelling. Some nouns have both masculine and feminine forms. Generally, to make a noun feminine, you add an e at the end:

a male friend	**un ami**	a female friend	**une amie**

Those that already have an e at the end don't change their spelling. It is only the article that tells you the gender of the noun:

a male student	**un élève**	a female student	**une élève**

There are some general rules for turning masculine nouns into feminine nouns and vice versa:

NOUN ENDINGS	
Masculine	**Feminine**
-oux	-ouse
-eur	-euse
-teur	-trice
-er	-ère
-ien	-ienne
-eau	-elle

	M	F
spouse	un époux	une épouse
dancer	un danseur	une danseuse
actor	un acteur	une actrice
nurse	un infirmier	une infirmière
guard	un gardien	une gardienne
twin	un jumeau	une jumelle

The following are less common ending changes. There is no easy pattern to the formation of these feminine nouns: they just have to be learned:

son	un fils	girl/daughter	une fille
hero	un héros	heroine	une héroïne
host	un hôte	hostess	une hôtesse

ARTHUR OR MARTHA?

You can often guess the gender of a noun by its ending.

- Common masculine endings:
  -acle, -age, -eau, -ème, -isme, -ment, -ier, -ien
- Common feminine endings:
  -aison, -nce, -nse, -ée, -ion, -ude, -ure, -elle, -ille

Plural

The general rule for making a noun plural is to add s. As the s is not pronounced, often the only way you can tell whether the noun is singular or plural in spoken French is by the article before it:

a house	*une* maison	*some* houses	*des* maisons

There are also some general rules you can follow for making singular nouns plural:

Singular	Plural
-al	-aux
-eau	-eaux
-eu	-eux
-ou	-ous
-ail	-ails/-aux

horse	un cheval	horses	des chevaux
water	une eau	waters	des eaux
fire	un feu	fires	des feux
neck	un cou	necks	des cous
rail	un rail	rails	des rails
work/job	un travail	works/jobs	des travaux

Again, there are exceptions to the rules for making nouns plural. The following are some words that do not follow the above patterns:

carnival	un carnaval	carnivals	des carnavals
tyre	un pneu	tyres	des pneus
pebble	un caillou	pebbles	des cailloux

Compound Plurals

Compound nouns are made up of two nouns joined together by a hyphen. To make a compound noun plural you generally make both parts of the word plural.

cauliflower	un chou-fleur	cauliflowers	des choux-fleurs
stronghold	un château-fort	strongholds	des châteaux-forts

ADJECTIVES

Gender

Adjectives must always reflect the gender and number of the nouns they describe, ie they reflect whether the noun is masculine or feminine, singular or plural. To form the feminine of most adjectives, just add an e to the end.

a big tree	un grand arbre (m)
a big house	*une* grand*e* maison (f)
a black cat	un chat noir (m)
a black car	*une* voiture noir*e* (f)

As with nouns, there are some patterns you can follow for turning masculine adjectives into feminine adjectives:

ADJECTIVE ENDINGS	
Masculine	**Feminine**
-er	-ère
-eux	-euse
-f	-ve
-el	-elle
-eil	-eille
-en	-enne
-on	-onne
-et	-ette
-s	-sse

However, some commonly used adjectives have unusual forms in the feminine. These just have to be learnt:

dry	sec	sèche
false	faux	fausse
favourite	favori	favorite
fresh	frais	fraîche
long	long	longue
old	vieux	vieille
white	blanc	blanche

the white truck — le camion blanc
the white car — la voiture blanche

the old horse — le vieux cheval
the old woman — la vieille femme

Like nouns, masculine adjectives ending in e do not change for the feminine. For example, jeune ('young') and riche ('rich').

He is young. — Il est jeune.
She is rich. — Elle est riche.

For ease of pronunciation some common adjectives have two masculine forms. One form is used before nouns beginning with a consonant and the other form is used before nouns beginning with a vowel or silent h.

	• Before a noun beginning with a consonant	• Before a noun beginning with a vowel or silent h.
beautiful	beau un beau chien	bel un bel éléphant
new	nouveau un nouveau roman	nouvel un nouvel article
old	vieux un vieux bâtiment	vieil un vieil homme

Plural Adjectives

In general, to make an adjective plural, you add an s. However some adjectives follow the same rules for making the plural as nouns (see table, page 21).

the ugly cat the ugly cats	le chat laid les chats laids
the beautiful dog the beautiful dogs	le beau chien les beaux chiens

Position of Adjectives

As a general rule, adjectives are placed after the noun, eg:

the white wall	le mur blanc (lit. 'the wall white')
the green book	le livre vert
cold water	l'eau froide
the sick woman	la femme malade

POSSESSION

Like other adjectives, possessive adjectives must agree in number and gender with the noun they refer to, not the person who it belongs to:

	Masculine	Feminine	Plural
my	mon	ma	mes
your	ton	ta	tes
his/her/its	son	sa	ses
our	notre	notre	nos
your	votre	votre	vos
their	leur	leur	leurs

my dog — *mon* chien
your skirt — *ta* jupe
our books — *nos* livres

Mon, ton and son are used with nouns beginning with a vowel or silent h regardless of whether they are masculine or feminine:

my team — *mon* équipe (f)
your odour — *ton* odeur (f)
his/her arrogance — *son* arrogance (f)

ADVERBS

The general rule is to add -ment (which corresponds to the English adverb ending '-ly') to the feminine form of the adjective:

happy heureux/heureuse happily heureusement

As usual, there are some exceptions:

nice gentil/gentille nicely gentiment
brief bref/brève briefly brièvement

If an adjective ends with a vowel, use the masculine form plus -ment:

real; true	vrai/vraie	really; truly	vraiment

If an adjective ends with -ant or -ent, change it to -amment or -emment respectively:

constant	constant	constantly	constamment
prudent	prudent	prudently	prudemment

There are a few common irregular adverbs that must be learned:

good	bon	well	bien
bad	mauvais	badly	mal
better	meilleur	best	mieux

PRONOUNS

Subject Pronouns	
I	je
you	tu (sg & inf)
he/it	il (m)
she/it	elle (f)
we	nous
you	vous (pl & pol)
they	ils (m)/elles (f)

Ils is the masculine plural pronoun but it is also used to refer to a mixture of males and females. Even if there is only one male among 100 females, ils must be used to refer to the group.

The subject pronoun on, meaning 'one', is considered formal and even old-fashioned in English but it is alive and well in French and is often used to refer to a non-specific subject. It is also often used in place of je ('I') or nous ('we'):

On parle français ici. (literally, 'one speaks French here')	French is spoken here.
On va au théâtre?	Are we going to the theatre? *or* Shall we go to the theatre?

Object Pronouns

These stand in place of an object and are placed before the verb in a sentence.

Direct Object Pronouns

me	**me**
you	**te** (sg & inf)
him/it	**le** (m)
her/it	**la** (f)
us	**nous**
you	**vous** (pl & pol)
them	**les**

I see the mountain.	Je vois *la montagne.*
I see it.	Je *la* vois.

Indirect Object Pronouns

to me	**me**
to you	**te**
to him/it	**lui**
to her/it	**lui**
to us	**nous**
to you	**vous**
to them	**leur**

I gave the ball to Jack.	J'ai donné la balle *à Jack.*
I gave him the ball.	Je *lui* ai donné la balle.

When using both direct and indirect objects in the one sentence, the direct object comes before the indirect object:

I gave it to him.	**Je *le lui* ai donné.**

Useful Little Words

Y

There is another pronoun that you will hear often. It is a useful one to know. The little word **y** stands for 'there/to [a place]/in [a place]' or 'to [something]/in [something]. Like most other pronouns it comes just before the verb:

I am going to the country.	**Je vais *à la campagne*.**
I am going there.	**J'*y* vais.**
They are in the bedroom.	**Elles sont *dans la chambre*.**
They are in there.	**Elles *y* sont.**
He is opposed to it.	**Il s'*y* oppose.**
I am interested in it.	**Je m'*y* intéresse.**

En

The little pronoun **en** stands for 'some' or 'of it/of them'. It is placed before the verb:

I have two cars.	**J'ai deux *voitures*.**
I have two of them.	**J'*en* ai deux.**
Do you want some cherries?	**Tu veux *des cerises*?**
Do you want some?	**Tu *en* veux?**
I need money.	**J'ai besoin *d'argent*.**
I need (some of) it.	**J'*en* ai besoin.**

DID YOU KNOW ...

The most frequent letter in French is **e** (there are 15 in Scrabble), yet the author, Georges Perec, managed to write a book *(La Disparition)* without a single **e**.

VERBS

Verbs can be divided into three groups, according to their ending in the infinitive:

	-ir	-er	-re
Infinitive	finir (to finish)	parler (to speak)	vendre (to sell)
Stem	fin-	parl-	vend-

Tenses are formed by adding endings to the verb stem. The verb stem is just the infinitive minus its -ir, -er or -re ending. The endings vary according to the subject. But French verbs can be regular or irregular, which means that the endings are not always the same for every verb. While regular verb conjugations are easy to learn, irregular and semi-irregular verbs must be learned individually. It would be too much for the scope of this book to give conjugations for all irregular verbs but for some common ones see Key Verbs, page 38.

Present Tense

This tense can be translated in two ways. For example je mange can mean 'I eat' or 'I am eating'.

Present Tense Endings

	-ir	-er	-re
je	fin*is*	parl*e*	vend*s*
tu	fin*is*	parl*es*	vend*s*
il/elle	fin*it*	parl*e*	vend
nous	fin*issons*	parl*ons*	vend*ons*
vous	fin*issez*	parl*ez*	vend*ez*
ils/elles	fin*issent*	parl*ent*	vend*ent*

Past Tense

This tense can be translated in three ways. So, elle a fini can mean 'she finished', 'she has finished' or 'she did finish'. It is a compound tense which means that it is made up of an auxiliary verb which is either avoir ('to have') or être ('to be') in the present tense plus a past participle.

Avoir – To Have	
I have	j'ai
you (sg & inf)	tu as
he/she has	il/elle a
we have	nous avons
you (pl & pol) have	vous avez
they have	ils/elles ont

Être – To Be	
I am	je suis
you (sg & inf) are	tu es
he/she is	il/elle est
we are	nous sommes
you (pl & pol) are	vous êtes
they are	ils/elles sont

To form a past participle, the ending of the verb is changed:

	Infinitive		Past Participle	
-er becomes -é	manger	(to eat)	mangé	(eaten)
-ir becomes -i	partir	(to leave)	parti	(left)
-re becomes -u	étendre	(to stretch)	étendu	(stretched)

IRREGULAR PAST PARTICIPLES

There are no easy ways to remember irregular past participles. They just have to be learned. Here are some common ones:

Infinitive		*Past Participle*	
avoir	to have	eu	had
être	to be	été	been
boire	to drink	bu	drunk
courir	to run	couru	run
craindre	to fear	craint	feared
croire	to believe	cru	believed
devoir	to have to; owe	dû	had to; owed
dire	to say	dit	said
écrire	to write	écrit	written
faire	to do; make	fait	done; made
ouvrir	to open	ouvert	opened
lire	to read	lu	read
mettre	to put	mis	put
mourir	to die	mort	dead
naître	to be born	né	born
ouvrir	to open	ouvert	open
pouvoir	to be able to	pu	was able to
prendre	to take	pris	taken
savoir	to know	su	known
suivre	to follow	suivi	followed
tenir	to hold	tenu	held
venir	to come	venu	come
voir	to see	vu	seen
vouloir	to want; wish	voulu	wanted; wished

Verbs Taking être In The Past Tense

Past participles of verbs taking être as their auxiliary verb must agree in number and gender with the subject, just as adjectives must agree in number and gender with the nouns they describe:

They went.	Ils sont allés.
I came.	Je (f) suis venue.
We arrived.	Nous (f) sommes arrivées.
She fell out of the tree.	Elle est tombée de l'arbre.
We were born on the same day.	Nous sommes nés le même jour.

ÊTRE VERBS

Here are some common verbs that take **être** as their auxiliary in the past tense:

aller	to go
arriver	to arrive
descendre	to go down
devenir	to become
entrer	to enter
monter	to go up
mourir	to die
naître	to be born
partir	to leave
rentrer	to come/go back (in)
rester	to stay
retourner	to return
revenir	to come back; to come again
sortir	to go out; to leave
tomber	to fall
venir	to come

About the Authors

Marie-Hélène Girard is a school librarian and Anny Monet teaches English at primary school level. Both live in Lille in the north of France.

From the Authors

Thanks to Annemarie Gorisse for her assistance.

From the Publisher

This book was produced from an original manuscript by Marie-Hélène Girard and Anny Monet. A number of dedicated people lent a hand in the process. Lou Callan spent many hours hovering over the book as editor, and wrote the pronunciation and grammar chapters; Sally Steward helped to plan the book and provided editorial guidance and champagne; Penelope Richardson plied pen, pencil and mouse to illustrate and design the pages within; Diana Saad eyed the book with much scrutiny as proofreader and, as wordsmith extraordinaire, put together the crosswords.

We are indebted to Véronique Lyttle who provided many translations, good ideas and advice. Many thanks to Monique Burston for her research on dialects; to everyone at Lonely Planet's French office for proofreading and for being so French; to Adrienne Costanzo for her help with that beast, French grammar; to Richard Plunkett who threw wit and wisdom together and came up with crossword clues and to Peter D'Onghia for creating all those little squares; to Emma Powell who assisted with layout; to Tony Wheeler for his suggestions and interest; and to Michelle de Kretser for her French expertise.

Particular thanks go to Michael Janes who, with meticulous aplomb, proofread this edition.

ADJECTIVES BEFORE THE NOUN

Many commonly used adjectives precede the noun.

autre	other	**mauvais/e**	bad
beau/belle	beautiful	**méchant/e**	naughty; wicked
bon/bonne	good	**même**	same
gentil/gentille	kind; nice	**moindre**	least
grand/e	big	**nouveau/ nouvelle**	new
gros/grosse	fat; big		
haut/e	high; tall	**petit/e**	small
jeune	young	**pire**	worse
joli/e	pretty	**vieux/vieille**	old
long/longue	long	**vilain/e**	nasty; ugly

the long river — **la longue rivière**
the big building — **le grand bâtiment**

Some adjectives change their meaning, according to whether they come before or after the noun:

a former student	un ancien élève
an ancient house	une maison ancienne
my dear friend	ma chère amie
an expensive present	un cadeau cher
their own car	leur propre voiture
a clean car	une voiture propre
my poor mother (ie sympathy/pity)	ma pauvre mère
some poor people (ie with little money)	des gens pauvres

Comparative Adjectives

plus [adjective] que ...	'more [adjective] than ...'
aussi [adjective] que ...	'as [adjective] as ....'
moins [adjective] que ...	'less [adjective] than ...'

I am naughtier than you.	Je suis *plus* méchant *que* toi.
Marie is as interested as Jeanne.	Marie est *aussi* intéressée *que* Jeanne.
Cats are less ferocious than lions.	Les chats sont *moins* féroces *que* les lions.

Superlative Adjectives

le/la [noun] le/la plus [adjective]
'the most [adjective + noun]'
le/la [noun] le/la moins [adjective]
'the least [adjective + noun]'

The most recent song.	*La* chanson *la plus* récente.
The least intelligent dog.	*Le* chien *le moins* intelligent.
The biggest birds.	*Les* oiseaux *les plus* grands.

Two of the most common adjectives have irregular forms for the comparative and superlative:

Adjective	Comparative	Superlative
bon/bonne (good)	meilleur/e (better)	le/la meilleur/e (best)
mauvais/e (bad)	pire/plus mauvais/e (worse)	le/la pire; le/la plus mauvais/e (worst)

Reflexive Verbs

All reflexive verbs take être in the past tense as well. These are verbs that reflect the action back onto the subject. You can recognise them because they all have the reflexive pronoun se in front of them, eg, se laver which means 'to wash oneself'.

We washed (ourselves)	Nous nous sommes lavés.
We washed the dogs.	Nous avons lavé les chiens.

Verbs Taking avoir in the Past Tense

Past participles of verbs taking avoir in the past tense do not agree with the subject, so they do not change.

They saw/have seen.	Elles ont vu.
You wrote/have written.	Tu as écrit.

However, they do have to agree when a direct object comes before the verb:

She took that route.	Elle a pris cette route.
She took it.	Elle l'a pris*e*.
The route that she took.	La route qu'elle a pris*e*.

Note that the verbs être ('to be') and avoir ('to have') both take avoir as their auxiliary verb in the past tense. See Key Verbs, page 38, for full conjugations of each.

DID YOU KNOW ... The French call their country the Hexagon (**L'Hexagone**) because of its shape. The first side borders Belgium and Germany; the second, Switzerland and Italy; the third, the Mediterranean Sea; the fourth, Spain; the fifth, the Bay of Biscay; and the sixth, the English Channel.

Imperfect Tense

The imperfect tense is used for an action in the past that continued over a period of time, and has no specific beginning and end. For example, take the sentence 'I was watching TV when John knocked at the door.' The verb 'to watch' is in the imperfect tense as it is an action that continued over a period of time while the verb 'to knock' is in the perfect tense as it is an action that began and ended.

The imperfect tense is formed by taking the **nous** form of the present tense of a verb, removing the **-ons** ending and adding the appropriate imperfect tense endings. The only exception to this rule is the verb **être** (see Key Verbs, page 39).

Subject	Ending	vendre (to sell)
je	-ais	vendais
tu	-ais	vendais
il/elle	-ait	vendait
nous	-ions	vendions
vous	-iez	vendiez
ils/elles	-aient	vendaient

The sun was shining. — **Le soleil brillait.**
Marie was reading her book when she heard the siren. — **Marie lisait son roman quand elle a entendu la sirène.**

The imperfect is also used to describe a habitual action in the past. In English we often use 'used to ...' to denote this habitual action.

We used to go to the park on Sundays. — **Nous allions au parc le dimanche.**
They used to dance all the time. — **Ils dansaient tout le temps.**

Future Tense

Future tense endings are added directly to the infinitive.

Subject	Ending	porter (to carry/wear)
je	-ai	porter**ai**
tu	-as	porter**as**
il/elle	-a	porter**a**
nous	-ons	porter**ons**
vous	-ez	porter**ez**
ils/elles	-ont	porter**ont**

But -re verbs drop the final e before adding the endings:

to take	**prendre**
I will take the money.	**Je prendrai l'argent.**

Near Future (Futur Proche)

The simplest way of expressing the future tense is to use the present tense of aller ('to go') plus an infinitive. We use this in English too so you won't have any trouble remembering. Firstly, you should learn the present tense of aller as it is irregular:

Aller – To Go

I go	je	vais
you (sg & inf) go	tu	vas
he/she goes	il/elle	va
we go	nous	allons
you (pl & pol) go	vous	allez
they go	ils/elles	vont

I am going to eat an apple.	**Je vais manger une pomme.**
She is going to buy six pens.	**Elle va acheter six stylos.**

KEY VERBS

Aimer *(to like/love)*

	present	past	imperfect	future
	I love	*I loved*	*I loved*	*I will love*
j'	aime	ai aimé	aimais	aimerai
tu	aimes	as aimé	aimais	aimeras
il/elle	aime	a aimé	aimait	aimera
nous	aimons	avons aimé	aimions	aimerons
vous	aimez	avez aimé	aimiez	aimerez
ils/elles	aiment	ont aimé	aimaient	aimeront

Aller *(to go)*

	present	past	imperfect	future
	I go	*I went*	*I was going*	*I will go*
je/j'	vais	suis allé/e	allais	irai
tu	vas	es allé/e	allais	iras
il/elle	va	est allé/e	allait	ira
nous	allons	sommes allés/es	allions	irons
vous	allez	êtes allé/e, allés/es	alliez	irez
ils/elles	vont	sont allés/es	allaient	iront

Avoir *(to have)*

	present	past	imperfect	future
	I have	*I had*	*I had*	*I will have*
j'	ai	ai eu	avais	aurai
tu	as	as eu	avais	auras
il/elle	a	a eu	avait	aura
nous	avons	avons eu	avions	aurons
vous	avez	avez eu	aviez	aurez
ils/elles	ont	ont eu	avaient	auront

Dire *(to say/tell)*

	present	past	imperfect	future
	I say	*I said*	*I was saying*	*I will say*
je/j'	dis	ai dit	disais	dirai
tu	dis	as dit	disais	diras
il/elle	dit	a dit	disait	dira
nous	disons	avons dit	disions	dirons
vous	dites	avez dit	disiez	direz
ils/elles	disent	ont dit	disaient	diront

Donner *(to give)*

	present	past	imperfect	future
	I give	*I gave*	*I was giving*	*I will give*
je/j'	donne	ai donné	donnais	donnerai
tu	donnes	as donné	donnais	donneras
il/elle	donne	a donné	donnait	donnera
nous	donnons	avons donné	donnions	donnerons
vous	donnez	avez donné	donniez	donnerez
ils/elles	donnent	ont donné	donnaient	donneront

Être *(to be)*

	present	past	imperfect	future
	I am	*I was*	*I was*	*I will be*
je/j'	suis	ai été	étais	serai
tu	es	as été	étais	seras
il/elle	est	a été	était	sera
nous	sommes	avons été	étions	serons
vous	êtes	avez été	étiez	serez
ils/elles	sont	ont été	étaient	seront

Faire *(to do/make)*

	present	past	imperfect	future
	I do/make	*I did/made*	*I was doing/ was making*	*I will do/ will make*
je/j'	fais	ai fait	faisais	ferai
tu	fais	as fait	faisais	feras
il/elle	fait	a fait	faisait	fera
nous	faisons	avons fait	faisions	ferons
vous	faites	avez fait	faisiez	ferez
ils/elles	font	ont fait	faisaient	feront

Pouvoir *(to be able/can)*

	present	past	imperfect	future
	I can	*I could have*	*I was able to*	*I will be able to*
je/j'	peux	ai pu	pouvais	pourrai
tu	peux	as pu	pouvais	pourras
il/elle	peut	a pu	pouvait	pourra
nous	pouvons	avons pu	pouvions	pourrons
vous	pouvez	avez pu	pouviez	pourrez
ils/elles	peuvent	ont pu	pouvaient	pourront

GRAMMAR

KEY VERBS

Savoir *(to know (something))*

	present	past	imperfect	future
	I know	*I knew*	*I knew*	*I will know*
je/j'	sais	ai su	savais	saurai
tu	sais	as su	savais	sauras
il/elle	sait	a su	savait	saura
nous	savons	avons su	savions	saurons
vous	savez	avez su	saviez	saurez
ils/elles	savent	ont su	savaient	sauront

Venir *(to come)*

	present	past	imperfect	future
	I come	*I came*	*I was coming*	*I will come*
je	viens	suis venu/e	venais	viendrai
tu	viens	es venu /e	venais	viendras
il/elle	vient	est venu/e	venait	viendra
nous	venons	sommes venus/es	venions	viendrons
vous	venez	êtes venu/e, venus/ues	veniez	viendrez
ils/elles	viennent	sont venus/es	venaient	viendront

Voir *(to see)*

	present	past	imperfect	future
	I see	*I saw*	*I used to see*	*I will see*
je/j'	vois	ai vu	voyais	verrais
tu	vois	as vu	voyais	verrais
il/elle	voit	a vu	voyait	verrait
nous	voyons	avons vu	voyions	verrons
vous	voyez	avez vu	voyiez	verrez
ils/elles	voient	ont vu	voyaient	verront

Vouloir *(to want/wish)*

	present	past	imperfect	future
	I want	*I wanted*	*I wanted*	*I will want*
je/j'	veux	ai voulu	voulais	voudrai
tu	veux	as voulu	voulais	voudras
il/elle	veut	a voulu	voulait	voudra
nous	voulons	avons voulu	voulions	voudrons
vous	voulez	avez voulu	vouliez	voudrez
ils/elles	veulent	ont voulu	voulaient	voudront

Imperative (Commands)

To give an order in French, just use the present tense of the verb without the subject. Commands exist only in the tu, vous and nous forms. With -er verbs, drop the final s of the tu ending:

Eat!	Mange! (sg & inf)
Go!	Allez! (pl & pol)
Let's sing!	Chantons!

To make a command negative, just put ne ... pas around it:

Don't speak!	Ne parlez pas!

The verb être has a very irregular form in the imperative:

Let's be nice!	Soyons gentils!
Don't be so angry!	Ne sois pas si fâché!

QUESTIONS

There are three ways of asking a question in French.

- The most common way is to use the intonation of your voice:

You have a car.	Tu as une voiture.
Do you have a car?	Tu as une voiture?

- Use Est-ce que ... (literally, 'is it that ...?') at the beginning of a sentence:

Do you have a car?	Est-ce que tu as une voiture?

- Invert the subject and the verb and link them with a hyphen:

Do you have a car?	As-tu une voiture?

When the question is in the affirmative and you want to answer 'yes', say Oui. But when the question is in the negative and you want to answer 'yes', say Si.

Don't you have a car?	Tu n'as pas de voiture?
Yes I do.	Si.

Question Words

• **Who?**	**Qui?**	Who is it? C'est qui? Qui est-ce?
• **What?**	**Quoi?**	What is it? C'est quoi? (inf) Qu'est-ce que c'est ?
• **Which?**	**Quel/Quelle**	Which boy is it? C'est quel garçon? Quel garçon est-ce?
• **Where?**	**Où?**	Where is she going? Où est-ce qu'elle va? Où va-t-elle?
• **When?**	**Quand?**	When are you leaving? Tu pars quand? (inf) Quand (est-ce que) tu pars? Quand pars-tu?
• **How?**	**Comment?**	How is he going? Il va comment? (inf) Comment (est-ce qu') il va? Comment va-t-il?

The third example above can have two meanings: 'How is he?' (meaning his health) or 'How is he going?' (ie, by what means?)

• **Why?**	**Pourquoi?**	Why do you do that? Tu fais ça pourquoi? (inf) Pourquoi (est-ce que) tu fais ça? Pourquoi fais-tu ça?

NEGATIVES

To form the negative in a sentence, place ne ... pas around the verb. In the case of a compound tense place them around the auxiliary verb.

She doesn't play.	Elle *ne* joue *pas.*
I didn't see the lions.	Je *n'*ai *pas* vu les lions.

In spoken French you'll notice that people will often omit the ne.

There are four verbs that do not have to include the pas especially in written French. These are cesser ('to stop/cease'), oser ('to dare'), pouvoir ('to be able to'), savoir ('to know').

I can't do it.	Je ne peux le faire
I don't know.	Je ne sais.

Other Negatives

I don't smile *any more.*	Je *ne* souris *plus.*
She *never* sleeps.	Elle *ne* dort *jamais.*
He *hardly* plays.	Il *ne* joue *guère.*

Pas, used alone, corresponds to the English word 'not' and is used when there is no verb:

Not yet.	Pas encore
Not bad.	Pas mal.
Not me.	Pas moi.

PREPOSITIONS

of/from	**de**
from the country	de la campagne
to/at	**à**
to/at a concert	à un concert

When used with the definite article in the masculine and in the plural, these prepositions change their form:

to/in Japan	au (à + le) Japon
from Japan	du (de + le) Japon
to/at the children	aux (à + les) enfants
of/from the children	des (de + les) enfants

OTHER USEFUL PREPOSITIONS

with	avec	in front of	devant
without	sans	between	entre
at the place of/at	chez	for	pour
against	contre	under	sous
in	dans/en	on	sur
behind	derrière	towards	vers

CONJUNCTIONS

Conjunctions link things in a sentence. These things could be nouns, phrases or clauses.

and	et
as	comme
because	parce que
but	mais
however	cependant
or	ou
since	depuis que
so	donc
when	quand; lorsque
while	pendant que
without	sans que

FAUX AMIS – FALSE FRIENDS

GETTING IT RIGHT

Be careful! Many French words are like English words but have a very different meaning. These are called *faux amis*. Here are some to watch out for:

to say ...	*use ...*	*don't use ...*	*which means ...*
actual	**vrai**	**actuel**	present; current
affluence	la **richesse**	une **affluence**	crowd
alien	un **étranger/** une **étrangère**	un/e **aliéné/e**	mental patient
to assist	**aider**	**assister**	to attend
to attend	**assister à**	**attendre**	to wait
bachelor/ spinster	le/la **célibataire**	le **bachelier/** la **bachelière**	high school graduate
benefit	un **avantage**	le **bénéfice**	profit
big	**grand/e**	**large**	wide
blouse	le **chemisier**	la **blouse**	overall
camera	un **appareil photo**	la **caméra**	cine-camera
car	la **voiture**	un **car**	coach, bus
caution	la **prudence**	la **caution**	deposit
chance	le **hasard**	la **chance**	luck
chips	des **pommes frites**	des **chips**	crips
complete	**entier/ entière**	**complet/ complète**	full
confused	**embrouillé/e**	**confus/e**	embarrassed
to cry	**pleurer**	**crier**	to shout
delay (n)	le **retard**	le **délai**	time; time-limit

FAUX AMIS – FALSE FRIENDS

to say ...	*use ...*	*don't use ...*	*which means ...*
to demand	**exiger**	**demander**	to ask
infant	le **bébé**	un/e **enfant**	child
information	les **renseignements**	les **informations**	the news
to introduce	**présenter**	**introduire**	to put in; to insert
journey	le **voyage**	la **journée**	day
library	la **bibliothèque**	la **librairie**	bookshop
location	un **lieu**	la **location**	hiring, renting
menu	la **carte**	le **menu**	set menu
occasion	un **jour spécial**; un **événement**	une **occasion**	bargain
petrol	l'**essence** (f)	le **pétrole**	oil
preservative	un **conservateur**	un **préservatif**	condom
prune	**un pruneau**	une **prune**	plum
refuse (n)	les **ordures**	le **refus**	refusal
Roman	**romain**	un **roman**	novel
sensible	**sensé/e**	**sensible**	sensitive
trivial	**banal**	**trivial**	vulgar
vacancy	le **poste vacant**	les **vacances**	holidays

MEETING PEOPLE

YOU SHOULD KNOW

Hello.	Bonjour; Salut. (inf)
Goodbye.	Au revoir; Salut; Tchao. (inf)
Yes/Yeah	Oui; Ouais.
No.	Non.
Excuse me.	Excusez-moi.
May I?/Do you mind?	Je peux?; Vous (me) permettez? Ça ne vous fait rien?
Sorry. (Excuse me/Forgive me)	Pardon.
Please.	S'il vous plaît.
Thank you (very much).	Merci (beaucoup).
That's fine/You're welcome.	De rien; Je vous en prie.

GREETINGS

Good morning/afternoon.	Bonjour.
Good evening/night.	Bonsoir.
How are you?	Comment allez-vous? (pol) Comment vas-tu? (inf) (Comment) ça va? (inf)
Well, thanks.	Bien, merci.
Not bad, (thanks).	Ça va, (merci).
So-so.	Ça peut aller; Bof. (inf)
And you?	Et vous? (pol) Et toi? (inf)

DID YOU KNOW ...

With people they know well, the French often exchange kisses – usually one peck on each cheek. The number of kisses depends on the person, and the region you're in.

FORMS OF ADDRESS

If in doubt as to whether to use Madame or Mademoiselle, stick to Madame.

Madam/Mrs	Madame (Mme)
Sir/Mr	Monsieur (M)
Ms/Miss	Mademoiselle (Mlle)

FIRST ENCOUNTERS

What's your name?	Comment vous appelez-vous? (pol)
	Tu t'appelles comment? (inf)
My name is ...	Je m'appelle ...
I'm a friend of ...	Je suis un/e ami/e de ...
I'd like to introduce you to ...	Je vous présente ...
His/Her name is ...	Il/Elle s'appelle ...
Pleased to meet you.	Enchanté/e.
Are you here on holiday?	Vous êtes ici pour les vacances? (pol)
	Tu es ici pour les vacances? (inf)

I'm here on ...	Je suis ici pour ...
a holiday	les vacances
business	le travail
to study	les études

Where are you staying?	Où logez-vous?
I'm staying at ...	Je loge à ...
We're staying at ...	Nous logeons à ...
How long have you been here?	Depuis quand êtes-vous ici? (pol)
	Tu es là depuis quand? (inf)
I've been here (three) days/weeks.	Je suis ici depuis (trois) jours/semaines.

See page 235 for numbers.

How long are you here for? — Vous restez ici combien de temps? (pol)
Tu restes ici combien de temps? (inf)

We're here for (two) weeks. — Nous restons ici (deux) semaines.

This is my first visit to France. — C'est mon premier séjour en France.

We like France very much. — Nous aimons beaucoup la France.

Do you like it here? — Ça vous plaît ici? (pol)
Tu aimes ici? (inf)

Are you travelling alone? — Vous voyagez seul/e?

No, I'm with ... — Non, je suis avec ...
- my friend — mon ami/e
- my boyfriend/girlfriend — mon petit ami/ma petite amie
- my business associate — mon associé/e
- my family — ma famille
- a group — un groupe

Well, enjoy your stay.
Eh bien, passez de bonnes vacances.

Goodbye, nice to meet you.
Au revoir, ravi/e de vous avoir rencontré/e.

Goodbye
Au revoir

See you.
A bientôt; A plus tard.

ARTHUR OR MARTHA?

Remember that in this book, the masculine form of a word appears first, separated from the feminine form by a slash. See page 10 for a full explanation.

NATIONALITIES

Where are you from?	Vous venez d'où? (pol) Tu viens d'où? (inf)
I come ...	Je viens ...
from Australia	d'Australie
from Africa	d'Afrique
from Canada	du Canada
from England	d'Angleterre
from France	de France

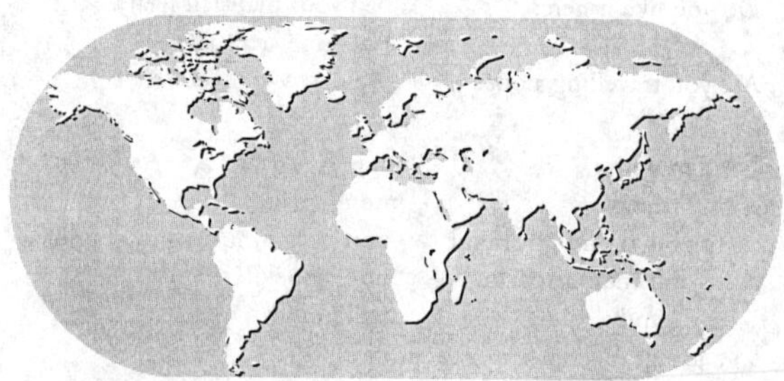

from Hong Kong	de Hong Kong
from Ireland	d'Irlande
from the Ivory Coast	de la Côte-d'Ivoire
from Japan	du Japon
from Korea	de Corée
from Mauritius	de l' le Maurice
from the Middle East	du Moyen-Orient
from New Caledonia	de Nouvelle-Calédonic
from New Zealand	de Nouvelle-Zélande
from Scotland	d'Écosse
from Seychelles	des Seychelles

from South Africa	d'Afrique du Sud
from South America	d'Amérique du Sud
from Switzerland	de Suisse
from the USA	des États-Unis
from Wales	du pays de Galles

You'll find that many country names in French are very similar to English. If your country is not listed above try saying it in English and you'll most likely be understood.

What nationality are you?	Vous êtes de quelle nationalité? (pol) Tu es de quelle nationalité? (inf)
Have you been to my country?	Vous connaissez mon pays? (pol) Tu connais mon pays? (inf)

CULTURAL DIFFERENCES

How do you do this in your country?	Comment fait-on cela dans votre pays?
In my country ...	Dans mon pays ...
Is this a local or national custom?	Est-ce que c'est une coutume locale ou nationale?
I don't want to offend you.	Je ne veux pas vous faire de la peine.
I'm sorry, it's not the custom in my country.	Je m'excuse, ce n'est pas la coutume dans mon pays.
I'm not accustomed to this.	Je ne suis pas habitué/e à cela.
I'd prefer not to participate.	Je préfère de ne pas participer.

My culture/religion doesn't allow me to ...	Ma culture/Ma religion ne me permet pas de ...
practise this	pratiquer cela
eat this	manger cela
drink this	boire cela

AGE

How old are you?	Vous avez quel âge? (pol) Tu as quel âge? (inf)
I'm ... years old.	J'ai ... ans.
You don't look it!	Vous ne les faites pas. (pol) Tu (ne) les fais pas. (inf)

LANGUAGE DIFFICULTIES

Do you speak English?	Vous parlez anglais?
Does anyone speak English?	Est-ce qu'il y a quelqu'un qui parle anglais?
I speak a little ...	Je parle un peu de ...
I don't speak ...	Je ne parle pas ...
I understand.	Je comprends.
I don't understand.	Je (ne) comprends pas.
Could you speak more slowly?	Est-ce que vous pourriez parler plus lentement?
Could you repeat that, please?	Pouvez-vous répéter, s'il vous plaît?
Can you spell that for me?	Vous pouvez épeler, s'il vous plaît?
How do you say ...?	Comment est-ce qu'on dit ...?
What does ... mean?	Que veut dire ...?
I speak ...	Je parle ...
English	anglais
French	français
German	allemand
Italian	italien
Spanish	espagnol

OCCUPATIONS

Where do you work?	Vous travaillez où? (pol)
	Tu travailles où? (inf)
What (work) do you do?	Vous faites quoi comme métier? (pol)
	Tu fais quoi comme métier? (inf)
I am (a/an) ...	Je suis ...
artist	un/e artiste
business person	un homme/une femme d'affaires
chef	cuisinier/cuisinière
doctor	médecin
engineer	ingénieur
farmer	agriculteur
journalist	journaliste
lawyer	avocat/avocate
mechanic	mécanicien/mécanicienne
nurse	infirmier/infirmière
office worker	employé/e de bureau
scientist	scientifique
teacher	professeur; prof (inf)
(in primary school)	instituteur/institutrice; maître/maîtresse
waiter	serveur/serveuse
writer	écrivain
I'm a homemaker.	Je suis homme/femme au foyer.
I'm a public servant.	Je travaille dans la fonction publique.
I'm retired.	Je suis retraité/e.
I'm unemployed.	Je suis chômeur/chômeuse.
	Je suis sans travail.

DID YOU KNOW ...

The RMI (Revenu Minimum d'Insertion) is a minimal income for those who can't claim the dole. You may hear someone say, therefore, Je suis RMIste.

Do you enjoy your work?	Vous aimez votre travail? (pol) Tu aimes ton travail? (inf)
How long have you been in your job?	Depuis quand faites-vous ce travail? (pol) Depuis quand fais-tu ce travail? (inf)

STUDYING

What are you studying?	Que faites-vous comme études? (pol) Que fais-tu comme études? (inf)
I'm studying ...	Je fais des études ...
art	artistiques
business	commerciales
education	pour devenir enseignant/e
engineering	d'ingénieur
humanities	en sciences humaines
languages	de langues
law	de droit
medicine	de médecine
science	scientifiques
social sciences	en sciences sociales
French	de lettres (French people) de français (foreigners)

college	un établissement d'enseignement supérieur; une école professionnelle; un institut universitaire
degree	un diplôme
dole	l'allocation; l'indemnité de chômage

DID YOU KNOW ...

French school students sit for their **baccalauréat** (or **bac**) to gain entrance into university.

school	une école
job	un travail; un emploi; un poste
professional	professionnel/le
salary	un salaire
specialist	un/e spécialiste
university	une université
office	un bureau; un service (ie department or section within a larger organisation)

RELIGION

Do you have a religion?	Vous avez une religion? (pol)
	Tu as une religion? (inf)
What is your religion?	Quelle est votre religion? (pol)
	Quelle est ta religion? (inf)
I am not religious.	Je ne suis pas croyant/e.
I am an agnostic.	Je suis agnostique.
I am an atheist.	Je suis athée.
I think I believe in God.	Je pense que je crois en Dieu.

I am ...	Je suis ...
Buddhist	bouddhiste
Catholic	catholique
Christian	chrétien/ne
Hindu	hindou/e
Jewish	juif/juive
Muslim	musulman/e
Protestant	protestant/e

FEELINGS

I like ...	J'aime ...
I don't like ...	Je n'aime pas.
Do you like ...?	... vous plaît? (pol)
	Tu aimes ...? (inf)
I'm sorry. (condolence)	Je suis désolé/e.
I'm grateful.	Je vous suis reconnaissant/e.

I am ...	J'ai ...
Are you ...?	Avez-vous ...? (pol)
	As-tu ...? (inf)
cold	froid
hot	chaud
hungry	faim
thirsty	soif
right	raison
sleepy	sommeil

I am ...	Je suis ...
Are you ...?	Etes-vous ...? (pol)
	Es-tu ...? (inf)
angry	fâché/e
happy	heureux/heureuse
in a hurry	pressé/e
sad	triste
tired	fatigué/e
well	bien

I'm fed up!	J'en ai assez! (pol)
	J'en ai marre! (inf)

USEFUL EXPRESSIONS

OK	D'accord; D'ac (inf); OK.
Of course!	Bien sûr; Naturellement; Bah ouais! (inf)
Sure	Bien sûr.
Good!	Tant mieux!
Good luck!	Bonne chance!
Good idea.	Bonne idée.
Wait!	Attendez!
Careful!	Attention!

USEFUL EXPRESSIONS

Let's go!	Allons-y!
Go on!	Vas-y!
Come on!	Allez, viens!
Hurry up!	Dépêchez-vous! (pl)/ Dépêche-toi! (sg) Grouille-toi! (inf)
Ready?	Prêt/e?; Vous y êtes?
I'm ready.	Je suis prêt/e.
Too bad!	Tant pis!
What a shame!	Quel dommage!
Doesn't matter.	C'est pas grave.
No problem.	Pas de problème.
What's up/the matter?	Qu'est-ce qu'il y a?
At last!	Enfin!
How lucky!	Quelle chance!
Just as well/Fortunately!	Heureusement!
It's strange/funny.	C'est marrant/rigolo/bizarre.
It's nothing/Don't mention it.	Ce n'est rien.
Better luck next time.	Ça ira mieux la prochaine fois.
Just a minute/moment.	Attendez une minute/un moment.
In a minute.	Tout à l'heure.
It's important.	C'est important.
It's not important.	Ce n'est pas important.
It's possible.	C'est possible.
It's (not) possible.	Ce n'est pas possible.
It's impossible to ...	Pas moyen de ...
I don't believe you.	Tu parles/rigoles; Mon œil! (inf)

CROSSWORD – MEETING PEOPLE

Across

2. A person who doesn't believe in God.
6. Evening greeting
7. What people do if not unemployed.
9. Time it took God to create universe (and take day off)

Down

1. Word for rural areas
3. One who writes
4. Female sibling
5. Institution for education
8. Solitary (masculine)
10. Male friend

Answers on page 309.

GETTING AROUND

DON'T MISS IT!

What time does ... leave/ arrive?	À quelle heure ... part/ arrive ...?
the plane	l'avion
the boat	le bateau
the boat (small)	l'embarcation
the boat (liner/ship)	le paquebot/le navire
the bus (city)	l'(auto)bus
the bus (intercity)	l'(auto)car; le bus
the train	le train
the tram	le tramway

FINDING YOUR WAY

Where is the ...?	Où est ...?
bus station	la gare routière
bus stop	l'arrêt d'autobus
city centre	le centre-ville
port	le port
taxi stand	la station de taxis
train station	la gare
subway/underground station	la station de métro
ticket office	le guichet

Where are we now?	Où sommes-nous maintenant?
We want to go to ...	Nous voulons aller à ...
How do I get to ...?	Pour aller à ..., s'il vous plaît?
What's the best way?	Quel est le chemin le plus direct?
Is it far from/near here?	C'est loin/près d'ici?
Can I walk there?	Je peux y aller à pied?
Can you show me (on the map)?	Pouvez-vous me le montrer (sur la carte)?
Are there other means of getting there?	Est-ce qu'il y a une autre façon d'y aller?

DIRECTIONS

Go straight ahead.	Continuez tout droit.
Cross the road.	Traversez la rue.
It's (two) blocks down.	C'est (deux) rues plus loin.
Turn left ...	Tournez à gauche ...
Turn right ...	Tournez à droite ...
at the next corner	au prochain coin
at the next intersection	au prochain carrefour
at the traffic lights	aux feux
at the roundabout	au rond-point

behind	derrière	north	nord (m)
in front of	devant	south	sud (m)
far	loin	cast	est (m)
near (to)	près de	west	ouest (m)
opposite	en face de		

Which ... is this?	**Quel/Quelle ... est-ce?**
avenue	**avenue (f)**
road	**route (f)**
street	**rue (f)**
boulevard	**boulevard (m)**
square	**place (f)**

BUYING TICKETS

SIGN	
GUICHET	TICKET OFFICE

Excuse me, where is the ticket office?	**Excusez-moi, où est le guichet?**
Where is the timetable?	**Où est le tableau des horaires?**
Where can I buy a ticket?	**Où peut-on acheter un billet?**
I want to go to ...	**Je veux aller à ...**
How much is the fare to ...?	**Quel est le prix du billet pour ...?**
What is the cheapest fare to ...?	**Quel est le tarif le moins cher pour ...?**
Do I need to book?	**Est-ce qu'il faut réserver une place?**
I'd like to book a seat to ...	**Je voudrais réserver une place pour ...**
Is it full?	**C'est complet?**
Can I get a stand-by ticket?	**Est-ce que je peux acheter un billet en stand-by?**

I'd like ...	**Je voudrais ...**
a one-way ticket	**un billet simple**
a return ticket	**un billet aller et retour**
(four) tickets	**(quatre) billets**
tickets for all of us	**des billets pour nous tous**
a concession fare	**une réduction; un tarif réduit**
for a child	**pour un enfant**

I'm a pensioner.	Je suis retraité/e.
I'm a student.	Je suis étudiant/e.
Are there any special fares?	Il y a des tarifs réduits?
I'd like ... my reservation.	Je voudrais ... ma réservation.
to cancel	annuler
to change	changer
to confirm	confirmer
1st class	première classe
2nd class	seconde/deuxième classe

THEY MAY SAY ...

Il faut réserver une place.
You need to book.

C'est complet.
It's full.

Billet simple?
One way?

Aller et retour?
Return?

Fumeur ou non-fumeur?
Smoking or non-smoking?

Special Requests

I'd like a window seat .
Je voudrais une place côté fenêtre.

I'd like an aisle seat.
Je voudrais une place côté couloir.

I'd like a non-smoking seat/carriage.
Je voudrais une place/un wagon non-fumeur.

I'd like a kosher/vegetarian meal.
Je voudrais un repas cascher/végétarien.

AT CUSTOMS

SIGNS

DOUANE	CUSTOMS
HORS TAXE; EXEMPTÉ DE DOUANE	DUTY-FREE
CONTRÔLE DES PASSEPORTS	PASSPORT CONTROL

I have something to declare.	J'ai quelque chose à déclarer.
I have nothing to declare.	Je n'ai rien à déclarer.
This is all I have.	C'est tout ce que j'ai.
Do I have to declare this?	Faut-il déclarer cela?
You must clear your luggage through customs.	Il faut dédouaner vos bagages.
I didn't know I had to declare this.	Je ne savais pas que je devais déclarer cela.

AIR

SIGNS

ARRIVÉES	ARRIVALS
DÉPARTS	DEPARTURES
ENREGISTREMENT	CHECK-IN COUNTER
LIVRAISON DES BAGAGES	BAGGAGE CLAIM

Is there a flight to ...?	Est-ce qu'il y a un vol pour ...?
When is the next flight to ...?	À quelle heure part le prochain avion pour ...?
How long does the flight take?	Le vol dure combien de temps?
What is the flight number?	Quel est le numéro de vol?
When do I have to check in?	À quelle heure dois-je me présenter à l'enregistrement?

You must check in at ...	Vous devez vous présenter à l'enregistrement à ...
My luggage hasn't arrived.	Mes bagages ne sont pas arrivés.
airport tax	taxes d'aéroport
boarding pass	carte d'embarquement
domestic	intérieur
international	international

BUS & TRAM

SIGNS

ARRÊT D'AUTOBUS	BUS STOP
ARRÊT DE TRAMWAY	TRAM STOP

Where is the bus/tram stop?	Où est l'arrêt d'autobus/de tramway?
Which bus goes to ...?	Quel bus va à ...?
Does this bus go to ...?	Est-ce que ce bus va à ...?
Where do I buy a ticket for the bus?	Où est-ce qu'on achète un billet pour le bus?
Do the buses come often?	Les bus passent souvent?
What time is the ... bus?	Le ... bus passe à quelle heure?
next	prochain
first	premier
last	dernier
every (ten) minutes	toutes les (dix) minutes
every (half) hour	toutes les (demi-) heures
Do you stop at ...?	Est-ce que vous vous arrêtez à ...?
Could you let me know when we get to ...?	Pouvez-vous me dire quand nous arrivons à ...?
I want to get off!	Je veux descendre!

TRAIN

France's train network is operated by the SNCF (Société Nationale des Chemins de Fer). The high-speed train is the TGV (Train à Grande Vitesse). Before boarding any train you must validate your ticket in one of the orange composteurs which you'll find somewhere between the ticket office and the platform.

SIGNS

GARE	TRAIN STATION
GRANDES LIGNES	MAIN LINE TRAINS
BANLIEUE	TRAINS TO SUBURBS
OBJETS TROUVÉS	LOST & FOUND

Where is the nearest train station? — Où est la gare la plus proche?

Is this the right platform for ...? — C'est le bon quai pour ...?

The train leaves from platform ... — Le train part du quai ...

Passengers must ... — Les voyageurs doivent ...
- change trains — changer de train
- change platforms — changer de quai

dining car
le wagon-restaurant

express
rapide

left-luggage lockers
consigne automatique

local
local

platform
le quai

sleeping car
un wagon-lit

NO

To make a sentence negative, place the word **ne** before the verb and **pas** after the verb:

I see. — Je vois.

I don't see. — Je *ne* vois *pas*.

METRO

The underground network in Paris consists of two systems: the **Métro** and the **RER**. The **RER (Réseau Express Régional)** is a network of suburban services which passes through the city centre.

There is one standard fare to anywhere on the Paris Metro. Tickets are normally bought 10 at a time. This is called a **carnet**.

SIGNS

DISTRIBUTEUR DE MONNAIE	CHANGE MACHINE
CORRESPONDANCE	TO OTHER LINES
SORTIE	WAY OUT

Which line goes to ...?	**Quelle ligne va à ...?**
Is this the line to ...?	**Est-ce que cette ligne va à ...?**
What is the next stop?	**Quelle est la prochaine station?**

TAXI

Where is a taxi stand?	**Où se trouve la station de taxi?**
Are you free?	**Vous êtes libre?**
Please take me to ...	**Conduisez-moi à ..., s'il vous plaît.**
How much does it cost to go to ...?	**C'est combien pour aller à ...?**
Does that include luggage?	**Les bagages sont compris?**
Do you have change of ... francs?	**Pouvez-vous me faire la monnaie de ... francs?**
Is this the most direct route?	**Est-ce que c'est le chemin le plus direct?**
This is not the most direct route.	**Ce n'est pas le chemin le plus direct.**

Instructions

Here is fine, thank you.	**Ici ça va, merci.**
The next corner, please.	**Au prochain coin de rue, s'il vous plaît.**
Straight on!	**Continuez!**
The next street to the left/ right.	**La prochaine rue à gauche/ droite.**
Stop here, please!	**Arrêtez-vous ici, s'il vous plaît!**
Please slow down.	**Roulez plus lentement, s'il vous plaît.**
Please wait here.	**Attendez ici, s'il vous plaît.**

USEFUL WORDS & PHRASES

The (train) is delayed.	**Le (train) a du retard.**
The (train) is cancelled.	**Le (train) a été annulé.**
How long will it be delayed?	**Il aura combien de retard?**
There is a delay of ... hours.	**Il y aura un retard de ... heures.**
Can I smoke?	**Je peux fumer?**
How long does the trip take?	**Le trajet dure combien de temps?**
Is it a direct train?	**C'est un train direct?**
I'm hitching a lift to Paris.	**Je fais du stop jusqu'à Paris.**
Is that seat taken?	**Est-ce que cette place est occupée?**
Do you mind if I put the window down/up?	**Ça ne vous dérange pas si j'ouvre/je ferme la fenêtre?**
I'm sorry, I can't find my ticket.	**Je suis désolé/e, je ne retrouve pas mon billet.**
I want to get off at ...	**Je veux descendre à ...**
Excuse me, may I sit here?	**Excusez-moi, puis-je m'asseoir ici?**

inspector	**le contrôleur**
driver	**le conducteur**
hitching	**l'auto-stop; le stop**
motorcycle	**la moto**
passenger	**le voyageur**
passport	**le passeport**
ticket	**le billet**
trip/journey	**le voyage**
visa	**le visa**
waiting room	**la salle d'attente**

L'

The definite articles **le** (m) and **la** (f) become **l'** before a noun beginning with a vowel or silent **h**.

CAR

Where can I rent a car?	**Où est-ce que je peux louer une voiture?**
How much is it daily/weekly?	**Quel est le tarif par jour/par semaine?**
Does that include insurance/mileage?	**Est-ce que l'assurance/le kilométrage est compris/e?**

SIGNS

DÉVIATION	DETOUR
DANGER	DANGER
ATTENTION	CAUTION
GARAGE/ STATION-SERVICE	GARAGE/ SERVICE STATION
CÉDEZ LE PASSAGE	GIVE WAY
ENTRÉE INTERDITE	NO ENTRY
RALENTIR	SLOW DOWN
DÉFENSE DE DOUBLER	DO NOT OVERTAKE
TRAVAUX	ROAD WORKS
STATIONNEMENT INTERDIT	NO PARKING
OUVERT 24 H SUR 24	24-HOUR ACCESS
SENS UNIQUE	ONE WAY
PIÉTONS	PEDESTRIANS
RESPECTEZ LA DISTANCE DE SÉCURITÉ	KEEP A SAFE DISTANCE

I'd like to rent a small/large car.	Je voudrais louer une petite/ grosse voiture.
Can I see it?	Je peux la voir?
Can I return it in another city?	Je peux la rendre dans une autre ville?
Where's the next petrol/gas station?	Où est la prochaine station-service?
Please fill the tank.	Le plein, s'il vous plaît.
... litres of petrol/gas, please.	... litres d'essence, s'il vous plaît.
Please check the oil and water.	Contrôlez l'huile et l'eau, s'il vous plaît.
Can I park here?	Je peux stationner ici?
How long can I park here?	Combien de temps est-ce que je peux stationner ici?
Is this the road to ...?	C'est la route pour ...?

air (for tyres)	le compresseur
automatic	automatique
battery	une batterie
brakes	les freins
clutch	l'embrayage
to cut in	faire une queue de poisson
diesel	diesel
driving/driver's licence	le permis de conduire
engine	le moteur
fanbelt	la courroie du ventilateur
indicator	le clignotant
inner/outer ring	le périphérique intérieur/extérieur
leaded	qui contient du plomb
lights	les phares
main road	la grande route
manual	manuel
mechanic	le mécanicien
mobile breath testing unit	l'alcotest; le ballon
motorway with tolls	une autoroute à péage
petrol/gas	l'essence
puncture	une crevaison
radiator	le radiateur
regular/premium *(petrol)*	normale
repairs	des réparations
ring road	un (boulevard) périphérique (BP)
road map	une carte routière
seatbelt	une ceinture de sécurité
self service	libre-service
speed limit	la limitation de vitesse
super *(petrol)*	super
toll	un péage
traffic jam	un bouchon
tyres	les pneus
unleaded	sans plomb
windscreen	le pare-brise

Car Problems

I need a mechanic.	J'ai besoin d'un mécanicien.
My car has broken down at ...	Ma voiture est tombée en panne à ...
What make is it?	C'est quelle marque?
I've run out of petrol.	Je suis en panne d'essence.
The battery is flat.	La batterie est à plat.
The radiator is leaking.	Le radiateur fuit.
I have a flat tyre.	Mon pneu est à plat.
I've had a blow out.	J'ai crevé.
It's overheating.	Le moteur chauffe.
It's not working.	Elle ne marche pas.
I've stalled the car.	J'ai calé.
I've locked my keys in the car.	J'ai enfermé mes clés dans la voiture.
I need a tow truck.	J'ai besoin d'une dépanneuse.
I need a push start.	J'ai besoin qu'on me pousse.
Do you have jump(er) leads/ jumper cables?	Vous avez des câbles de démarrage?

BICYCLE

Where can I hire a bicycle?	Où est-ce que je peux louer un vélo?
How much is it for an hour/ a day?	C'est combien l'heure/la journée?
Do I have to wear a helmet?	Il faut porter un casque?
Where can I leave my bike?	Où puis-je laisser mon vélo?
Where's a bicycle repair shop?	Où y a-t-il un réparateur de vélos?
Is this road OK for bikes?	Est-ce qu'on peut rouler à vélo ici?
Is there a cycling track near here?	Y a-t-il une piste cyclable près d'ici?

bicycle pump	une pompe à vélo
bicycle/bike	une bicyclette/un vélo
brakes	les freins
chain	une chaîne
frame	un cadre
handlebars	un guidon
mountain bike	un vélo tout-terrain (VTT)
padlock	un cadenas
puncture	une crevaison
racing bike	un vélo de course
seat	une selle
spokes	les rayons
stunt-bike	un vélo-cross
tyres	les pneus
wheels	les roues

CROSSWORD – GETTING AROUND

Across

5. French brands include Renault and Citroen
8. Distant
9. Documented proof you paid for your seat
10. Best place to board a train

Down

1. —— d'Orsay
2. Hole in a tyre
3. Brands include Airbus and Boeing
4. Place to get your 'billet'
6. Term for city or town
7. Outlying residential area

Answers on page 309.

ACCOMMODATION

FINDING ACCOMMODATION

I'm looking for ...	Je cherche ...
Where is ...?	Où est-ce qu'on peut trouver ...?
a cheap hotel	un hôtel bon marché
a good hotel	un bon hôtel
a nearby hotel	un hôtel pas loin d'ici
a clean hotel	un hôtel propre
What is the address?	Quelle est l'adresse?
Could you write the address, please?	Est-ce vous pouvez écrire l'adresse, s'il vous plaît?

SIGNS

CAMPING	CAMPING GROUND
PENSION (DE FAMILLE)	GUESTHOUSE
HÔTEL	HOTEL
MOTEL	MOTEL
AUBERGE DE JEUNESSE	YOUTH HOSTEL
GÎTE	SELF-CATERING ACCOMMODATION
CHAMBRE LIBRE	VACANCY
COMPLET	NO VACANCY

BOOKING AHEAD

Do you have any rooms available?	Est-ce que vous avez des chambres libres?
I'd like to book a room ...	Je voudrais réserver une chambre ...
for one person	pour une personne
for two people	pour deux personnes
from next (Tuesday)	à partir de (mardi) prochain

I'm going to stay for ...	Je resterai ...
one night	une nuit
five nights	cinq nuits
one week	une semaine

I'd like ...	Je voudrais ...
a single room	une chambre à un lit
a double room	une chambre double
to share a dorm	coucher dans un dortoir

I want a room with ...	Je veux une chambre avec ...
a bathroom	une salle de bain
a double bed	un grand lit
a shower	une douche
a television	une télévision
twin beds	des lits jumeaux
a view	une vue
a sca view	une vue sur la mer
a balcony	un balcon
a window	une fenêtre

CHECKING IN

We have a reservation.	Nous avons une réservation.
How much is it per night/ per person?	Quel est le prix par nuit/ par personne?
Is there a tax?	Est-ce qu'il y a une taxe de séjour?
Can I see it?	Je peux la voir?
Is there anything else?	Il n'y a rien d'autre?
Are there any cheaper/ quieter rooms?	Vous n'avez pas de chambres moins chères/bruyantes?
Can I see the bathroom?	Je peux voir la salle de bain?
Is there a reduction for students/children?	Est-ce que vous avez un tarif réduit pour les étudiants/ les enfants?
Is breakfast included?	Le petit déjeuner est compris?
Is there hot water all day?	Il y a de l'eau chaude pendant toute la journée?
Can I pay by credit card?	Je peux payer avec une carte de crédit?
Can I pay with travellers' cheques?	Je peux payer avec des chèques de voyage?
Do you require a deposit?	Il faut payer une caution?
Do I have to hire the bed linen or is it included?	Je dois payer les draps ou c'est compris dans la location?
Is there a lift/elevator?	Est-ce qu'il y a un ascenseur?
Where is the bathroom?	Où est la salle de bain?
It's fine/OK.	D'accord.
I'll take it.	C'est bien, je la prends.
We're not sure how long we're staying.	Nous ne savons pas exactement combien de temps nous resterons.

THEY MAY SAY ...

Est-ce que vous avez une pièce d'identité?
Do you have identification?

Votre carte d'adhérent, s'il vous plaît.
Your membership card, please.

Désolé/e, mais c'est complet.
Sorry, we're full.

Vous resterez combien de temps?
How long will you be staying?

Combien de nuits?
How many nights?

Le prix est de ... par nuit/par personne.
It's ... per night/per person.

REQUESTS & QUERIES

I need ...	J'ai besoin de ...
The key for room (331) please.	La clé de la chambre (331), s'il vous plaît.
Can you adjust the heating/ air-conditioning in my room?	Pouvez-vous régler le chauffage/la climatisation de ma chambre?
Do you have a safe where I can leave my valuables?	Est-ce que vous avez un coffre-fort pour déposer mes objets de valeur?
Is there somewhere to wash clothes?	Est-ce qu'il y a un endroit où on peut faire la lessive?
Can I use the kitchen?	Est-ce que je peux me servir de la cuisine?
What time is breakfast served?	A quelle heure sert-on le petit déjeuner?
Can we have breakfast served in our room?	On peut prendre le petit déjeuner dans la chambre?

Can I use the telephone?	Est-ce que je peux utiliser le téléphone?
If ... calls, please tell him/her I'm not here.	Si ... téléphone, dites-lui que je ne suis pas là.
Please wake me up at ...	Réveillez-moi à ..., s'il vous plaît.
The room needs to be cleaned.	Il faut nettoyer la chambre.
Please change the sheets.	Changez les draps, s'il vous plaît.
Can we have a cot?	On peut avoir un lit d'enfant?
Do you have a message for me?	Vous avez un message pour moi?
Can I leave a message for someone?	Je peux laisser un mot pour quelqu'un?

COMPLAINTS

The window is stuck.	La fenêtre est bloquée.
I've locked myself out of my room.	Je me suis enfermé/e dehors.
The toilet won't flush.	La chasse d'eau ne marche pas.
There is no hot water.	Il n'y a pas d'eau chaude.
I don't like this room.	Cette chambre ne me plaît pas.
It's too hot/cold in my room.	Il fait trop chaud/froid dans ma chambre.

HOLD YOUR TONGUE

Consonants at the end of a word are generally only pronounced when the following word begins with a vowel or a silent **h**. One exception is the letter **c** at the end of a word, eg **sec** is pronounced 'sek'.

It's too small.
Elle est trop petite.
It's noisy.
Elle est bruyante.
It's too dark.
Elle est trop sombre.
It's (too) expensive.
C'est (trop) cher.

CHECKING OUT

What's checkout time?	Quand faut-il régler (la note)?
Can I have a late checkout?	Pourrais-je régler plus tard?
I am/We are leaving now.	Je pars/Nous partons maintenant.
I would like to pay the bill.	Je voudrais régler (la note).
What is this charge for? (pointing)	Qu'est-ce que c'est?
Can I leave my luggage here until (tonight)?	Puis-je laisser mes bagages jusqu'à (ce soir)?
Please call me a taxi.	Appelez-moi un taxi, s'il vous plaît.

RENTING

The abbreviations F1, F2, F3, etc in a rental advertisement refer to the number of rooms in an apartment.

I would like to rent a house by the month/week.	Je voudrais louer une maison au mois/à la semaine.

I want to rent a (two-) bedroom apartment.	Je cherche à louer un appartement à (deux) pièces.
I'm looking for a furnished place.	Je cherche un meublé.
Do you have any rooms/ apartments for rent?	Avez-vous des chambres/ appartements à louer?
I'm looking for something close to ...	Je cherche quelque chose près ...
the city centre	du centre
the beach	de la plage
the railway station	de la gare
the shopping centre	du centre commercial
I'd like to look at the room/ apartment you have for rent.	Je voudrais voir la chambre/ l'appartement que vous louez.
Is there anything cheaper?	Y a-t-il quelque chose de moins cher?
Could I see it?	Je pourrais le/la voir?
I'd like to rent it for (one) month/week.	Je voudrais le/la louer pour (un) mois/(une) semaine.
How much is it per month/ week?	Combien cela coûte-t-il par mois/semaine?
Do you require a deposit?	Vous demandez une caution?
Do I get it back?	Je vais la récupérer?
Do I require fire and water damage insurance?	Est-ce que je dois prendre une assurance-incendie?

CROSSWORD – ACCOMMODATION

Across
2. No bath? Try this
4. Very unquiet
6. Device to open doors
8. Glass-filled hole in wall
10. Deposit

Down
1. Room
3. You'll want this in winter
5. Ideal place to sleep
7. To rent
9. Dark time of day

Answers on page 309.

AROUND TOWN

LOOKING FOR ...

I'm looking for ...	Je cherche ...
the art gallery	le musée (state); la galerie (private)
a bank	une banque
the church	l'église
the city centre	le centre-ville
the ... embassy	l'ambassade de ...
my hotel	mon hôtel
the market	le marché
the museum	le musée
the police station	le commissariat de police
the post office	le bureau de poste
a public toilet	des toilettes; WC
a telephone box	une cabine téléphonique
the tourist information office	l'office de tourisme; le syndicat d'initiative

What time does it open?	Quelle est l'heure d'ouverture?
What time does it close?	Quelle est l'heure de fermeture?
What street is this?	C'est quelle rue?
What suburb is this?	C'est quel quartier ici?

For directions see Getting Around, page 60.

AT THE BANK

Can I change money/travellers cheques here?	Est-ce que je peux changer de l'argent/des chèques de voyage ici?
I want to exchange some money/traveller's cheques.	Je veux changer de l'argent/des chèques de voyage.
What is the exchange rate?	Quel est le taux de change?

How many francs per dollar?	Quel est le cours du dollar?
What is your commission?	Quelle est votre commission?
Can I have smaller notes, please?	Je pourrais avoir de plus petites coupures, s'il vous plaît?
I'd like to open an account.	Je voudrais ouvrir un compte.
The ATM has swallowed my credit card.	Le guichet automatique/Le distributeur a avalé ma carte de crédit.
Can I use my credit card to withdraw money?	Pourrais-je utiliser ma carte de crédit pour retirer de l'argent?
Can I have money transferred here from my bank?	Est-ce que je peux faire un virement de mon compte en banque ici?
How long will I have to wait?	Combien de temps est-ce qu'il faudra attendre?
Has my money arrived?	Est-ce que mon argent est arrivé?

DID YOU KNOW ...

Metropolitan France is divided into **départements**. These départements are numbered alphabetically, that is, the département that comes first alphabetically is No. 1 and the département that comes last alphabetically is No. 95. Their numbers appear not only in every postcode but also on car number plates. This enables people from the provinces to exclaim **Encore des parisiens!** whenever they see a 75 number plate.

account — un compte
automatic teller machine; ATM — un distributeur (de billets); DAB
bank draft — une traite bancaire
bank notes — des billets de banque
coins — des pièces
credit card — une carte de crédit; une carte bleue; une carte bancaire
deposit — un dépôt
exchange — l'échange
identification — une pièce d'identité
loose change — de la petite monnaie
PIN number — code confidentiel
signature — la signature
teller; cashier — le caissier/la caissière
withdrawal — un retrait

AT THE POST OFFICE

I'd like to send ... — Je voudrais envoyer ...
an aerogram — un aérogramme
a letter — une lettre
a postcard — une carte postale
a parcel — un colis

I'd like some stamps. — Je voudrais des timbres.
How much does it cost to send this to ...? — À combien est-ce qu'il faut affranchir ceci pour ...?
Where is the poste restante section? — Où est le service de poste restante?
Is there any mail for ...? — Y a-t-il du courrier pour ...?

air mail — par avion
envelope — une enveloppe
express mail — par express
mail box — une boîte aux lettres
registered mail — en recommandé
surface mail — par voie de terre; par voie maritime

ON THE STREET

What is this?	Qu'est-ce que c'est?
What's happening?	Qu'est-ce qui se passe?
What has happened?	Qu'est-ce qui s'est passé?; Qu'est-ce qui est arrivé?
What's he/she doing?	Qu'est-ce qu'il/elle fait?
Can I have one, please?	Je peux en avoir un/e, s'il vous plaît?

People

artist	un artiste
beggar	un mendiant
busker	un musicien des rues
clown	un clown
dropout	un zonard
flower seller	un/e marchand/e de fleurs
fortune teller	une diseuse de bonne aventure
magician	un magicien
performing artist	un artiste
portrait sketcher	un dessinateur de rues
second-hand bookseller	un bouquiniste (in Paris)
street vendor	un marchand ambulant

Things

newspaper kiosk	le kiosque à journaux
festival	la fête
parade	le défilé (procession); la parade (ceremony)
street	la rue
street market	une braderie
second-hand market	une brocante
suburb	la banlieue

TELECOMMUNICATIONS

I want to ring ...	Je voudrais appeler ...
The number is ...	Le numéro est ...
I want to speak for threc minutes.	Je veux parler trois minutes.
How much does a three-minute call cost?	Quel est le prix d'une communication de trois minutes?
How much does each extra minute cost?	Quel est le prix de chaque minute supplémentaire?
I want to make a reverse-charges/collect call.	Je veux téléphoner en PCV.
I want to make a direct (person-to-person) call to ...	Je veux téléphoner avec préavis à ...
It's engaged.	La ligne est occupée.
I've been cut off.	J'ai été coupé.
Could you try again please?	Pouvez-vous essayer encore une fois, s'il vous plaît?
Is it OK to use my mobile phone here?	Je peux utiliser mon portable ici?
I'd like to rent a mobile phone.	Je voudrais louer un portable.
I want to send a fax.	Je veux envoyer un fax.
How much per page?	C'est combien la page?
Where can I use email?	Où est-ce que je peux utiliser le courrier électronique/ le e-mail?
Where can I use the Internet?	Où est-ce que je peux utiliser le Net?

answering machine	un répondeur automatique
operator	un opérateur/une opératrice
telephone card	une télécarte
telephone box	une cabine téléphonique
telephone book	un annuaire (du téléphone)
directory assistance	(le service des) renseignements

THEY MAY SAY ...

Oui, il/elle est là.	Yes, he/she is here.
Non, il/elle n'est pas là.	No, he/she is not here.
Un instant, s'il vous plaît.	One moment, please.
Je peux prendre un message?	Can I take a message?

Making a Call

Hello?	Allô?
Do you speak English?	Vous parlez anglais?
I would like to speak to ...	Je voudrais parler à ...
Is ... there?	Est-ce que ... est là?
Can I leave a message?	Je peux laisser un message?
When should I call again?	Quand pourrais-je rappeler?
Could you ask him/her to call me, please?	Pourriez-vous lui dire de me rappeler, s'il vous plaît?
My number is ...	Mon numéro est le ...
Thank you, goodbye.	Merci, au revoir.

PEOPLE

He/She dresses like a ...	Il/Elle est habillé/e comme ...
He/She is done up like a	Il/Elle est sapé/e comme ...
	Il/Elle est fringué/e comme ...
She/He is ...	C'est ...
a hippy	un/e hippy
a punk	un/e punk
a skinhead	un skinhead
a yuppy	un/e yuppie; un jeune cadre dynamique
a mohawk	un iroquois/une iriquoise
a tagger	un tagueur/une tagueuse
a tramp/bum	un clochard/une clocharde

SIGHTSEEING

Where is the tourist office?	Où est l'office de tourisme/le syndicat d'initiative?
Do you have a guidebook/ local map?	Est-ce que vous avez un guide touristique/une carte de la région?
What are the main attractions?	Quels sont les endroits les plus intéressants?
What time does it open?	Quelle est l'heure d'ouverture?
What time does it close?	Quelle est l'heure de fermeture?
Is there an admission charge?	Il faut payer l'entrée?
Is there a free day?	Est-ce qu'il y a un jour où l'entrée est gratuite?
Is there a discount for ...?	Il y a une réduction pour les ...?
pensioners	personnes du troisième âge
students	étudiants
children	enfants
What is that?	Qu'est-ce que c'est?; C'est quoi?
How old is it?	De quand date-t-il/elle?
Can I take photographs?	Je peux prendre des photos?

ancient	antique
archaeological	archéologique
beach	une plage
bridge	un pont
building	un bâtiment
castle	un château
cathedral	une cathédrale
caves	des grottes
church	une église
city walls	les remparts

COMBO

The vowel combination ai is not pronounced as the 'ai' in 'bait' but more like the 'e' in 'bet'. (See Pronunciation, page 15.)

concert hall	une salle de concert
convent	un couvent
library	une bibliothèque
main square	une place centrale
market	un marché
monastery	un monastère
monument	un monument
mosque	une mosquée
museum	un musée
old city	la vieille ville
palace	un palais
park	un parc

parliament	le parlement	statues	des statues
opera house	(le théâtre de) l'opéra	synagogue	une synagogue
		temple	un temple
ruins	des ruines	university	une université
stadium	un stade	zoo	un zoo

VERLAN

In the 1970s and 80s **verlan** arrived from the suburbs of big cities. Young people use this language, a sort of back slang where the second part of a word is put before the first part:

zicmu	(music)	music
un céfran	(français)	French
chébron	(branché)	with it; connected
delbor	(bordélique)	chaotic; shambolic
une meuf	(femme)	woman
un keum	(mec)	guy; chap
un keuf	(flic)	cop
un ripou	(pourri)	bent cop
une teuf	(fête)	party
vegra	(grave)	serious
un Beur	(Arabe)	Arab person
Laisse béton!	(tomber)	Give up!

CROSSWORD – AROUND TOWN

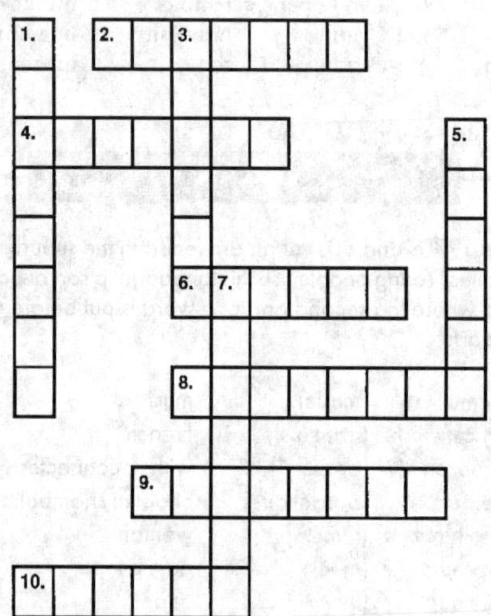

Across

2. Fix these to letters
4. Withdraw
6. Place of Christian worship
8. Mail
9. In-person meeting, say for a job
10. Home of royalty

Down

1. Type of phone beloved by yuppies
3. Old-fashioned retail area
5. To speak
7. Where speleologists venture

Answers on page 309.

GOING OUT

WHERE TO GO

In Paris you'll find information on cultural events, music, theatre, films, exhibitions, festivals, etc in two weekly publications: *Pariscope* and *L'Officiel des Spectacles*. They are available from most newsstands.

What's there to do in the evenings?	Qu'est-ce qu'on peut faire le soir?
Where can I find out what's on?	Où puis-je me renseigner sur ce qu'il y a à faire?
Is there an entertainment guide?	Il y a un guide des spectacles?
What's everyone doing tonight/this weekend?	Qu'est-ce que vous faites tous ce soir/ce week-end?
What's on tonight?	
(theatre, music)	Qu'est-ce qu'on joue ce soir?
(cinema)	Qu'est-ce qu'on passe ce soir?
I'd like to go ...	Je voudrais aller ...
to the cinema	au cinéma
to a concert	à un concert
to a disco	en boîte; dans une discothèque
to a restaurant	dans un restau(rant)
to the theatre	au théâtre

See page 119 for more on cinema and theatre.

INVITES

What are you doing tonight/this weekend?	Que fais-tu ce soir/ce week-end?
Let's go to the theatre/cinema.	Si on allait au théâtre/cinéma?

Do you want to go dancing?	Si nous allions danser?
Would you like to listen to a jazz band?	Aimerais-tu entendre un orchestre de jazz?
Do you prefer an opera, a concert or a ballet?	Tu préfères un opéra, un concert ou de la danse?
I'd love to come.	Je viendrai avec plaisir.

SWEARING

Shoot!/Damn!	Punaise!
Damn it/Dash!	Zut!; Mince!
Shit!	Merde!
Darn it/Bugger it!	Nom d'une pipe!; Nom d'un chien!
Bloody hell!	Putain! (which literally means 'whore')
Bastard!	Con; Connard!
God damn it!/God almighty!	Nom de Dieu!
to argue	se disputer (to quarrel); discuter; argumenter (to debate)
to swear	jurer
to swear like a trooper	jurer comme un charretier

NIGHTCLUBS & BARS

Are there any nightclubs here?	Est-ce qu'il y a des boîtes (de nuit) ici?
Are there places where you can hear local music?	Est-ce qu'il y a des endroits où on peut écouter de la musique locale?
How much is it to get in?	Quel est le prix de l'entrée?
What time should I get there?	A quelle heure dois-je être là?
What should I wear?	Comment dois-je m'habiller?
Can I go like this?	Je peux y aller comme ça?

Is there a door charge?	Est-ce qu'il faut payer l'entrée?
What sort of music do they play there?	Quel genre de musique on y joue?
Which is the best night to go?	Est-ce qu'il y a un soir mieux que les autres?
What band is playing tonight?	Quel groupe joue ce soir?
No performance tonight.	Ce soir, relâche.
What time does it open/shut?	À quelle heure ça ouvre/ferme?
Is it OK to go there on my own?	Je peux y aller tout/e seul/e.
It's great fun!	On s'éclate!
I feel great!	J'ai la pêche!

concert	un concert
dance floor	la piste (de danse)
disc jockey	un disc-jockey; un DJ ('dee-jay')
gig	un concert
nightclub	une discothèque; une boîte
to go clubbing	sortir en boîte
party; night out	une soirée
performance	un spectacle
pub; bar	un bar
rave	une rave
show	un spectacle; un show
ticket office	un guichet

ARRANGING TO MEET

What time will you be there?	À quelle heure y seras-tu?
What time shall we meet?	On se retrouve à quelle heure?
Where shall we meet?	On se retrouve où?
Let's meet at (eight o'clock) outside the ...	On peut se retrouver à (huit heures) devant la porte de ...
OK, I'll see you then.	D'accord, j'y serai.

I'll be there at (six). J'y serai à (six heures).
I'll pick you up at (seven). Je viendrai te chercher à (sept heures).
I'll try to be on time. J'essaierai d'être à l'heure.
If I'm not there by (nine) don't wait for me. Si je ne suis pas là avant (neuf heures) ne m'attends pas.
I'll be along later. Where will you be? J'arriverai plus tard. Où seras-tu?
See you later. À plus tard; À tout à l'heure.
See you on Friday. À vendredi.
Sorry I'm late. Désolé/e, je suis en retard.
Never mind. Ce n'est pas grave.
That's OK. Ça va.
Make yourself at home. Fais comme chez toi.
Come any time. Tu viens quand tu veux.
Come for a drink. Viens prendre l'apéro.

Afterwards

It was nice talking to you.
C'était sympa de parler avec toi.
It was nice to meet you.
C'était sympa de faire ta connaissance.
I have to go now.
Je dois m'en aller maintenant.

DANGEROUS LIAISONS

When one word ends in a consonant and the next word begins with a vowel, run the sounds together as if they were one word: **Vous avez** ('you have') sounds like 'voozavay'.

I had a great day/night. C'était vraiment une journée/une soirée sympa.
I hope to see you again soon. J'espère te revoir bientôt.
I'll give you a call. Je t'appellerai.
See you soon. À bientôt.
We must do this again. On doit refaire .

DATING & ROMANCE

Breaking the Ice

Do you mind if I sit here?	Je peux m'asseoir ici?
What about a drink?	Si on buvait quelque chose?
Do you want to dance?	Tu veux danser?
Shall we get some fresh air?	Nous allons prendre l'air?
Do you have a girlfriend/ boyfriend?	Tu as une petite amie/ un petit ami?
Here's my telephone number.	Voici mon numéro de téléphone.
May I call you?	Je peux t'appeler?
Can I take you home?	Je peux te ramener chez toi?

CLASSIC PICK-UP LINES

Haven't we met before?	Je crois qu'on se connaît?
Would you like a cigarette?	Tu veux une cigarette?
Would you like a drink?	Tu veux boire quelque chose?
Do you have a light?	Tu as du feu?
Your place or mine?	Chez toi ou chez moi?

Rejections

No, thank you.	Non, merci.
I'm waiting for someone.	J'attends quelqu'un.
You are very nosey.	Vous êtes vraiment indiscret/ indiscrète.
I'm happy on my own, thank you.	Je suis bien tout/e seul/e, merci.
I'd rather be alone, thank you.	Je préférerais rester seul/e, merci.
That's none of your business.	Ça ne vous regarde pas.

I'm not interested.	Ça ne m'intéresse pas.
Leave me alone!	Laissez-moi (tranquille), s'il vous plaît.
I don't find you attractive.	Je ne vous trouve pas attirant/e.
Don't touch me!	Ne me touchez pas!

CLASSIC REJECTION LINES

Get lost!	**Allez-vous-en!; Dégagez!**
I have plans tonight.	**Je suis occupé/e ce soir.**
I'm not on my own.	**Je ne suis pas seul/e.**
You're not my type.	**Vous n'êtes pas mon genre.**
I don't want to get involved.	**Je ne veux pas m'engager.**
I'm gay.	**Je suis homosexuel/ lesbienne.**

The Date

Are you free this evening?	Es-tu libre ce soir?
What are you doing tonight/ this weekend.	Que fais-tu ce soir/ ce week-end?
Would you like to go out somewhere?	Tu veux qu'on aille quelque part?
May I take you to dinner?	Je peux t'inviter à dîner?
Yes, I'd love to.	Oui, j'aimerais bien.
No, I'm sorry, I can't.	Non, je suis désolé/e, je ne peux pas.
Where would you like to go?	Où aimerais-tu aller?
What would you like to do?	Qu'est-ce que tu aimerais faire?
What about tomorrow/ Saturday?	Si on disait demain/samedi?

DID YOU KNOW ...

If someone is staring at you, you could say **On se connaît?** ('Have we met?') or, if you want to be slightly more aggressive, **Vous voulez ma photo?** ('Do you want my photo?')

What's your phone number?	Quel est ton numéro de téléphone?
I'll pick you up at the hotel.	Je passerai te prendre à ton hôtel.
Will you take me home?	Tu veux bien me ramener (chez moi)?
Do you want to come back to my place?	Tu veux venir chez moi?
I'd like to go now.	J'aimerais partir maintenant.
I'd like to go back to your place.	Je voudrais aller chez toi.
Please call me a taxi.	Appelle-moi un taxi, s'il te plaît.
Thanks for a lovely evening.	Merci pour cette agréable soirée.
Can I see you again tomorrow?	On se revoit demain?
Can I call you tomorrow?	Je peux t'appeler demain?
Do you want to come inside for a while?	Tu veux entrer un instant?

For more phrases on going out, see page 91.

Useful Words

affair
une liaison
an intimate dinner for two
un dîner en tête-à-tête
boyfriend
un petit ami; un copain
date (n)
un rendez-vous

THEY MAY SAY ...

On se téléphone, on se fait une bouffe!

I'll ring you, we'll have dinner together sometime.

girlfriend	une petite amie; une copine
one-night stand	une passade; une aventure
single	célibataire
to be engaged	être fiancé/e

to chat up	baratiner; draguer
to court	faire la cour à; courtiser
to date; to go out together	se fréquenter
to fall in love	tomber amoureux
to get engaged	se fiancer
to go out with; to date	sortir avec

In the Bedroom

I want you.	Je te désire; Je te veux; J'ai envie de toi.
I want to make love to you.	Je veux faire l'amour avec toi.
Let's go to bed.	Allons au lit.
Do you have a condom?	Tu as un préservatif?
I'd like you to use a condom.	Je voudrais que tu utilises un préservatif.
I won't do it without a condom.	Je ne vais pas le faire sans préservatif.
I take the proper precaution.	Je me protège.
I think we should stop now.	Il faut arrêter maintenant.

INTIMATE FRENCH

Do you like this?	Tu aimes ça?
Kiss me.	Embrasse-moi.
I like that.	J'aime ça.
I don't like that.	Je n'aime pas ça.
That feels good.	Ça fait du bien; C'est bon.
Please stop.	Arrête, s'il te plaît.
Please don't stop.	N'arrête pas, s'il te plaît.
Tie me up.	Attache-moi!
I'm coming.	Ça vient!
Touch me here/there.	Touche-moi ici/là.
You're fantastic.	Tu es fantastique/super.
You're hot stuff.	Tu es canon.

FRISKY FRENCH

caress	une caresse
condom	un préservatif
fetish	un fétiche
French letter	une capote (anglaise)
to fuck	baiser
kiss	un baiser
to kiss	embrasser
lover	un amant/une amante
orgasm	un orgasme
safe sex	des rapports sexuels protégés
to get laid	s'envoyer en l'air

I really like your ...	J'aime ...
body	ton corps
breasts	tes seins
bum/ass	ton derrière; ton cul
eyes	tes yeux
hair	tes cheveux
lips	tes lèvres
mouth	ta bouche
skin	ta peau

But Don't Forget ...

AIDS	le SIDA
HIV	le VIH (virus immunodéficitaire humaine)
STD	une MST (maladie sexuellement transmissible)

DID YOU KNOW ...

The noun **un baiser** means 'a kiss'. Be careful that you don't confuse this with the verb **baiser** which means 'to fuck'!

evening star	l'étoile du berger
full moon	la pleine lune
galaxy	une galaxie
light-year	une année-lumière
milky way	la voie lactée
moon/sun eclipse	une éclipse de lune/de soleil
nebula	une nébuleuse
new moon	la nouvelle lune
northern hemisphere	l'hémisphère nord
planet	une planète
pole star	l'étoile polaire
shooting star	une étoile filante
solar system	le système solaire
southern hemisphere	l'hémisphère sud
space probe	une sonde
space program	un programme spatial
space rocket	une fusée interplanétaire
star	une étoile
telescope	une lunette astronomique; un télescope
universe	l'univers

The Unknown

Do you believe in ...?	Croyez-vous ...?
UFOs	aux OVNI (objets volants non identifiés)
extraterrestrials	aux extra-terrestres
ghosts	aux fantômes
life after death	à la vie après la mort
life on Mars	à la vie sur Mars
reincarnation	à la réincarnation
telepathy	à la télépathie
withcraft/sorcery	à la sorcellerie

passive	passifs
shy	timides
stubborn	obstinés; têtus
jealous	jaloux
warm	chaleureux
sensual	sensuels

Do you want me to do your horoscope?
    Veux-tu que je fasse ton horoscope?
Do you know your astrological chart?
    Tu connais ton thème astral?

M or F?

If you are having trouble deciding whether a word is masculine or feminine, you can often guess by the ending of the word. See page 20.

Astronomy

The names of the planets are the same as in English, with the exception of La Terre (Earth).

Is there an observatory near here?	Est-ce qu'il y a un observatoire près d'ici?

astrodynamics	l'astrodynamique
astrophysics	l'astrophysique
atom	un atome
big bang theory	la théorie du big bang
black hole	un trou noir
comet	une comète
constellation	une constellation
cosmology	la cosmologie
cosmos	le cosmos

Afterwards

That was great.	C'était super/génial.
How was it for you?	Comment c'était pour toi?
You're a great lover.	Tu es un/e amant/e génial/e.
Let's do it again!	Encore une fois; On recommence!
I'm knackered/wiped out.	Je suis crevé/e.
Do you want a cigarette?	Tu veux une cigarette?
Can I stay the night?	Est-ce que je peux rester la nuit?
You can't stay here tonight.	Tu ne peux pas rester ici ce soir.
When can I see you again?	Je peux te revoir quand?
I'll call you.	Je t'appelle.
Do you want to keep seeing each other?	Tu veux qu'on continue à se voir?

MY LITTLE CABBAGE

Here are some affectionate names used in French with their literal meanings in English.

mon chéri/ma chérie	my darling
mon amour	my love
ma biche/bichette	my doe (yes, the animal)
mon coco	my little egg
ma cocotte	my little hen
mon (petit) chou	my little cabbage
mon (petit) canard	my little duck
mon (petit) chaton	my little kitten
ma (petite) caille	my little quail
ma (petite) puce	my little flea

Love

I think I'm falling in love. — Je crois que je tombe amoureux/amoureuse.
I love you. — Je t'aime.
My darling. — Mon chéri/Ma chérie.
I'll never forget you. — Je ne t'oublierai jamais.
It's love at first sight. — C'est le coup de foudre.
I'm in love. — Je suis amoureux/amoureuse.
Do you love me? — Tu m'aimes?

Do you want to go out with me? — Veux-tu sortir avec moi?
Let's move in together! — Vivons ensemble!
Will you marry me? — Veux-tu m'épouser?
Why not? — Pourquoi pas?
Don't laugh, I'm not kidding. — Ne ris pas, je suis sérieux/sérieuse.

OUT OF SIGHT

Love is blind. — L'amour est aveugle.
Out of sight, out of mind. — Loin des yeux, loin du cœur.

Leaving & Breaking Up

I have to leave tomorrow. — Je dois partir demain.
I'll miss you. — Tu me manqueras.

When the French want to say that they miss someone or something, they say that someone or something misses them, ie the person or thing that is missed is the subject. So, the above sentence literally means 'You will miss (to) me.'

I'll come and visit you. — Je viendrai te voir.
Can I have your address/phone number? — Tu peux me donner ton adresse/numéro?

Come back with me.	Rentre avec moi.
I really want to keep in touch with you.	Je tiens à rester en contact avec toi.
Will I see you again?	Est-ce que je vais te revoir?
I don't think it's working out.	Je ne pense pas que ça marche.
I want to end the relationship.	Je veux arrêter notre relation; Je veux rompre avec toi.
I want to stay friends.	Je veux que nous restions amis.
I'll never forget you.	Je ne t'oublierai jamais.
Don't forget me!	Ne m'oublie pas!
I don't love you.	Je ne t'aime pas.
I don't love you any more.	Je ne t'aime plus.
Is there someone else?	Il y a quelqu'un d'autre?
I've met someone else.	J'ai rencontré quelqu'un d'autre.

WEATHER

It's ...	Il fait ...
cold	froid
hot	chaud
sunny	beau
windy	du vent
It's cloudy.	Le temps est couvert; Il y a des nuages.
It's raining.	Il pleut.
It's snowing.	Il neige.
It's nice today.	Il fait beau aujourd'hui.
Will it be ... tomorrow?	Est-ce qu'il fera ... demain?

CROSSWORD – GOING OUT

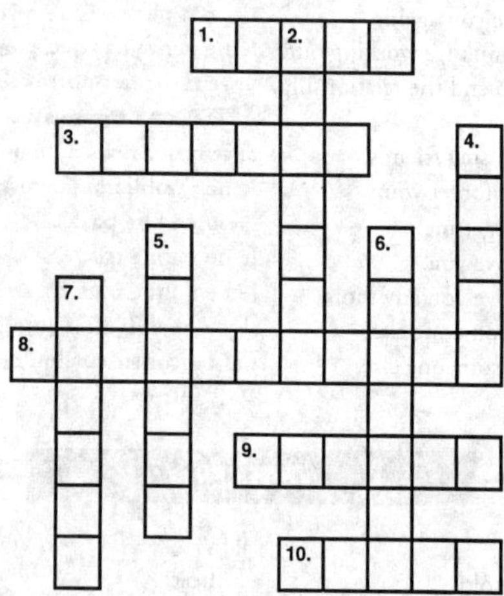

Across

1. Free
3. To chat up
8. Unmarried
9. 'French' version includes tongues
10. Evening meal

Down

2. Will happen before long
4. Floor on which to shake your booty
5. Period between afternoon and the dead of night.
6. Social lubricant
7. He is sorry

Answers on page 309.

THE FAMILY

QUESTIONS

Are you married?	Vous êtes marié/e? (pol) Tu es marié/e? (inf)
Do you have any children?	Vous avez des enfants? (pol) Tu as des enfants? (inf)
How many children do you have?	Vous avez combien d'enfants? (pol) Tu as combien d'enfants? (inf)
How old are they?	Quel âge ont-ils (m)/ ont-elles (f)?
Do you live with your family?	Vous habitez chez vos parents? (pol) Tu habites chez tes parents? (inf)
Do you live alone?	Vous vivez seul/e? (pol) Tu vis seul/e? (inf)
How many sisters/brothers do you have?	Vous avez combien de sœurs/ frères? (pol) Tu as combien de sœurs/ frères? (inf)
Is your husband/wife here?	Est-ce que votre mari/femme est là?
Do you have a boyfriend/ girlfriend?	Vous avez un petit ami/une petite amie? (pol) Tu as un petit ami/une petite amie? (inf)

REPLIES

I'm single.	Je suis célibataire.
I'm married.	Je suis marié/e.
I'm separated.	Je suis séparé/e.

I'm divorced.	Je suis divorcé/e.
I'm a widower/widow.	Je suis veuf/veuve.
I'm engaged.	Je suis fiancé/e.
I don't have any children.	Je n'ai pas d'enfants.
I have a daughter/a son.	J'ai une fille/un fils.
I have a partner/boyfriend/ girlfriend.	J'ai un/e (petit/e) ami/e.
My partner and I live together but we're not married.	Mon ami/e et moi nous vivons ensemble, mais nous ne sommes pas mariés.

FAMILY MEMBERS

baby	un bébé
boy	un garçon
brother	un frère
children	des enfants
daughter	une fille
family	une famille
father	un père
girl	une fille
grandparents	des grands-parents
grandfather	un grand-père
grandmother	une grand-mère
husband	un mari; un époux
mother	une mère
sister	une sœur
son	un fils
wife	une femme; une épouse

The same word is used to mean both 'half brother/sister' and 'step brother/sister' – demi-frère/sœur. The word beau/belle (literally, 'beautiful') is used with names of family members to mean '...-in-law'. When used in front of père, mère, fille and fils, it can also mean 'step-...'.

TALKING WITH CHILDREN

What an adorable little girl!	Quelle adorable petite fille!
What an adorable little boy!	Quel adorable petit garçon!
How old are you?	Quel âge as-tu?
Have you started school yet?	Tu vas déjà à l'école?
Do you like school?	L'école te plaît?
Is your teacher nice?	Ta maîtresse est gentille?

Children aged three to 10 have a maîtresse, older ones have a professeur (or prof).

Do you have a pet at home?	Tu as un animal à la maison?
Do you do sport?	Tu fais du sport?
What do you do after school?	Que fais-tu après l'école?

DID YOU KNOW ...

When kids lose their teeth, you say **Est-ce que la petite souris est passée?**, literally, 'Did the little mouse come?'.

When's your birthday?	C'est quand ton anniversaire?
Have you got brothers and sisters?	Tu as des frères et des sœurs?
Do you learn English?	Tu apprends l'anglais?
What did she bring you?	Qu'est-ce qu'elle t'a apporté?

TONGUE TWISTERS

Some popular kids' tongue twisters:

Un chasseur sachant chasser sait chasser sans son chien.	'A hunter able to hunt can hunt without his dog.'
Les chaussettes de l'archi-duchesse sont-elles sèches, archisèches?	'Are the archduchess's socks dry, completely dry?'

Mum	Maman
Dad	Papa
Granny	Mamie; Mémé
Grandad	Papi; Pépé
Aunt; Auntie	Tante; Tatie; Tata
Uncle	Oncle; Tonton
first name	prénom
nickname	surnom
surname	nom de famille
sweet little face	une frimousse
pain	un bobo
to be hurt; have a pain	avoir bobo
swear word; naughty word	un gros mot
beddy-byes	dodo
doggie	un toutou
gee-gee	un dada
Giddy up!	Hue (dada)!

TALKING WITH PARENTS

What a cute baby!	Qu'il est mignon! Qu'elle est mignonne!
He's/She's a real darling!	C'est un amour!
How old is she?	Quel âge a-t-elle?
What's his name?	Comment s'appelle-t-il?
How old is the eldest?	Quel âge a l'aîné/e?
How old is the youngest?	Quel âge a le dernier/ la dernière?

Cadet/cadette also means the youngest but often you will hear people use the word benjamin/benjamine as well.

She is very like you.	Elle vous ressemble beaucoup.
He is very like his mother.	Il ressemble beaucoup à sa mère.
Do they go to school or kindergarten?	Ils/Elles vont à l'école ou au jardin d'enfants?
Who looks after the children?	Qui s'occupe des enfants?
When is the baby due?	C'est pour quand?

PETS

Do you like animals?
Vous aimez les animaux?

Do you have any pets?
Avez-vous des animaux?

What a cute puppy!
Qu'il est mignon!

SEA IS FOR KAT

The letter **c** is pronounced as the English 'k' before **a**, **o** and **u**, but like the 's' as in 'sun' before **e**, **i** and **y**.

Which breed is it?	Il/Elle est de quelle race?
Is it male or female?	C'est un mâle ou une femelle?
Does it bite?	Est-ce qu'il/elle mord?

ANIMALS IN EXPRESSIONS

In God's name!	Nom d'un chien! – *in the name of a dog*
He has bats in the belfry.	Il a une araignée au plafond. – *he has a spider on the ceiling*
It's there to be used.	Ce n'est pas fait pour les chiens. – *it isn't done for dogs*
I have other fish to fry.	J'ai d'autres chats à fouetter. – *I have other cats to whip*
Don't count your chickens before they're hatched.	Ne vendez pas la peau de l'ours avant de l'avoir tué. – *don't sell the bear's skin before killing it*
When pigs fly!	Quand les poules auront des dents! – *when hens have teeth*
to murder the French language	parler français comme une vache espagnole – *to speak French like a Spanish cow*
to be bad-tempered	avoir un caractère de chien – *to have the nature of a dog*
to fight like cat and dog	s'entendre comme chien et chat
a dog's life	une vie de chien
foul/lousy weather	un temps de chien – *dog's weather*
in the twilight	entre chien et loup – *between dog and wolf*

SIGNS

(ATTENTION) CHIEN MÉCHANT	BEWARE OF THE DOG
SPA (Société Protectrice des Animaux)	(R)SPCA

I have a/an ...	J'ai ...
animal	un animal
bird	un oiseau
cat	un chat
dog	un chien
fish	un poisson
goldfish	un poisson rouge
guide dog	un chien d'aveugle
ordinary/alley cat	un chat de gouttière
insect	un insecte
kitten	un chaton
mutt; pooch	un cabot; un clébard
pet	un animal familier
puppy	un chiot
pussycat	un minet; un minou

CROSSWORD – THE FAMILY

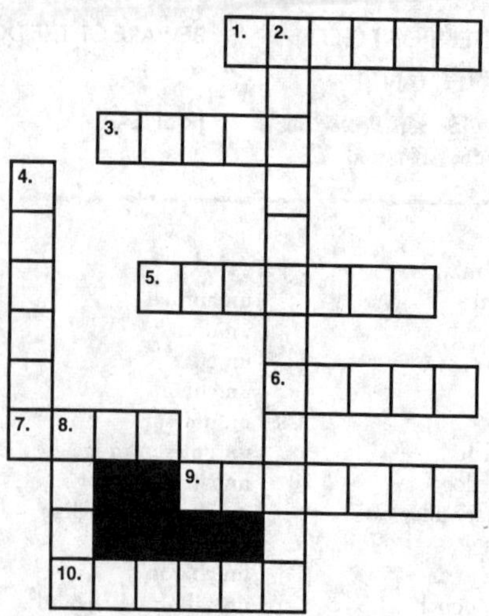

Across

1. Prepubescent male
3. Man's best friend
5. Airborne creatures
6. Female sibling
7. This person always has a wife
9. Animal happiest in water

10 Indispensable to a husband

Down

2. Everyone celebrates theirs just once a year
4. Also called Christian name
8. Eldest son

Answers on page 309.

COMMON INTERESTS

An enthusiast or fan of a sport, hobby or particular interest is called un amateur

What do you do in your spare time?	Que fais-tu pendant tes loisirs?
Do you like ...?	Aimes-tu ...?
I like ...	J'aime ...
I don't like ...	Je n'aime pas ...
dancing	la danse
films	le cinéma
good food	la bonne cuisine; la bonne bouffe (inf)
football	le football
going out	sortir
going to the beach	aller à la plage
keeping fit	faire de l'exercice
hiking	la marche; la randonnée
music	la musique
photography	la photographie
reading	lire
playing sport	faire du sport
watching sport on TV	regarder le sport à la télé
shopping	faire des courses/du shopping
travelling	voyager
meeting people	rencontrer des gens

DID YOU KNOW ...

A library is une bibliothèque, a bookshop is une librairie.

STAYING IN TOUCH – THE LETTER

For official letters, such as job or visa applications, write your address in the top left-hand corner and your correspondent's address in the top right. Abbreviations are not used and the writing style is rather elaborate.

How are you?	Comment allez-vous? (pol) Comment vas-tu? (inf)
Thanks for ...	Je vous (pol)/te (inf) remercie de ...
Sorry for writing so late.	Je suis désolé/e de répondre si tard.

BEGINNING A LETTER

Informal	*Formal*
Cher Marc	Cher Monsieur
Chère Sophie	Chère Madame

ENDING A LETTER

Informal	*Formal*
Grosses bises (big kisses)	Cordialement (kind regards)
Je t'embrasse (I kiss you)	Amicalement (best wishes)
Bisous (kisses)	Amitiés (very best wishes)

VERY FORMAL LETTERS

Je vous prie d'agréer Madame/Monsieur (l'expression de) mes sentiments distingués
(Yours sincerely; Yours faithfully)

Dans l'attente de vous lire
(looking forward to your reply)

STAYING IN TOUCH

Tomorrow's my last day here.	Demain je passe ma dernière journée ici.
I'd like to write to you.	Je voudrais t'écrire.
I'll write to you.	Je t'écrirai.
I'll send you some photos.	Je t'enverrai des photos.
Let's swap addresses.	Échangeons nos adresses.
Do you have a pen and paper?	Tu as un stylo et du papier?
What's your address?	Quelle est ton adresse?
Here's my address.	Voici mon adresse.
If you ever visit (Scotland) you must come and visit us.	Si un jour tu voyages en (Ecosse) il faut nous rendre visite.
Whenever you come to (Melbourne), you've got a place to stay.	Quand tu viendras à (Melbourne) tu auras une chambre à toi.
Do you have an email address?	As-tu une adresse électronique/un e-mail?

ART

There are two major art magazines in France: *Beaux-Arts* (painting, sculpture, architecture, photography) and *L'estampille, l'objet d'art* (mainly technologically-based art).

I'd like to visit a city of artistic interest.	J'aimerais visiter une ville d'art.
Where can I see (Cézanne's) works?	Où pourrais-je voir des œuvres de (Cézanne)?
Which works are exhibited here?	Quelles œuvres sont exposées ici?
Whose works are exhibited here?	De qui sont les œuvres exposées ici?
I'm interested in (19th-century) art.	Je m'intéresse à l'art du (dix-neuvième) siècle.
I can't get into abstract art.	L'art abstrait, j'ai du mal à accrocher.

EVERYONE'S A CRITIC I

What do you think of (the work of) ...?	Qu'est-ce que tu penses (des œuvres) de ...?
It's ...	C'est ...
awful	affreux
beautiful	beau
interesting	intéressant
unusual	pas commun
It's reminiscent of ...	Ça me rappelle ...

Useful Words

abstract art	l'art abstrait
architecture	l'architecture
art gallery	un musée (state-owned); une galerie (private)
artist	un/e artiste
canvas	une toile
computer-aided	assisté par ordinateur
contemporary art	l'art contemporain
cyber art	l'art cybernétique
engraver	un graveur
exhibition	une exposition
figurativre art	l'art figuratif
graphic art	les arts graphiques
kinetic art	l'art cinétique
masterpiece	un chef d'œuvre
movement	un mouvement (artistique)
multimedia	le multimédia
painter	un/e peintre
painting	la peinture (the art); un tableau (a picture)
oil painting	une peinture à l'huile

watercolour	une aquarelle
sculptor	un sculpteur
sculpture	la sculpture
studio	un atelier (d'artiste)
style	un style
technological art	l'art technologique
work (n)	une œuvre

MUSIC

Talking About It

Do you like music?	Tu aimes la musique?
What sort of music do you like?	Quel genre de musique aimes-tu?
Which bands do you like?	Quels groupes aimes-tu?
Have you heard ...?	As-tu déjà entendu ... ?
I like ...	J'aime ...

Names of types of modern music are the same as in English.

I like classical music.	J'aime la musique classique.
Where can I hear live music/ an original band?	Où puis-je écouter de la musique live/un groupe original?
Which radio stations plays ...?	Quelle station de radio passe ...?
Where can I buy this music?	Où puis-je trouver ce type de musique?
Where can I buy sheet music?	Où puis-je acheter des partitions?
Where can I get music lessons?	Où puis-je prendre des leçons de musique?
It's elevator music!	C'est de la musique de supermarché!

Playing It

Do you play an instrument?	Tu joues d'un instrument?
What do you play?	De quel instrument joues-tu?

I play ...	Je joue ...
bass guitar	de la (guitare) basse
bassoon	du basson
cello	du violoncelle
clarinet	de la clarinette
drums	de la batterie
flute	de la flûte
guitar	de la guitare
keyboard	du clavier
lead guitar	de la guitare principale
oboe	du hautbois
percussion	des percussions
rhythm guitar	de la guitare rythmique
sax	du saxophone; du saxo
violin	du violon

ZZZZZZ!

The letter **s** between two vowels is pronounced as a 'z'.

For example **poésie** ('poetry') is pronounced 'poh-ay-zee'.

Useful Words

band	un groupe; un orchestre
gig	un concert
manager	un imprésario
music shop	un disquaire
orchestra	un orchestre
record producer	un producteur de disques
recording studio	un studio d'enregistrement
rock group	un groupe rock
score	une partition
show	un spectacle
singer	un chanteur/une chanteuse
songwriter	un auteur-compositeur
song	une chanson
sound engineer	un ingénieur du son
tune	un air
voice	une voix

For more phrases on music see On Tour, page 226.

CINEMA & THEATRE

If you want to see a foreign film that is not dubbed into French, look for the letters VO or VOST (version originale sous-titrée français – 'original version, French subtitles') in film listings or on advertising posters. A film dubbed into French will have the letters VF (version française).

What sort of films do you like? Quel genre de films aimes-tu?

I like ...	J'aime ...
I don't like ...	Je n'aime pas ...
action films	les films d'action
animation	l'animation
art films	les films d'art et d'essai
avant-garde films	les films d'avant-garde
comedies	les films comiques

documentaries	les documentaires
dramas	les comédies dramatiques
fantasy films	les films fantastiques
films noir	les films noirs
horror films	les films d'horreur
melodramas	les mélodrames
psychodramas	les drames psychologiques
science-fiction films	les films de science-fiction
short films	les courts métrages
thrillers	les (films) policiers; les polars

EVERYONE'S A CRITIC II

Did you like it?	Tu l'as aimé?
I liked it very much.	Je l'ai beaucoup aimé.
I didn't like it very much.	Je ne l'ai pas beaucoup aimé.
I thought it was ...	J'ai trouvé ça ...
boring	ennuyeux
excellent	excellent
funny	drôle
interesting	intéressant
It wasn't bad.	Ce n'était pas mal.
I had a few problems with the language.	J'ai eu quelques problèmes avec la langue.

Who is your favourite director?	Qui est ton cinéaste préféré?
Where can I see ...?	Où pourrais-je voir ...?
I feel like seeing a/an ...	J'aimerais bien voir un/e ...
What's on tonight?	Qu'est-ce qui passe ce soir?

Where can I find a cinema guide?	Où pourrais-je trouver un programme des films?
Is it in English?	C'est en anglais?
Is it dubbed or subtitled?	C'est doublé ou sous-titré?
Are there any tickets left for ...?	Il y a encore des places pour ...?
Sorry, we're sold out.	Désolé/e, nous n'en avons plus.
Have you seen the latest Téchiné film?	As-tu vu le dernier Téchiné?
Who's in it?	Qui joue dans ce film?
Who directed it?	Qui a réalisé ce film?

Useful Words

actor	un acteur/une actrice
angle	un angle
ballet	un ballet
box-office success	un film à succès
camera work	une prise de vue
cinema	le cinéma; le ciné (inf); le cinoche (inf); le septième art (lit: 'the seventh art')
close-up	un gros plan
director	un/e cinéaste
intermission	l'entracte
long shot	un plan d'ensemble
musical	une comédie musicale
opera	l'opéra
play	une pièce (de théâtre)
producer	un producteur
production	une production
silent/talking film	un film muet/parlant
stage	la scène
subtitles	les sous-titres
theatre	le théâtre

LITERATURE

What kind of books do you read?	Quel genre de livres lis-tu?
Who is your favourite author?	Quel est ton auteur préféré?
I like ...	J'aime ...
biography; autobiography	les biographies; les autobiographies
comics	les bandes dessinées (BD)
crime/detective novels	les romans policiers
erotic literature	la littérature érotique
fantasy	la littérature fantastique
fiction	la fiction
historical novels	les romans historiques
horror	les romans d'épouvante
mysteries	les romans policiers
novels	les romans
poetry	la poésie
romance	le roman d'amour; le roman à l'eau de rose
science fiction	la science-fiction
short stories	les nouvelles
the classics	les classiques
thrillers	les romans à suspense
travel writing	les récits de voyage

DID YOU KNOW ...

The longest French books are *Les hommes de bonne volonté* by Jules Romains which has 17 volumes, and *À la recherche du temps perdu* by Marcel Proust which has seven volumes and a total of 1,310,000 words.

Do you read in other languages? — Tu lis dans d'autres langues?
Can you recommend a good book? — Tu peux me recommander un bon livre?

For more phrases on buying books, see Shopping, page 143.

EVERYONE'S A CRITIC III

Have you read ...?	As-tu lu ...?
What did you think of ...?	Que penses-tu de ...?
I thought it was ...	J'ai trouvé que c'était ...
badly written	mal écrit
boring	ennuyeux
interesting	intéressant
excellent	excellent
well-written	bien écrit
better/worse than his/her previous book	mieux/pire que son livre précédent
It was a real page turner.	Je l'ai lu d'une traite.

HOBBIES

Do you have any hobbies? — Est-ce que tu as des hobbies/des passe-temps?

Are there any games clubs here? — Y a-t-il des clubs de jeux ici?
I like ... — J'aime bien ...
I practise ... — Je fais du (m)/de la (f) ...
I collect ... — Je fais collection de ...

bird-watching — l'ornithologie
body building — le culturisme
book collector — un/e bibliophile

caving	la spéléologie
choir	une chorale
clay	l'argile
coin collector	un/e numismate
collect	collectionner
collector of model cars/ railways/planes etc	un collectionneur/une collectionneuse de modèles réduits
comics	la BD
cooking	la cuisine
dancing	la danse
decorating	la décoration
DIY	le bricolage
embroidery	la broderie
fencing	l'escrime
fishing	la pêche
framing	l'encadrement
gardening	le jardinage
genealogy	la généalogie
knitting	le tricot
martial arts	les arts martiaux
naturism	naturisme
needlework	les travaux d'aiguille
potter	un potier
pottery	la poterie
seashells	coquillages
sewing	la couture
sewing pattern	un patron
singing	le chant
stamp collector	un/e philatéliste
train spotting	l'observation des trains
travelling	les voyages
video game	un jeu vidéo
weaving	le tissage
woodwork	menuiserie
xylography	la xylographie; la gravure sur bois

TRAVEL

Do you travel often?	Vous voyagez souvent?
I love to travel.	J'adore voyager.
What do you think of ...?	Qu'est-ce que vous pensez de ...?
I think it's ...	Je pense que c'est ...
boring	ennuyeux
exciting	génial; super
expensive	cher
Are there too many tourists?	Il y a trop de touristes?
Is it unsafe to go alone?	C'est risqué d'y aller seul/e?
When is the best time to go?	Quelle est la meilleure période pour partir?
Is it expensive?	C'est cher?
How long have you been away from home?	Depuis quand êtes-vous parti de chez vous?
I'd like to travel round the world.	J'aimerais faire le tour du monde.

TALKING WITH OTHER TRAVELLERS

Are you staying long here?	Vous restez longtemps ici?
I'm staying here for ... days/weeks.	Je reste ici ... jours/semaines.
Where have you been on this trip?	Où êtes-vous allé pendant votre séjour?
Where are you going next?	Où allez-vous après?
We are going to ... next.	Après nous allons à ...
Do you know anyone here/there?	Vous connaissez quelqu'un ici/là?

I prefer to travel light.
Je préfère voyager avec un minimum de bagages.
I had a very nice trip.
J'ai fait un beau voyage.

THEY MAY SAY ...

Les voyages forment la jeunesse.
Travel broadens the mind.

literally, 'travel develops the youth'

STARS

Astrology

What is your star sign? — Tu est de quel signe?

I'm a/an ...	Je suis ...
Capricorn	Capricorne
Aquarius	Verseau
Pisces	Poisson
Aries	Bélier
Taurus	Taureau
Gemini	Gémeaux
Cancer	Cancer
Leo	Lion
Virgo	Vierge
Libra	Balance
Scorpio	Scorpion
Sagittarius	Sagittaire

(Leos) are very ...	Les (Lions) sont très ...
affectionate	affectueux
aggressive	agressifs
loving	aimants
loyal	loyaux
outgoing	ouverts

Have you ever seen one?	En as-tu déjà vu un/e?
I believe in destiny/fate.	Je crois au destin.
I'm ...	Je suis ...
People in my country tend to be ...	Les gens chez nous ont tendance à être ...
superstitious	superstitieux
realistic	réalistes
scientific	scientifiques
imaginative	imaginatifs
sceptical	sceptiques

CROSSWORD - INTERESTS

Across

4. Celine Dion does this better than Plastic Bertrand
8. Show of an artist's work
9. Must be literate to do this
10. State art gallery
11. Seriously uninteresting

Down

1. Trekking, rambling
2. Artist's place of work
3. Fictional works longer than a novella
5. Distant sun
6. Collected works of an artist
7. Person listed on film credits under 'Un film de'

Answers on page 309.

POLITICS

Politics always creates heated discussion, no matter where you are in the world. And the French are no different. They love to talk politics, so here are a few conversational phrases to arm yourself with.

What do you think of the current government?	**Que penses-tu du gouvernement actuel?**
What do you think of our government?	**Que penses-tu de notre gouvernement?**
I agree with their policy on ...	**Je suis d'accord avec leur politique en matière ...**
I don't agree with their policy on ...	**Je ne suis pas d'accord avec leur politique en matière ...**
drugs	**de drogue**
the economy	**d'économie**
education	**d'éducation**
the environment	**d'environnement**
military service	**de service militaire**
privatisation	**de privatisation**
social welfare	**d'aide sociale**

MAJOR POLITICAL PARTIES

FN	**Front National** (extreme right wing)
RPR	**Rassemblement pour la République** (right wing)
UDF	**Union pour la Démocratie Française** (right wing)
PS	**Parti Socialiste**
PC	**Parti Communiste**
	Les Verts ('the Greens')
	Génération écologie (literally, 'ecology generation')

SOCIAL ISSUES

ARGUING

I don't agree with you.	Je ne suis pas d'accord avec vous.
You're wrong.	Vous vous trompez/Vous avez tort.
I don't think it's a good idea.	Je ne crois pas que ce soit une bonne idée.
You must be crazy!	Non mais ça va pas (la tête)!
Fair enough!	Admettons!
Now you're going too far!	Alors là, tu abuses!
No way!	Alors là, (je ne suis) pas d'accord!
As I see it .../In my opinion ...	À mon avis ...
I feel/find that ...	Je trouve que ...
I imagine/daresay that ...	J'imagine que ...
As far as I am concerned...	En ce qui me concerne...
It's true that ... but ...	Il est vrai que ... mais ...
Keep talking!	Cause toujours, tu m'intéresses!
Don't get into a state over it!	Tu (ne) vas pas en faire une maladie/un fromage!
I mean ...	J'veux dire ...
I'm telling you.	J'vais t'dire.

I'm against/in favour of ...	Je suis contre/pour ...
Who do you vote for?	Pour qui votez-vous?
I'm a supporter of ...	Je suis partisan ...
capitalism	du capitalisme
communism	du communisme
democracy	de la démocratie
dictatorship	de la dictature
socialism	du socialisme

Useful Words

anarchy	l'anarchie
bribery	corruption électorale
candidate's speech	le discours du candidat
constituents	les électeurs
corruption	la corruption
dictator	un dictateur
electoral roll	une liste électorale
electorate	l'électorat
executive power	le pouvoir exécutif
foreign policy	la politique extérieure
government	le gouvernement
green politics	la politique écologique
independent	un/e indépendent/e; un/e élu/e sans étiquette
left-wing	de gauche
legislative power	le pouvoir législatif
local councillors	conseillers municipaux
majority	la majorité
mayor	le maire

THE MINISTRY

President of the French Republic	le président de la République française
Prime Minister	le Premier ministre
Finance Minister	le ministre des Finances
Home Office	le ministère de l'Intérieur
Foreign Office	le ministère des Affaires Étrangères
Home Secretary	le ministre de l'Intérieur
Treasurer	le ministre des Finances
National Assembly	l'Assemblée nationale

members of parliament	les députés
monarchy	la monarchie
opposition	l'opposition
parliament	le parlement
party	un parti
policy	la politique
politician	un homme/une femme politique
polls	le scrutin
public opinion	l'opinion publique
rally	un rassemblement; un meeting
republic	une république
right-wing	de droite
senate	le sénat
speech	un discours
state-controlled	étatisé
summit meeting	une conférence au sommet
term of office	un mandat

DID YOU KNOW ...

Marianne is the symbol of **La République française**. Cartoonists use Marianne to symbolise France and French public opinion. Her profile is also on French stamps; but you'll recognise her profile as that of the actress, Catherine Deneuve. Deneuve, and formerly Brigitte Bardot, were also models for busts of Marianne which are found in various official buildings.

ENVIRONMENT

In France, there are six national parks (parcs nationaux), mostly in the Alps, and about 120 nature reserves (réserves naturelles) which are run by local organisations under the responsibility of the state.

Does Montpellier have a recycling program?	Est-ce que Montpellier a une politique de recyclage?
Are there any protected species here?	Y a-t-il des espèces protégées ici?
Is la Vanoise a national nature reserve?	Est-ce que la Vanoise est un parc naturel national?
This beach is classified C. (This means it is sometimes polluted.)	Cette plage est classée C.

Useful Words

acid rain	les pluies acides
antinuclear groups	des antinucléaires
asbestos	l'amiante
atmospheric pollution	la pollution atmosphérique
catalytic converter	le pot catalytique
deforestation	le déboisement; la déforestation
endangered species	des espèces en voie de disparition
environment	l'environnement
greenhouse effect	l'effet de serre
industrial waste	les déchets industriels
kitchen waste	les déchets ménagers
nature reserve	une réserve naturelle
noise pollution	la pollution acoustique
nuclear energy	l'énergie nucléaire
nuclear test	un essai nucléaire
oil slick	une marée noire
ozone layer	la couche d'ozone
ozone-friendly	(qui) préserve la couche d'ozone
polluting agents; pollutants	les (agents) polluants
pollution	la pollution
radioactive waste	les déchets radioactifs
recycled paper	le papier recyclé
recycling bin	un bac de récupération
recycling	le recyclage

rubbish dump	la décharge (publique); le dépôt d'ordures
toxic waste	les déchets toxiques
water pollution	la pollution des eaux
wildlife park	un parc animalier

SOCIAL ISSUES

What's the government's policy on ...?	Quelle est la politique du gouvernement en ce qui concerne ...?
What do you think of ...?	Que penses-tu de ...?
I support	Je suis pour ...
I don't support ...	Je suis contre ...
abortion	l'avortement
animal rights	les droits des animaux
equal opportunity	l'égalité des chances
euthanasia	l'euthanasie
immigration	l'immigration
unions	les syndicats
nuclear power	l'énergie nucléaire
Do you have adequate social welfare here?	Vous avez un bon système de protection sociale chez vous?
Is there an unemployment problem?	Est-ce qu'il y a beaucoup de chômage?

Useful Words

atomic bomb	la bombe atomique
capital punishment	la peine de mort
citizenship	la citoyenneté
class system	un système de classes
lower classes	le prolétariat
middle classes	la bourgeoisie
upper classes	la haute société

delinquency	la délinquance
demonstrate	manifester
dole	l'allocation chômage
ecologist	un/e écologiste
equality	l'égalité
ghetto	un ghetto
homeless person	un/e sans abri; un/e SDF (sans domicile fixe)
human rights	les droits de l'homme
illegal immigrant	un/e clandestin/e un/e sans-papiers
income	les revenus
inequality	l'inégalité
job centre	l'ANPE (l'Agence Nationale Pour l'Emploi)
to break the law	violer/enfreindre la loi
majority	la majorité
minority	une minorité
petition	une pétition
political exile	un/e exilé/e politique
protest march	une manifestation; une manif
racism	le racisme (SOS Racisme is a French association committed to eliminating racism)
social outcasts	les exclus
social security	la Sécurité Sociale
social security benefits	les prestations (sociales)
street kids	les gosses des rues
to go on strike	se mettre en grève
taxes	les impôts; les taxes
terrorism	le terrorisme
unemployment	le chômage
to be unemployed	être au chômage
welfare	l'aide sociale

DRUGS

All drugs are illegal in France, although small amounts kept for personal use may be tolerated. If you find yourself in a situation where drugs are being discussed, the following phrases may help you understand the conversation, but if referring to your own interests, use discretion.

Do you smoke?	Tu fumes?
Do you want to smoke?	Tu veux fumer?
I'm stoned.	Je suis défoncé/e.
He/She is out of it.	Il/Elle plane.
I'm addicted to ...	Je m'adonne ...
marijuana	à la marijuana
hash	au haschich
heroin	à l'héroïne
cocaine	à la cocaïne
amphetamines	aux amphétamines
acid	à l'acide
drugs	aux drogues
I take ... occasionally.	Je prends du (m)/de la (f) ... occasionnellement.
My friend has taken an overdose.	Mon ami/e est en overdose.
My friend has collapsed.	Mon ami/e est tombé/e dans les pommes.
Where can I find clean syringes?	Où puis-je trouver des seringues à usage unique?
Do you sell syringes?	Vous vendez des seringues?
I don't take drugs.	Je ne touches pas à la drogue.
I'm not interested.	Ça ne m'intéresse pas.
I don't do it any more.	Je n'y touche plus.
I'm trying to get off it.	J'essaie d'arrêter.
I'm on the methadone programme.	Je suis un traitement à la méthadone.

I need help.	J'ai besoin d'aide.
Where can I get help?	Où puis-je trouver de l'aide?
Do you have a methadone programme in this country?	Existe-t-il des traitements à la méthadone dans ce pays?
Can I register?	Je peux m'inscrire (dans un centre spécialisé)?
This is just for personal use.	C'est uniquement pour mon usage personnel.

DOPE – COLLOQUIAL TERMS

One problem with being in another country is that it is often difficult to assess situations and people as easily as you can back home, especially when you are unfamiliar with the language. So you'll know what's going on around you, here are some colloquial terms common amongst drug users.

grass	l'herbe; la marie-jeanne
hash	le teush
ecstasy	l'ecstasy
heroin	la poudre; la blanche
horse	le cheval
cocaine	la neige
speed	le speed
acid	l'acide; le LSD
trip	un trip
dope	la dope
joint	un joint; un pétard

Useful Words

addiction	la dépendance
cold turkey	la crise de manque
dealer	un dealer
detox	désintoxication

drug addict	un/e toxico(mane); un/e drogué/e; un/e camé/e
drug pusher	un revendeur; une revendeuse
hallucinate	avoir des hallucinations
inject	injecter
methadone	la méthadone
overdose	une overdose
pure	pur/e
to smoke	fumer
to sniff	sniffer
to take	prendre
to be high; to be out of it	être raide; être défoncé/e
to be on drugs	être drogué/e
to feel withdrawal symptoms	être en manque
coming off drugs; weaning off	le sevrage

ABBREVIATIONS

la UE	EU
l'ONU	UN
PTT	on post boxes and post offices
RATP	Paris Metro
SARL; SA	Inc; Ltd; Pty Ltd; plc
SNCF	National railways
TTC	all inclusive; tax included
h	o'clock
TVA	VAT
HT	no tax
f	francs
HS	Out of Order (**En Panne** is also common)

CROSSWORD – SOCIAL ISSUES

Across

1. Goes with liberty and fraternity
3. Why drug abusers don't quit
6. One of life's certainties, along with death
8. Chief official of town or city
10. Product which promotes plant growth

Down

1. The people of an electorate
2. Process of clearing trees in a grand scale
4. Caused by lack of work
5. To smoke
7. Organisation representing workers
9. Break this, and maybe face jail

Answers on page 309.

SHOPS

antique shop	un antiquaire
bookshop	une librairie
camera shop	un magasin de photos
clothing store	un magasin de vêtements
department store	un grand magasin
flea market	un marché aux puces
flower shop; florist	un fleuriste
grocery	une épicerie
jewellery shop	une bijouterie
junk shop	une brocante
hairdresser; barber	un coiffeur
hardware shop	un marchand de couleurs; une quincaillerie
laundrette	une laverie automatique
market	un marché
newsagency	un marchand de journaux
newsstand	un kiosque
pharmacy	une pharmacie
record shop	un disquaire
secondhand clothes shop	une friperie
shoeshop	un magasin de chaussures
souvenir shop	un magasin de souvenirs
stationers	une papeterie
supermarket	un supermarché
toy shop	un magasin de jouets
travel agency	une agence de voyages

DID YOU KNOW ...

In French, 'to go window shopping' is **faire du lèche-vitrines** which literally means 'to go window licking'.

MAKING A PURCHASE

I'd like to buy ...	Je voudrais ...
How much is it?	C'est combien?
Do you have others?	Est-ce que vous en avez d'autres?
I don't like it.	Cela ne me plaît pas.
Can I look at it?	Est-ce que je peux le/la voir?
I'm just looking.	Je regarde.
Can you write down the price?	Est-ce que vous pouvez écrire le prix?
Can I pay with my credit card?	Est-ce je peux payer avec ma carte de crédit?
Can I pay with travellers cheques?	Est-ce que je peux payer avec des chèques de voyage?

Can I have a receipt, please?
Je peux avoir un reçu, s'il vous plaît?

Does it have a guarantee?
Il/Elle est garanti/e?

I'd like to exchange this.
Je voudrais échanger ceci.

It's faulty.
Il/Elle est défectueux/ défectueuse.

I'd like a refund.
Je voudrais être remboursé/e.

THEY MAY SAY ...

Vous désirez?/ Je peux vous aider?
May I help you?

Autre chose?
Anything else?

Je vous l'emballe?
Would you like it wrapped?

Désolé/e il n'y a que celui-ci/celle-ci.
Sorry this is the only one.

Vous en désirez combien?
How much/many do you want?

BARGAINING

It's a real bargain!
C'est une bonne affaire!

How much for (two)?
Combien ça fait pour (deux)?

That's very expensive.	C'est très cher.
Could you lower the price?	Vous pouvez baisser le prix?
Is that your lowest price?	C'est le prix le plus bas?
I don't have much money.	Je n'ai pas beaucoup d'argent.
I don't have enough.	Je n'en ai pas assez.
I'll give you ... francs.	Je vous donne ... francs.
OK, 30 francs!	Va pour 30 francs!
I'd like (three).	J'en voudrais (trois).
Satisfaction guaranteed!	Satisfaction garantie!
to bargain with somebody	marchander avec quelqu'un
flea market	un marché aux puces; les puces
flower market	marché aux fleurs
open air market	marché en plein air
secondhand clothes	des vêtements d'occasion; des fripes
secondhand clothes dealer	un fripier

ESSENTIAL GROCERIES

batteries	des piles
bread	du pain;
cereal	des céréales
chocolate	du chocolat
coffee	du café
washing-up liquid	un (produit) lave-vaisselle
fruit juice	du jus de fruit

gas cylinder	une bouteille de gaz
matches	des allumettes
milk	du lait
mineral water	de l'eau minérale; de l'eau de source
sugar	du sucre
tea	du thé
tissues	des kleenex; des mouchoirs en papier
toothpaste	du dentifrice
washing powder	de la lessive

SOUVENIRS

earrings	des boucles d'oreilles
handicrafts	des objets artisanaux
jewellery	des bijoux
embroidery	la broderie
gems	des pierres précieuses
lace	de la dentelle
miniature statue	une statuette
necklace	un collier
poster	un poster; une affiche
pottery	des poteries
ring	une bague
rug	un tapis
tablecoths	des nappes

CLOTHING

blouse	un chemisier
boots	des bottes
clothing	des vêtements
coat	un manteau
dress	une robe
hat	un chapeau

NOT AS IT SEEMS

Remember that to pronounce the French **u**, purse your lips and push them forward as if you were saying 'oo' but say the sound 'ee' instead.

jacket	une veste
jumper (sweater)	un pull-over
lingerie	de la lingerie
overalls	une salopette
raincoat	un imperméable
shirt	une chemise
shoes	des chaussures
skirt	une jupe
socks	des chaussettes
stockings	des bas
swimsuit	un maillot de bain
T-shirt	un T-shirt
trousers	un pantalon
underwear	des sous-vêtements

Can I try it on?	Je peux l'essayer?
My size is ...	Je fais du ...
It doesn't fit.	Ce n'est pas la bonne taille.

It's too ...	C'est trop ...
big	grand
small	petit
long	long
short	court
tight	serré; étroit
loose	large

Fashion

I buy unlabelled designer clothes.	J'achète des vêtements dégriffés.
I'm looking for a designer seconds store.	Je cherche un magasin de dégriffés.
The sales are on.	C'est la saison des soldes.
It's the latest fashion!	C'est le dernier cri!; C'est la dernière mode!

in fashion	à la mode
out of fashion	passé de mode; démodé
to set the fashion	lancer la mode
fashion parade	un défilé de mannequins
on sale	en solde
sale price	un prix soldé

Shoe Repairs

Is there a shoe repairer near here?	Est-ce qu'il ya a un cordonnier près d'ici?
I'd like to have my shoes resoled.	Je voudrais faire ressemeler mes chaussures.
When will they be ready?	Quand est-ce qu'elles seront prêtes?

heels	les talons
to reheel	remettre un talon à
soles	les semelles
shoelaces	les lacets
shoe polish	le cirage

MATERIALS

brass	en cuivre	leather	en cuir
ceramic	en céramique	metal	en métal
cotton	en coton	linen	en lin
glass	en verre	silver	en argent
gold	en or	silk	en soie
handmade	fait à la main	wool	en laine

COLOURS

black	noir/e	orange	orange
blue	bleu/e	red	rouge
brown	brun/e; marron	white	blanc/blanche
green	vert/e	yellow	jaune
pink	rose	dark	foncé/e
purple	violet/te	light	clair/e

AT THE HAIRDRESSER

Where can I get a haircut?	Où est-ce que je peux avoir une coupe?
I want a haircut.	Je voudrais une coupe.
I like your haircut.	J'aime ta coupe de cheveux.
I want it cut like this.	Je voudrais une coupe comme cela.
I want it short.	Je voudrais une coupe courte.
I just want a trim.	Je voudrais une coupe d'entretien.
I want a colour in my hair.	Je voudrais qu'on me fasse un shampooing colorant.

hairdresser's	un salon de coiffure
haircut	une coupe
to have a haircut	se faire couper les cheveux
blow dry	un brushing
blonde (hair)	blonds (cheveux)
more/less blonde	plus/moins blonds
dark	bruns
more/less dark	plus/moins bruns

DID YOU KNOW ...

As in English, some brand names have become the popular name of a particular product:

un bic instead of **un stylo-bille** (ball-point pen);

un k-way instead of **un coupe-vent** (jacket; windcheater).

un frigidaire instead of **un réfrigérateur** (refrigerator);

un kleenex, instead of **un mouchoir jetable** (tissue).

TOILETRIES

aftershave	un après-rasage
antiperspirant	un déodorant
comb	un peigne
condoms	des préservatifs
dental floss	du fil dentaire
deodorant	un déodorant
hairbrush	une brosse à cheveux
moisturiser	de la crème hydratante
panty liners	des protège-slips
razor	un rasoir
razor blades	des lames de rasoir
sanitary napkins	des serviettes hygiéniques
shampoo	du shampooing
shaving cream	de la mousse à raser
soap	du savon
scissors	des ciseaux
sunblock	de la crème écran total
tampons	des tampons
tissues	des mouchoirs en papier
toilet paper	du papier hygiénique
toothbrush	une brosse à dents
toothpaste	du dentifrice

See also At the Chemist, page 216.

FOR THE BABY

baby chair	une chaise haute
stroller/buggy	une poussette
playpen	un parc
potty	un pot
baby food	l'alimentation pour bébé
baby powder	du talc
bib	un bavoir
disposable nappies	des couches jetables; des couches-culottes

dummy	une tétine
baby bottle	un biberon
nappy rash cream	une crème contre les rougeurs
teat	une tétine

STATIONERY & PUBLICATIONS

Is there an English-language bookshop nearby?	Y a-t-il une librairie anglaise près d'ici?
Where is the English-language section?	Où est le rayon anglais?
Do you have the latest novel by ...?	Est-ce que vous avez le dernier roman de ...?
Do you have a copy of ...?	Est-ce que vous avez un exemplaire de ...?
Can you recommend a novel by a contemporary French author?	Pouvez-vous me conseiller un roman d'un écrivain français contemporain?
Is there an English translation of this?	Est-ce qu'il existe une traduction anglaise de ceci?
Do you have a local entertainment guide?	Est-ce que vous avez un guide des spectacles locaux?

dictionary	un dictionnaire
envelope	une enveloppe
magazine	un magazine
... map	un plan ...
city	de la ville
underground	du métro
newspaper	un journal
newspaper in English	un journal en anglais
novels in English	des romans en anglais
paper	du papier
pen (ballpoint)	un stylo; un bic
stamps	des timbres

MUSIC

I'm looking for a CD/ cassette by ...	Je cherche un CD/une cassette de ...
What is his/her best recording?	Quel est son meilleur enregistrement?
What's the latest recording by ...?	Quel est le dernier enregistrement de ...?
What's the most popular French group/male vocalist?	Quel est le groupe/chanteur français le plus connu?
What's the most popular French female vocalist?	Quelle est la chanteuse française la plus connue?
Do you have this on ...	Est-ce que vous avez ça en ...?
CD	CD ('say-day')
record	disque
cassette	cassette
Can I listen to it here?	Je peux l'écouter ici?
I'd like to buy a blank tape/ cassette.	Je voudrais acheter une cassette audio/vidéo vierge.

See also, Music, page 117, for more musical phrases.

PHOTOGRAPHY

How much is it to process this film?	C'est combien pour développer ce film?
When will it be ready?	Quand est-ce que cela sera prêt?
I'd like a film for this camera.	Je voudrais une pellicule pour cet appareil photo.
Do you have disposable cameras?	Vous avez des appareils jetables?
Do you have underwater disposable cameras?	Vous avez des appareils jetables étanches?

Do you have one-hour processing?	Vous faites le développement en une heure?
I'd like to have some passport photos taken.	Je voudrais faire des photos d'identité.

battery	des piles
B&W (film)	noir et blanc
camera	un appareil photo
colour (film)	couleur
film	une pellicule; un film
film speed	ASA (pronounced as one word)
flash	un flash
lens	un objectif
light meter	un posemètre
film for slides	une pellicule diapos
video tape	une bande vidéo

SMOKING

You can buy tobacco at un débit de tabac, un bureau de tabac, un café-tabac and un bar-tabac

SIGNS

DÉFENSE DE FUMER	NO SMOKING
INTERDIT DE FUMER	NO SMOKING

A packet of cigarettes, please.	Un paquet de cigarettes, s'il vous plaît.
Are these cigarettes strong/mild?	Est-ce que ces cigarettes sont fortes/légères?
Do you have a light?	Vous avez du feu?
I don't smoke.	Je ne fume pas.
I gave up.	J'ai arrêté.
I'm trying to give up.	J'essaie d'arrêter.
Do you mind if I smoke?	Ça vous dérange si je fume?
Please don't smoke.	Ne fumez pas s'il vous plaît.
May I smoke here?	On peut fumer ici?
May I have an ashtray?	Je peux avoir un cendrier?

cigarettes	des cigarettes
cigarette papers	du papier à cigarettes
cigarette (vending) machine	un distributeur des cigarettes
fags/smokes	des clopes
filtered	avec filtre
lighter	un briquet
matches	des allumettes
menthol	mentholées
pipe	une pipe
roll-your-owns; rollies	des clopes roulées à la main
tobacco (pipe)	du tabac (pour la pipe)

SIZES & COMPARISONS

small	petit/e
smaller	plus petit/e
smallest	le/la plus petit/e
big	grand/e
bigger	plus grand/e
biggest	le/la plus grand/e
as big as	aussi grand/e que
heavy	lourd/e
light	léger/légère
more	plus
less	moins
least	le moins
most	le plus
many	beaucoup
too much/ too many	trop
none	aucun/e
some	quelque(s)
few	peu
a little bit	un peu
enough	assez

CROSSWORD – SHOPPING

Across

2. To pay
6. Torso garment
8. Precious metal
9. Transparent silicon material
12. Neck ornament
13. Comes in loaves
14. Cow juice

Down

1. Primary colour
3. Style favored by the socially handicapped
4. Not a bargain
5. Daily publication
7. Fiendishly difficult to grasp in bath
10. What you'll end up paying
11. Not loose
12. Material sorely missed by animals

Answers on page 309.

The cuisine of France is remarkably varied, with many differences based on the produce and gastronomy of each region. Even if you don't eat in restaurants and brasseries, you can enjoy France's epicurean delights by buying food at markets and speciality shops, trying the local delicacies and avoiding the standard fare of the tourist menus.

MEALS

breakfast	le petit déjeuner
lunch	le déjeuner
dinner	le dîner
Dinner/Lunch is ready!	À table!

FRENCH CUISINE

- **Haute cuisine**
  Originated in the spectacular feasts of French kings; typifed by super-rich, elaborately prepared and beautifully presented multicourse meals
- **Cuisine bourgeoise**
  French home cooking of the highest quality
- **Cuisine des provinces**
  Also known as **cuisine campagnarde**; uses the finest ingredients and most refined techniques to prepare traditional rural dishes
- **Nouvelle cuisine**
  Made a big splash at home and abroad in the diet-conscious 1970s and 80s; features rather small portions served with light sauces. Nouvelle cuisine is prepared and presented in such a way as to emphasise the inherent textures and colours of the ingredients.

VEGETARIAN & SPECIAL MEALS

I'm a vegetarian.	Je suis végétarien/végétarienne.
I don't eat meat.	Je ne mange pas de viande.
I don't eat ...	Je ne mange pas de ...
beef	bœuf
chicken	poulet
fish	poisson
ham	jambon
seafood	fruits de mer
I require a ... meal.	Je voudrais un repas ...
kosher	casher; kascher
vegetarian	végétarien
I'm allergic to ...	Je suis allergique ..
shellfish	aux cructacés
seafood	aux fruits de mer
wheat flour	à la farine de blé
I'm lactose intolerant.	Je ne supporte pas les produits laitiers.

BREAKFAST

cereal	des céréales
croissant	un croissant
bread	du pain
butter	du beurre
jam	de la confiture
eggs	des œufs
soft-boiled	à la coque
hard-boiled	durs
poached	pochés
scrambled	brouillés
fried	sur le plat

SNACKS — CASSE-CROÛTE

un cornet de frites	paper cone of chips.
une crêpe ...	thin pancake with ...
au sucre	sugar
au citron	lemon
au miel	honey
à la confiture	jam
un sandwich au fromage et jambon	cheese and ham sandwich
un croque-monsieur	grilled cheese (Welsh rarebit) and ham sandwich
un croque-madame	grilled cheese (Welsh rarebit) and ham sandwich with a fried egg
marrons chauds	roast chestnuts
une assiette anglaise	cold meat selection

EATING OUT

Service is usually included in the bill, but if you pay cash you should leave coins. And don't call the waiter garçon – this is only done in the movies!

Is there a ... restaurant near here?	Est-ce qu'il y a un restaurant ... près d'ici?
African	africain
Caribbean	antillais
Chinese	chinois
Japanese	japonais
Middle Eastern	du Moyen-Orient
Thai	tha landais
Vietnamese	vietnamien
Table for ... please.	Une table pour ... personnes, s'il vous plaît.
In the smoking area?	Dans l'espace fumeurs?
In the non-smoking area?	Dans l'espace non-fumeurs?
Can I see the menu please?	Est-ce que je peux voir la carte, s'il vous plaît?
Do you have a set menu?	Avez-vous un menu à prix fixe?
What do you recommend?	Qu'est-ce que vous me conseillez?

DID YOU KNOW ...

In French, menu refers to a set meal. If you want to choose dishes from a menu ask for la carte. A set menu is also sometimes referred to as une formule

I'd like the set menu please.
Je prends le menu, s'il vous plaît.
I don't want the set menu.
Je ne veux pas le menu à prix fixe.
What does it include?
Qu'est-ce que ça comprend?
Is service included in the bill?
Le service est compris?
Not too spicy, please.
Pas trop épicé, s'il vous plaît.

ARTHUR OR MARTHA?

Remember that in this book, the masculine form of a word appears first, separated from the feminine form by a slash. See page 10 for a full explanation.

ashtray	un cendrier
bill	l'addition
cup	une tasse
drink	une boisson
drinks included	boisson comprise
fizzy (drink)	gazeuse
fork	une fourchette
fresh	frais/fraîche
glass	un verre
jug (for wine)	un pichet
jug (for water)	une carafe
knife	un couteau
plate	une assiette (the object)
	un plat (dish)
service charge	le service
spicy	épicé
spoon	une cuillère
stale	pas frais/fraîche
sweet	sucré
teaspoon	une petite cuillère
tip	le pourboire

WELL-DONE!

steak	bifteck
rib steak	entrecôte
sirloin steak	faux-filet

Expect steaks to be cooked less than they might be back home – 'rare', for example, literally means 'bleeding'.

- bleu — nearly raw
- saignant — rare
- à point — medium (usually still pink)
- bien cuit — well-done

FOOD

MENU DECODER

à la vapeur	steamed
abricot	apricot
agneau	lamb
agneau de lait	baby lamb
ail	garlic
aloyau	sirloin
amandes	almonds
ananas	pineapple
anchois	anchovies
andouille	sausage made of intestines
aneth	dill
anguille	eel
artichaut	artichoke
asperges	asparagus
assiette/variés	assorted
au poivre	with pepper sauce
aubergine	aubergine; eggplant
avec	with
avocat	avocado
banane	banana
bar/loup de mer	bass
beignet	fritter
betterave	beetroot

bifteck	beefsteak
bisque	shellfish soup
bœuf	beef
bœuf bourguignon	beef stew with onions and mushrooms in a burgundy sauce
bouillabaisse	Marseillais fish soup
bouilli	boiled
bouillon	broth
bourride	Provençal white fish soup
braisé	braised
brème	bream
brochet	pike
cacahuètes	peanuts
caille	quail
calmar	squid
canard	duck
canard sauvage	wild duck
caneton	duckling
carbonnade	selection of char-grilled meats
carottes	carrots
carré d'agneau	loin of lamb
carrelet	plaice
cassis	blackcurrant
céleri	celery
cerfeuil	chervil
cerises	cherries
cervelle	brains
champignons	mushrooms
châtaignes; marrons	chestnuts
chevreuil; venaison	venison
chou	cabbage
chou-fleur	cauliflower
choucroute	pickled cabbage; sauerkraut

MENU DECODER

ciboulette	chives
citron	lemon
citrouille/potiron	pumpkin
cochon de lait	suckling pig
concombre	cucumber
consommé	clear soup
contre-filet	sirloin (steak)
coq au vin	chicken cooked with wine, onions and mushrooms
coquilles Saint-Jacques	scallops
cornichon	gherkin
côtelette	cutlet
coulis	purée, usually of fruit or vegetable
courgettes	courgettes; zucchini
crevettes grises	shrimps
crevettes roses	prawns
cru	raw
crudités	raw vegetables with dressings
cuisses de grenouilles	frog's legs
cuit	cooked
cuit au four	baked
cuit/e	cooked
darne	fish cutlet
datte	date
daurade	sea bream
dinde; dindon	turkey
dindonneau	young turkey
doux/douce	mild/sweet
du jour	of the day
écrevisses	crayfish
émincé	thinly sliced
entrecôte	ribsteak
épaule	shoulder
épinards	spinach
escargots	snails
estouffade	stew
estragon	tarragon
faisan	pheasant
fait à la maison	homemade
farci	stuffed
fenouil	fennel
fèves	broad beans
figue	fig
filet	fillet
flamiche	leek a quiche
foie	liver
fraises	strawberries
framboises	raspberries
fromage	cheese
fricassée	stewed meat and vegetables in creamy sauce
fumé	smoked
gambas	king prawns
garniture	garnish
gelée	jelly
gibiers	game
gigot	leg
glacé	glazed/iced
grillades	mixed grill
grillé	grilled
groseilles	gooseberries

MENU DECODER

hachis	hash (chopped vegetables, mince meat, etc)
haricots verts	French or string beans
homard	lobster
huîtres	oysters
jambon	ham
jarret de veau	knuckle of veal
laitance	roe
laitue	lettuce
langoustines	scampi or Dublin Bay prawns
langue	tongue
lapin	rabbit
lard	bacon
laurier	bay leaf
légumes	vegetables
lentilles	lentils
lièvre	hare
longe	loin
lotte	monkfish
maïs	corn
maison	of the house
mange-tout	sugar-peas; snowpeas
maquereau	mackerel
mariné	marinated
marjolaine	marjoram
menthe	mint
menu dégustation	tasting menu
merguez	spicy red sausage
merlan	whiting
moelle	marrow
moules	mussels
moules marinières	mussels with shallots in white-wine sauce
moutarde	mustard
mouton	mutton
mûres	blackberries
noisettes	hazelnuts
noix	walnuts
noix de coco	coconut
nouilles	noodles
oie	goose
oignon	onion
olives	olives
orange	orange
oseille	sorrel
palourdes	clams
pamplemousse	grapefruit
pané	crumbed
pastèque	watermelon
patate douce	sweet potato
pâte	batter/paste
pâté	pâté/pie
pâtes	pasta
pêche	peach
persil	parsley
petits pois	peas
piquant	spicy hot
pistou	pesto
poché	poached
poêle	frying pan
poêlé	pan-fried
poire	pear
poireau	leek
pois chiches	chickpeas
poisson	fish
poitrine de porc	pork belly
poitrine de veau/ mouton	breast of veal/ mutton
poivre	pepper
poivron	capsicum; pepper
pomme	apple
pomme de terre	potato
porc	pork

MENU DECODER

potage	thick soup, usually vegetable
poularde	fatted chicken
poulet	chicken
poulpe	octopus
prune/mirabelle	plum
pruneau	prune
queue de bœuf	oxtail
radis	radish
ragoût	stew of meat or poultry and vegetables
raifort	horseradish
raisins	grapes
ratatouille	eggplant, zucchini, tomato and garlic dish
rillettes	potted meat (pork or goose)
riz	rice
rognons	kidneys
romarin	rosemary
rôti	roast
roulé	rolled
saint-pierre	John Dory
sanglier	wild boar
sardines	sardines
sauge	sage
saumon	salmon
séché	dried
sel	salt
selle	saddle (of meat)
steak frites	steak with chips
steak tartare	raw minced beef, raw onion and egg yolk
thon	tuna
thym	thyme
topinambours	Jerusalem artichokes

tournedos	thick slices of fillet
tourte	pie
tranché	sliced
tripes	tripe
truffes	truffles
truite	trout
veau	veal
velouté	white sauce
vinaigre	vinegar
viande	meat
volaille	poultry /fowl

REGIONAL DISHES

North

flamiche au Maroilles	Maroilles cheese pie
flamiche aux poireaux	leek pie
lapin aux pruneaux	rabbit with prunes
salade d'endives	chicory salad
tarte au sucre	sugar tart

Normandy

tripes à la mode	tripe in butter, calvados, onion and cider
sole normande	sole in a sauce of butter, onino, white wine, mushrooms, cider, calvados and fresh cream
plateau de fromages	cheese platter and the famous calvados (apple brandy)

Alsace

bäckaoffa; baekehoffe	Alsatian stew (potatoes, vegetables and meat marinated in white wine)
choucroute	cabbage with pork meat and potatoes and sauerkraut
kougelhopf; kouglof	famous Alsatian cake made from a risen dough

The South East

Lyon's gastronomy is well known. You can taste it in one of the bouchons (typical restaurants).

quenelles	dumplings
charcuterie	cooked pork meats
fondue savoyarde	cheese fondue
raclette	melted cheese on a baguette

The South

soupe au pistou	vegetable soup with basil and garlic
pissaladière	bread dough with onion purée, anchovies and black olives
tapenade	capers, black olives, anchovies and tuna with lemon and olive oil

Brittany

une crêpe (au froment)	wheat pancake (sweet filling)
une galette (de sarrasin)	buckwheat pancake (savoury filling)
cidre	cider

A TYPICAL MENU FROM TOULOUSE

Entrées

confit de canard	conserve of duck
terrine de poisson	fish pâté
salade multicolore au basilic	salad with peppers, tomatoes, radishes, cucumber, egg, corn and basil
salade au bleu	salad with blue cheese and walnuts
salade de crudités	raw vegetable salad

Main Dishes	Plats Principaux
andouillette sauce au poivre	tripe sausage with pepper sauce
brochette de cœurs	heart kebab
entrecôte grillée avec sauce au bleu	grilled rib steak with blue cheese sauce
cotriade	fillet of fish with seafood and a saffron sauce
brochette de volailles au citron	poultry kebab with lemon

A TYPICAL MENU FROM PARIS

Entrées	
concombre à la crème-ciboulette	cucumber with cream and chives
salade de tomates avec basilic huile vierge	tomato salad with basil and virgin olive oil
sushi de poisson cru sur lit de soja croquant	raw fish sushi on a bed of crunchy soya bean sprouts
fromage blanc battu aux fines herbes	cream cheese blended with sweet herbs
méli-mélo de légumes vapeur	mixed steamed vegetables
boudin antillais en feuille de chêne et pommes de terres en robe des champs	West-Indian blood sausage with lettuce and potatoes in their jackets

Main Course	Plats Principaux
filets de rascasse grillés aux tagliatelles safranées	grilled fillets of scorpion fish with tagliatelli seasoned with saffron
émincé de haddock fumé avec pommes mousseline	slivers of smoked haddock with balls of mashed potato in a light pastry case
moelleux de porc au curry avec riz sauvage	tender pork curry with wild rice
demi-cannette rôtie avec pommes château	half a roast duckling with potatoes sautéed in butter
émincé de poulet mariné aux grains de coriandre en salade	slivers of marinated chicken with coriander seeds and salad

Desserts

charlotte	custard and fruit in lining of almond fingers
clafoutis	fruit tart, usually with berries
fromage blanc	cream cheese
glace	ice cream
île flottante crème vanille	soft meringues floating on custard with vanilla cream
mousse au chocolat crème anglaise	chocolate mousse with custard
parfait	frozen mousse
poires Belle Hélène	pears and ice cream in a chocolate sauce
sorbet au choix	choice of sorbets
tarte aux pommes fines	apple tart

SELF CATERING

bakery	une boulangerie
butcher	une boucherie
cake/pastry shop	une pâtisserie
cheese shop	une fromagerie; une crémerie
chocolate/sweet shop	une confiserie
delicatessen	une charcuterie
fish shop	une poissonnerie
fruit and vegetable shop	un magasin de fruits et légumes
greengrocer	un marchand de légumes
market	un marché
small grocer	une épicerie; une alimentation générale
supermarket	un supermarché
giant supermarket	un hypermarché
a carton of ...	une barquette ...
a portion of ...	une part de ...
a slice of ...	une tranche de ...
bean salad	des haricots en salade
bread	du pain
butter	du beurre
cheese	du fromage
gherkins	des cornichons
ham	du jambon
honey	du miel
liver/farmhouse pâté	pâté de foie/de campagne
mayonnaise	de la mayonnaise
milk	du lait
mixed salad	de la salade composée
oil	de l'huile
salt	du sel
sugar	du sucre
vinegar	du vinaigre

See At the Market, page 171, for key foodstuffs.

AT THE MARKET

Meat & Poultry — Viandes & Volailles

bacon	lard
beef	bœuf
brains	cervelle
chicken	poulet
duck	canard
goose	oie
ham	jambon
kidneys	rognons
lamb	agneau
liver	foie
mutton	mouton
pheasant	faisan
pork	porc
quail	caille
rabbit	lapin
tongue	langue
tripe	tripes
turkey	dinde; dindon
veal	veau
venison	chevreuil; venaison
young turkey	dindonneau

Fish & Seafood — Poisson & Fruits de Mer

anchovies	anchois
bass	bar; loup de mer
bream	brème
clams	palourdes
crayfish	écrevisses
eels	anguilles
John Dory	saint-pierre
king prawns	gambas
lobster	homard
mackerel	maquereau
monkfish	lotte
mussels	moules
octopus	poulpe
oysters	huîtres
pike	brochet
plaice	carrelet
prawns	crevettes roses
salmon	saumon
sardines	sardines
scallops	coquilles Saint-Jacques
shrimps	crevettes grises
squid	calmar
trout	truite
tuna	thon
whiting	merlan

JEE IS FOR GOOSE

The letter **g** is hard as in 'goose' before **a**, **o** and **u** but soft as in 'ginger' before **e**, **i** and **y**.

Vegetables — Légumes

Vegetables	Légumes
artichoke	artichaut
asparagus	asperges
avocado	avocat
beetroot	betterave
broad beans	fèves
cabbage	chou
capsicum/ pepper	poivron
carrots	carottes
cauliflower	chou-fleur
celery	céleri
chickpeas	pois chiches
corn	maïs
cucumber	concombre
eggplant	aubergine
fennel	fenouil
French/ string beans	haricots verts
gherkin	cornichon
leek	poireau
lentils	lentilles
lettuce	laitue
mushrooms	champignons
olives	olives
onion	oignon
peas	petits pois
potato	pomme de terre
pumpkin	citrouille; potiron
radish	radis
snowpeas	mange-tout
spinach	épinards
sweet potato	patate douce
truffles	truffes
zucchini	courgettes

Fruit & Nuts — Fruits & Noix

Fruit & Nuts	Fruits & Noix
almonds	amandes
apple	pomme
apricot	abricot
banana	banane
blackberries	mûres
blackcurrant	cassis
cherries	cerises
chestnuts	châtaignes; marrons
coconut	noix de coco
date	datte
fig	figue
gooseberries	groseilles
grapefruit	pamplemousse
grapes	raisins
hazelnuts	noisettes
lemon	citron
orange	orange
peach	pêche
peanuts	cacahuètes
pear	poire
pineapple	ananas
plum	prune; mirabelle
prune	pruneau
raspberries	framboises
strawberries	fraises
walnuts	noix
watermelon	pastèque

Condiments, Herbs & Spices

mustard	moutarde	marjoram	marjolaine
parsley	persil	dill	aneth
sage	sauge	fennel	fenouil
horseradish	raifort	sorrel	oseille
vinegar	vinaigre	salt	sel
mint	menthe	pepper	poivre
tarragon	estragon	rosemary	romarin
bay leaf	laurier	garlic	ail
chives	ciboulette	thyme	thym
chervil	cerfeuil		

DRINKS BOISSONS

Nonalcoholic

mineral water	de l'eau minérale; de l'eau de source
tap water	de l'eau du robinet
freshly-squeezed orange juice	une orange pressée
grapefruit juice	un jus de pamplemousse
orange juice	un jus d'orange
milk	du lait
soya milk	du lait de soja
coffee	un café

decaffeinated
  un décaféiné; un déca
tea
  un thé
herbal tea
  une tisane
tea with lemon
  thé au citron
white tea
  thé au lait
hot chocolate
  un chocolat chaud

See page 175 for how to order coffee the way you like it.

Alcoholic

If you want to order a drink at the bar, say **Je voudrais ...** plus the name of your favourite drink. If it is not in the list below, try saying it in English and you will most likely be understood.

beer	**une bière**
champagne	**du champagne**
sparkling wine	**du mousseux**
cider	**du cidre**
cocktail	**un cocktail**
brandy	**un cognac**
martini	**un martini**
rum	**un rhum**
shandy	**un panaché**
sherry	**un sherry; un xérès**
whisky	**un whisky**
vodka	**une vodka**
gin	**un gin**

You might want to try the following drinks which are commonly ordered in bars.

un kir	blackcurrant liqueur and white wine
un kir royal	blackcurrant liqueur and champagne
un pastis	aniseed liqueur served with water
un picon bière	beer mixed with a sweet liqueur
un pineau	cognac and grape juice
une suze	fermented gentian
un muscat	muscatel wine
un porto	port wine
un punch	punch

DID YOU KNOW ...

Un apéritif is a drink taken before a meal; **un digestif** is a drink taken after a meal.

THE CAFÉ

The French café is an institution. Sitting in a café to read, write or talk with friends is an integral part of everyday life in France. Cafés or café-restaurants serve simple meals and snacks as well as drinks. Café-tabac and Bar-tabac serve coffee and spirits and sell tobacco, stamps and sometimes magazines and lottery tickets.

café	un café; un troquet; un bistrot
counter	le comptoir; le zinc
bar manager	le patron/la patronne de café
waiter	un serveur/une serveuse
drink	une consommation; un pot un verre

coffee with milk
 un café au lait
coffee with cream
 un (café) crème
decaffeinated coffee
 un café décaféiné;
 un déca
expresso coffee
 un (café) express;
 un expresso
coffee ice cream
 un café liégeois
black coffee
 un (petit) noir

THEY MAY SAY ...

Buvons un coup!
Let's have a drink!

Qu'est-ce que vous prenez?
What will you have?

On ferme!
Closing time!

WINE

The main wine-growing regions of France are Alsace, Beaujolais, Bordeaux, Bourgogne, Champagne, Côte du Rhône, Jura, Languedoc, Loire, Provence and Savoie. Wine production in France in strictly supervised by the government. Under French law, wines are divided into four categories based on their quality.

WINE CATEGORIES

- **Appellation d'origine contrôlée (AOC)**
  almost always good, at the very least, and may be superb. The makers of AOC wines are the elite of the French wine industry.
- **Vin délimité de qualité supérieure (VDQS)**
  good wines; the second rank of French quality control
- **Vin de pays** ('country wine')
  reasonable quality and generally drinkable
- **Vin de table** or **vin ordinaire**
  very cheap, lower quality wine

We'd like to try a local wine.	Nous aimerions goûter un vin de pays.
Not too expensive.	Pas trop cher.
We'd like the house wine.	Nous aimerions la cuvée du patron.
May I see the wine list?	Je peux voir la carte des vins?
What is a good year?	Vous pouvez nous recommander une bonne année?
What wine do you recommend?	Quel vin me conseillez-vous?
We'd like to visit a local vineyard.	Nous aimerions visiter un vignoble local.
We'd like to do some wine-tasting.	Nous aimerions goûter des vins.
What sort of grapes grow in this area?	Quels cépages sont cultivés dans cette région?
What sort of wine is produced here?	Quel genre de vins est produit ici?
Which region produces the best ...	Quelle région produit le/la meilleur/e ...

body	le corps
bouquet	le bouquet
colour	la robe
corked wine	un vin qui a un goût de bouchon
dry	sec
full-bodied	qui a du corps; corsé
grapes	du raisin
harvest	les vendanges
light	léger
new wine	le vin nouveau
oak barrels	des tonneaux en chêne
red	rouge
sparkling	mousseux
sweet	demi-sec
sweet and strong	liquoreux
table wine	vin de table; vin ordinaire
very dry	brut
very sweet	doux
vineyards	des vignobles
vintage	la récolte (harvesting)
	le millésime (year)
white	blanc
wine cellar	une cave
wine grower	vigneron
wine tasting	dégustation
year	l'année

DID YOU KNOW ...

Sauternes is one of the most famous sweet wines (**vins liquoreux**). A microscopic mushroom, found in the crop, gives the wine its maturity.

CHEESE

There are over 400 kinds of cheese in France, with a wonderful range of textures and flavours. Like wines, some cheeses are particular to certain regions. Also like wines, some very good cheeses have an appellation d'origine. Here are just some of the more popular cheeses:

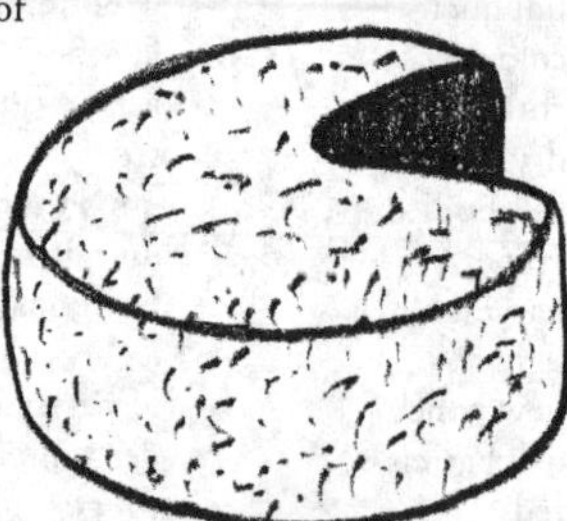

TYPES OF CHEESE

Pressed Cheeses
Beaufort
Cantal
Comté
Emmental
Gruyère
Morbier
Port-Salut
Pyrénées
Saint Nectaire

Soft Cheeses
Boursin
Brie
Neufchâtel
Camembert

Blue Cheeses
Bleu d'Auvergne
Bleu de Bresse
Bleu des Causses
Bleu du Haut-Jura
Fourme d'Ambert

Sheep's Milk Cheese
Roquefort

Goat's Milk Cheeses
Bougon
Banon
Valençay
Crottin de Chavignol
Mâconnais

hard cheese
fromage à pâte dure
soft cheese
fromage à pâte molle
goat's milk cheese
fromage de chèvre
sheep's milk cheese
fromage de brebis
cheese (made where the milk is produced)
fromage fermier

THEY MAY SAY ...

On ne va pas en faire un fromage.
Don't get into a state over it.
literally, 'we are not going to make cheese out of it'

mild	doux
sharp	fort
cream cheese	fromage blanc
cheese platter	le plâteau de fromages

CROSSWORD – FOOD

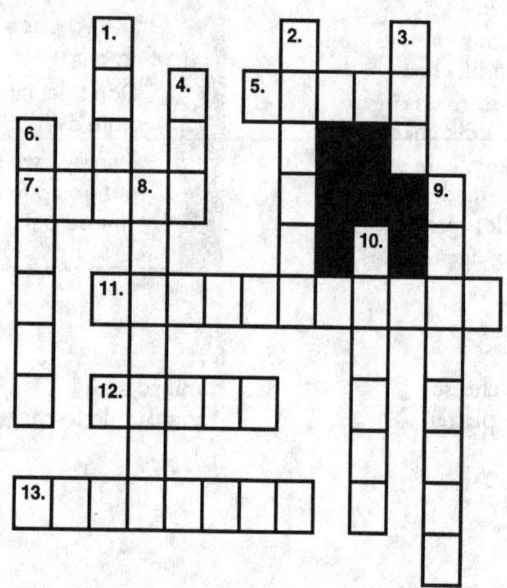

Across

5. Biggest-selling alcoholic beverage
7. Bird ovum
11. Where bread is made
12. Receptacle for fluids
13. Middle meal of the day

Down

1. Main ingredient of sauerkraut
2. Bitter citrus fruit
3. Condiment extracted from the sea
4. Liquid from fruit
6. Animal beloved of roosters
8. Product of bacteria and milk
9. Goes with knife and fork
10. The softer the bread, the harder this is.

Answers on page 310.

IN THE COUNTRY

CAMPING

Camping is very popular in France and there are many camp sites throughout the country. Hostels with lots of land sometimes let travellers pitch tents in the back yard. Another option is camping on someone's farm (camping à la ferme), but this usually means that there will be no amenities. Camping is generally permitted only in designated camp sites; camping sauvage is usually illegal.

May we camp here?	Est-ce qu'on peut camper ici?
Is there a camp site nearby?	Est-ce qu'il y a un camping près d'ici?
Is it possible to camp on a farm?	Est-ce qu'on peut faire du camping à la ferme?
How much is it per night?	Quel est le prix/tarif pour une nuit?
Where can I hire a tent?	Où puis-je louer une tente?
Where are the showers?	Où sont les douches?
Are the showers free?	Les douches sont-elles gratuites?
Where can I get drinking water?	Où puis-je trouver de l'eau potable?

backpack/rucksack	le sac à dos
can opener	l'ouvre-boîtes
firewood	du bois de chauffage
gas cartridge	une cartouche de gaz
hammock	le hamac
mallet	le maillet
mattress	le matelas
penknife	le canif
provisions/food supplies	les provisions

rope	la corde
sleeping bag	le sac de couchage
stove	le réchaud
tent	la tente
tent pegs	les piquets de tente
torch (flashlight)	la lampe de poche
water bottle	la gourde

HIKING

Hiking tracks throughout France are marked GR (sentiers de grande randonnée). Mountain huts or shelters (refuges) are sometimes available in uninhabited mountainous areas. Most of them have a telephone and sometimes meals are prepared by the attendant (gardien). Gîtes d'étapes, better equipped and more comfortable than refuges, are found in less remote areas.

What hiking routes are in this region?	Qu'est-ce qu'il y a comme sentiers de randonnée dans cette région?
Are there any guided treks?	Est-ce qu'il y a des marches organisées?
How long is the walk/trek?	Il faut compter combien de temps?
Is it a difficult walk?	C'est une marche difficile?
Is it a scenic walk?	La vue est belle pendant cette marche?
Does this path go to ...?	Est-ce que ce chemin mène à ...?
How many kilometres/hours to ...?	Nous sommes à combien de km/d'heures de ...?
Where can we spend the night?	Où peut-on passer la nuit?
How do we get there?	Comment y va-t-on?
We've lost our way.	Nous sommes perdus/perdues.

marked walking paths — sentiers balisés
national park — un parc national
nature reserve — une réserve naturelle
private road — un chemin privé
to ramble — randonner
tracks/trails/footpaths — les chemins (de randonnée)
trek — un trekking; un trek
view — la vue

MOUNTAINEERING

Is it a difficult climb? — C'est une ascension difficile?
Which is the shortest/easiest route? — Quel est le chemin le plus court/le plus facile?
Where have you come from? — D'où arrivez-vous?
Which way? — Quelle direction?
How long did it take you? — Ça vous a pris combien de temps?

altimeter
un altimètre
altitude
l'altitude
carabiner/crab
un mousqueton
to climb
grimper
climbing boots
les chaussures de montagne/de varappe
climbing wall
un mur d'escalade
compass
la boussole
crampons
les crampons

THEY MAY SAY ...

Je suis parti/e!;
Je grimpe!
Climbing!

Je tombe!
Falling!

Relais!
Off belay!

Du mou!
Slack!

Sec!
Tension!

downhill	en descente
gaiters	les guêtres
glacier	un glacier
gloves	les gants
harness/crossbelt	un baudrier
ice-axe/icepick	un piolet
incline	une pente
to link up	s'encorder
mountaineer	alpiniste
mountaineering	l'alpinisme
peg	un piton
to rappel down	descendre en rappel
rock climbing	la varappe; l'escalade; la grimpe
rope	une corde
runner	une sangle
steep	escarpé; raide; à pic (cliff)
uphill	en amont

AT THE BEACH

SIGN

BAIGNADE INTERDITE — NO SWIMMING

Is there a (public) beach near here?	Y a-t-il une plage (publique) près d'ici?
Do I have to pay?	Il faut payer?
Is it safe to swim?	On peut nager sans danger?
What time is low tide?	À quelle heure est la marée basse?
What time is high tide?	À quelle heure est la marée haute?
How much for a chair/ umbrella?	Combien coûte une chaise longue/un parasol?

coast	la côte	sea	la mer
coral	le corail	sunblock	un écran (solaire) total
lagoon	la lagune		
lagoon (coral)	le lagon	sunglasses	des lunettes de soleil
ocean	un océan		
reef	le récif	towel	une serviette de bain
rock	un rocher	waves	les vagues
sand	le sable		

See page 196 for more on aquatic sports.

AQUATIC CREATURES

crab	le crabe	whale	la baleine
dolphin	le dauphin	sea urchin	l'oursin
fish (pl)	les poissons	eel	l'anguille
lobster	le homard	seagull	la mouette
moray eel	la murène	seal	le phoque
ray	la raie	shellfish	le crustacé; le coquillage
shark	le requin		
turtle	la tortue marine		

GEOGRAPHICAL TERMS

agriculture	l'agriculture
bridge	un pont
caves	des cavernes; des grottes
cliff	une falaise
creek	une crique
crops	des cultures
farm	une ferme
forest	une forêt
hill	une colline
lake	un lac
mountains	des montagnes
mountain pass	un col
nature reserve	une réserve naturelle
peak	une cime; un sommet
pond	un étang; une mare (stagnant)
river	une rivière; un fleuve (major)
scenery	un paysage
trail	un sentier; un chemin
waterfall	une chute d'eau; une cascade
wildlife park	un parc d'animaux sauvages

DID YOU KNOW ...

Though you'd never know it from the name, France's national anthem, *La Marseillaise*, was actually written in Strasbourg. It was commissioned in 1792 after it was decided that the Revolutionary army should have a catchy and patriotic tune to sing while marching off to spread the blessings of liberty throughout the rest of Europe.

FAUNA

What animal is that?	Qu'est-ce que c'est, cet animal?

ant	une fourmi	peacock	un paon
bee	une abeille	pheasant	un faisan
bird	un oiseau	roebuck	un chevreuil
butterfly	un papillon	snail	un escargot
fly	une mouche	snake	un serpent
fox	un renard	spider	une araignée
frog	une grenouille	squirrel	un écureuil
game	le gibier	thrush	une grive
hare	un lièvre	toad	un crapaud
monkey	un singe	wasp	une guêpe
mosquito	un moustique	wild boar	un sanglier
mouse	une souris		

Farm Animals

calf	un veau	hen	une poule
chicken	un poulet	horse	un cheval
cow	une vache	ox	un bœuf
donkey	un âne	pig	un cochon
duck	un canard	rooster	un coq
goat	une chèvre	sheep	un mouton

See page 110, for some popular expressions with animals.

WILDLIFE

Alsace

stork	une cigogne

The Mountains

marmot	une marmotte
chamois	un chamois
bear	un ours
wolf	un loup
eagle	un aigle

Camargue

flamingo
un flamant rose

Camargue horse
un cheval camarguais

Camargue bull
un taureau camarguais

FLORA

What plant is that? — Quelle est cette plante?

carnation	un œillet
chestnut	le châtaignier
cypress	le cyprès
hydrangea	un hortensia
ivy	un lierre
fir	le sapin
lavender	de la lavande
lilac	du lilas
mimosa	le mimosa
pine	le pin
plane	le platane
poplar	le peuplier
privet	un troène
rose	une rose
sunflower	un tournesol
wisteria	une glycine

What are they growing here? — Qu'est-ce qu'on cultive ici?

barley	de l'orge
corn	du maïs
grapes	du raisin; de la vigne
hay	du foin
oats	de l'avoine
potatoes	des pommes de terre
sunflowers	des tournesols
wheat	du blé

CROSSWORD – IN THE COUNTRY

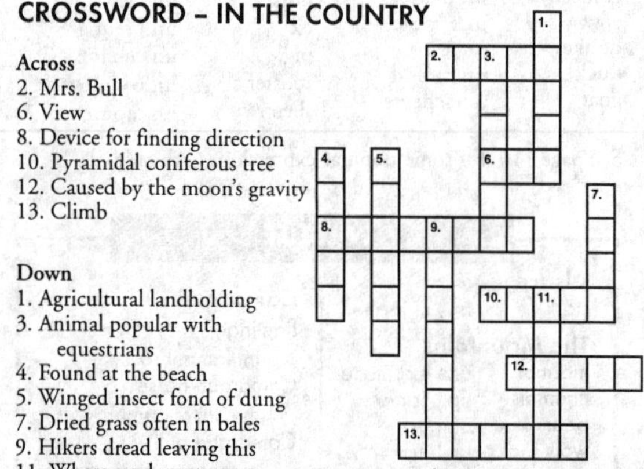

Across
2. Mrs. Bull
6. View
8. Device for finding direction
10. Pyramidal coniferous tree
12. Caused by the moon's gravity
13. Climb

Down
1. Agricultural landholding
3. Animal popular with equestrians
4. Found at the beach
5. Winged insect fond of dung
7. Dried grass often in bales
9. Hikers dread leaving this
11. Where sand meets sea

Answers on page 310.

TYPES OF SPORT

Do you play ...?	Vous faites ...?
Where can I play (indoor) ...?	Où pourrais-je faire ... (à l'intérieur)?
Let's play ... sometime.	Allons faire ... un de ces jours.

aerobics	de l'aérobic
athletics	de l'athlétisme
baseball	du base-ball
basketball	du basket(-ball)
boxing	de la boxe
cricket	du cricket
cycling	du cyclisme
diving	de la plongée (sous-marine)
fencing	de l'escrime
football (American)	du football américain
handball	du hand(-ball)
hockey	du hockey sur gazon
ice hockey	du hockey sur glace
martial arts	des arts martiaux
rowing	de l'aviron
rugby	du rugby
skiing	du ski
soccer	du foot(ball)
squash	du squash
surfing	du surf
swimming	de la natation
tennis	du tennis
gymnastics	de la gym(nastique)
volleyball	du volley(-ball)
weightlifting	de l'haltérophilie

TALKING ABOUT SPORT

Do you like sport?	Vous aimez le sport?
I like playing sport.	J'aime faire du sport.
I like to keep fit.	J'aime rester en forme.
I just like watching sport.	Je préfère regarder le sport.
What is your favourite sport?	Quel est votre sport préféré ?
What sports do you follow?	À quels sports vous intéressez-vous?
I follow ...	Je m'intéresse à ...
What team do you support?	Quelle équipe soutenez-vous?
I support ...	Je soutiens ...
Can I bet on it?	Je peux miser/parier là-dessus?
I'd like to place a bet.	Je voudrais parier.

GOING TO THE MATCH

I'd like to see a (rugby match).	Je voudrais voir un (match de rugby).
What's the admission charge?	Combien coûte l'entrée?
Where is it being held?	Où est-ce que cela a lieu?
What time does it start?	À quelle heure ça commence?
Who's playing?	Qui joue?
Who's winning?	Qui est en train de gagner?
Who do you think will win?	Qui va gagner à votre avis?
Who are you supporting?	Qui soutenez-vous?
I'm supporting ...	Je soutiens ...
What's the score?	Quel est le score?

What a ...!	Quel/Quelle ... !
goal	but
hit	coup
kick	tir
pass	passe (f)
game	match
performance	performance (f)

PELOTA (LA PELOTE BASQUE)

Pelota is the name given to a group of games native to the Basque Country. It is played with a hard ball and either bare hands or a scoop-like racket made of wicker, leather or wood.

ball	une balle
pelota player	un pelotari
pelota racket	un/une chistera
striker	un buteur
wall	un fronton

CYCLING

Cycling is very popular in France. Some GR trails (hiking trails) are open to mountain bikes. See page 71 for more phrases on getting around by bike.

bicycle path	une piste cyclable
cycling	le cyclisme
cyclist	un/e cycliste
cycle race	une course cycliste

The Tour de France is the biggest cycling event in the world. Annually up to 15 million people watch the race live (on the side of the road), and another 45 million on TV. The race is often called '23 days in July', and is usually made up of a prologue, 21 road race stages and a rest day.

yellow jersey (of the leading rider for that day)	le maillot jaune
bunch	un peloton
a stage (usually a day's run)	une étape
leading rider	le tête de la course

SKIING

With over 400 ski resorts, France has some of the best skiing in the world. The ski season generally lasts from December to March or

What was the final score?
Quel est le score final?
It was a draw.
Ils ont fait match nul.
That was a really good game.
C'était vraiment un beau match.
What a boring game.
Quel match ennuyeux!
They played badly.
Ils ont mal joué.
They played well.
Ils ont bien joué.

THEY MAY SAY ...

Allez-y; Vas-y; Allez!
Come on; Go!

But!
Goal!

Continue!
Play on!

Presque!
Nearly; Close!

Oui, c'est ça!; Ça y est!
Yes, that's it!

À vos marques, prêts, partez!
On your marks, get set, go!

SOCCER

The score is three-nil.
Le score est de trois à zéro.
Ten plays seven.
Dix à sept.
Metz is playing Lille on Saturday.
Metz joue contre Lille samedi.

ball	un ballon (de football)
centre-forward	un avant-centre
centre-half	un milieu de terrain
extra time	une prolongation
football ground	un terrain de foot(ball)
footballer	un footballeur/une footballeuse
foul	une faute
free kick	un coup franc
goal	un but
goalkeeper	un gardien de but

halftime	une mi-temps
to kick-off	donner le coup d'envoi
kick-off	un coup d'envoi
offside	un hors-jeu
to score a goal	marquer un but
to shoot	shooter; tirer; frapper
shot	un tir; une frappe

RUGBY

Rugby is especially popular in the south-west of France.

conversion	une transformation
forwards	les avants
fullback	un arrière
line-out	une remise en jeu
rugby ball	un ballon de rugby; un ballon ovale
rugby field	un terrain de rugby
rugby league	le rugby à treize
rugby player	un rugbyman
rugby union	le rugby à quinze
scrum half	un demi de mêlée
scrum	une mêlée
tackle	un plaquage
three-quarters	les trois-quarts
to touch down	marquer un essai
try (n)	un essai
winger	un ailier

TENNIS

Is there a tennis court near here?	Y a-t-il un terrain de tennis près d'ici?
What type of surface does it have?	De quelle surface s'agit-il?

ace	un ace
advantage	l'avantage
clay	la terre battue
deuce	égalité
fault	une faute
grass	le gazon
match point	une balle de match
net	le filet
point	un point
serve (v)	servir
tennis court	un terrain de tennis
tennis player	un tennisman; un/e jouer/joueuse de tennis
grand slam	le grand chelem

ballboy/girl
un ramasseur/
une ramasseuse de balles

THEY MAY SAY ...

Premier service!
First service!

Zéro: 15!
Love: 15!

Jeu!
Game!

Set!
Set!

Match!
Match!

Jeu, set et match!
Game, set and match!

April. Alpine skiing is mainly done in the Alpes and in the Pyrenées. The best cross-country resorts are in the Vosges and the Jura.

How much is a pass for these slopes?	Combien coûte un forfait pour ces pistes?
What are the skiing conditions like at ...?	Quelles sont les conditions pour skier à ...?
Is it possible to go cross-country skiing at ...?	C'est possible de faire du ski de fond à ...?
At what levels are the slopes?	À quelle altitude sont les pistes?
Which are the hardest/easiest slopes?	Quelles sont les pistes les plus difficiles/faciles?

Alpine skiing	le ski alpin
cable car	un téléphérique
chairlift	un télésiège
cross-country skiing	le ski de fond/de randonnée
downhill skiing	le ski de descente
instructor	un moniteur
monoski	le monoski
to ski	skier; faire du ski
ski jumping	le saut à skis
ski lodge	un refuge
ski poles	des bâtons de ski
ski resort	une station de ski
ski suit	une combinaison de ski
ski-lift	un remonte-pente
ski-tow	un téléski; un tire-fesses (inf)
skis	des skis
sledge/toboggan	une luge
slope	une piste
snowboarding	le surf (des neiges)
snowboots/moonboots	des après-skis
snowshoes	des raquettes
sunscreen	un écran solaire

AQUATIC SPORTS

to dive	plonger
diving equipment	un équipement de plongée
fins	les palmes
mask	le masque
mast	un mât
sail	une voile
sailing (the sport)	la voile
scuba diving	la plongée sous-marine
snorkel	le tube (respiratoire); le tuba
surfboard	une planche de surf
to surf	surfer
to go swimming	aller nager; se baigner
water sports	les sports nautiques
waterskiing	le ski nautique
wetsuit	une combinaison de plongée
windsurfing	la planche à voile
windsurfer (the object)	une planche à voile

See also At the Beach on page 184 for some other terms. The French diving organisation CMAS is the equivalent of the English-speaking world's PADI.

KEEPING FIT

Is there ... nearby?	Y-a-t-il ... près d'ici?
a gym	un gymnase; une salle de sport
a swimming pool	une piscine
Do I have to be a member?	Faut-il être membre?
Can I see it?	Je peux le/la voir?
What is the casual rate?	Quel est le tarif ordinaire?
Where can I do aerobics/yoga?	Où pourrais-je faire de l'aérobic/du yoga?
Where can we go jogging?	Où pouvons-nous courir/faire du jogging?

FOR HIRE

Can I hire ...?	Puis-je louer ...?
a bicycle	un vélo
diving equipment	un équipement de plongée
a racket	une raquette
shoes	des chaussures
skis	des skis
a surfboard	une planche de surf
a wetsuit	une combinaison de plongée
What's the charge per ...?	Quel est le prix ...?
day	par jour
game	de la séance
hour	de l'heure

HORSE RACING

French people usually have a bet on the horses on Sundays. Off-course betting takes place in certain cafés where you see the abbreviation PMU (Pari Mutuel Urbain). The most common bet is the trifecta – the three placed horses (le tiercé gagnant).

I'd like to have a bet on number (12).	Je voudrais parier sur le numéro (douze).
Here are the three winners.	Voici le tiercé gagnant.

bookie	un book(maker)
dividend	un gain
each-way bet	dans l'ordre et dans le désordre
gambler	un/e turfiste
horseracing	une course de chevaux
odds	la cote
1st four horses in a race	un quarté

1st five horses in a race	un quinté
racecourse	un hippodrome; un champ de course
racehorse	un cheval de course
thoroughbred	un pur-sang
to back a horse	jouer un cheval
to win a bet	gagner un pari
totalizer; tote	un pari mutuel
trifecta (1st three horses)	un tiercé

HORSE RIDING

Where can we go horse riding?	Où est-ce qu'on peut monter à cheval?
Where can we hire some horses?	Où peut-on louer des chevaux?
How long is the ride?	La balade à cheval dure combien de temps?
Do you have horses for beginners?	Avez-vous des chevaux pour débutants?
I want to wear a hard hat.	Je veux porter un casque.
I'm an experienced rider.	Je monte bien à cheval.
I prefer quiet horses.	Je préfère les chevaux tranquilles.
I prefer lively horses.	Je préfère les chevaux fougueux.

canter	un petit galop
to gallop	galoper
to trot	trotter
horse riding	l'équitation
pony trekking	une randonnée équestre
to ride	monter à cheval
riding lessons	un cours d'équitation
riding school	un manège; un centre équestre

GAMES

Do you play ...	Vous jouez ...?
How do you play ...?	Comment joue-t-on ...?
billiards; snooker; pool	**au billard; au snooker; au billard américain**
board games	**aux jeux de société**
cards	**aux cartes**
chess	**aux échecs**
computer games	**aux jeux électroniques**
darts	**aux fléchettes**
dominoes	**aux dominos**
draughts	**au jeu de dames**

noughts & crosses/
tic-tac-toe
au morpion
table soccer
au baby-foot
pinball/pinnies
au flipper
dice
un dés

THEY MAY SAY ...

C'est à qui (le tour)?
Whose turn?

C'est à moi (le tour).
It's my turn.

I don't know how to play it.	**Je ne sais pas y jouer.**

Cards

Let's have a game of ...	**Faisons une partie de ...**
bridge	**bridge**
poker	**poker**
gin rummy	**rami**
solo	**solo**
snap	**bataille**
twenty-one/blackjack	**vingt-et-un**
canasta	**canasta**
belote (popular French card game)	**belote**

cards	les cartes
to deal the cards	distribuer les cartes
to shuffle the cards	battre les cartes
to play solitaire/patience	faire une réussitee
trump card	l'atout
ace	l'as
jack	le valet
king	le roi
queen	la reine
clubs	les trèfles
diamonds	les carreaux
hearts	les cœurs
spades	les piques
to play a trump	jouer un atout
to take a trick	faire un pli
to have a good hand	avoir un bon jeu
to cheat	tricher

Chess

chess	les échecs
chessboard	un échiquier
Check!	Echec!
Checkmate!	Echec et mat!
castling king's side	petit roque
castling queen's side	grand roque
bishop	le fou
king	le roi
knight	le cavalier
pawn	le pion
queen	la dame
rook/castle	la tour
to be in check	être en échec
to castle	roquer

French Bowls

The popular traditional games pétanque and boules are usually played by village men on a rough gravel pitch (known as a boulodrome), scratched out wherever a bit of flat and shady ground can be found.

French bowls	la pétanque
shooter	un tireur
thrower	un pointeur
jack	le cochonnet
three-player team	une triplette
four-player team	une quadrette
to shoot	tirer
to plot	pointer
to bowl	lancer la boule

USEFUL WORDS

amateur	un amateur
ball	une balle
bat	une batte
championship	un championnat
coach	un entraîneur
competition	une compétition
to lose	perdre
loser	un/e perdant/e
Olympic Games	les Jeux Olympiques
opponent	un adversaire
racket	une raquette
referee/umpire	un arbitre
rules	les règles
scoreboard	le tableau (d'affichage)
sports equipment	un équipement sportif
sports ground	le terrain de sport
sportsperson	un sportif/une sportive
stadium	un stade
team	une équipe

team spirit	l'esprit d'équipe
tie/draw	une égalité
to be a good/bad loser	être bon/mauvais joueur (m) être bonne/mauvaise joueuse (f)
tournament	un tournoi
to win	gagner
winner	un/e gagnant/e
world title	un titre mondial

TV & VIDEO

There are several TV magazines in France. The least expensive is *Télé Z* and the most comprehensive is *Télérama,* which includes literature, music, cinema and radio reviews.

WHAT'S ON THE BOX?

broadcast	une émission
cable TV	le c ble
cartoons	des dessins animés
current affairs	magazines d'actualité
documentary	un documentaire
game show	un jeu télévisé
host/hostess	
(quiz shows)	un animateur/une animatrice
(news)	un présentateur/une présentatrice
kids' programs	des programmes pour la jeunesse
news	le journal
news & weather	les actualités et la météo
pay TV	la télévision payante
serial; soap	un feuilleton; une sitcom
talk show	une causerie télévisé
television	la télévision; la télé; le petit écran
TV film	un téléfilm

Do you mind if I put the TV on?	Ça ne vous dérange pas que j'allume la télé?
Do you mind if I turn it up/down?	Je peux augmenter/baisser le son?
Could you please turn it down?	Pouvez-vous baisser le son, s'il vous plaît?
What's on?	Qu'est-ce qu'il y a à la télé?
Is there a channel/news program in English?	Est-ce qu'il y a une chaîne/ des informations en anglais?
Can I change the channel?	Puis-je changer de chaîne?
Where can I hire a video?	Où pourrais-je louer une cassette (vidéo)?
Do you hire out videos?	Est-ce que vous louez les vidéos?
Do I have to be a member to hire a video?	Je dois être adhérent pour louer une cassette?
Can I join?	Je peux adhérer?
Is this film for daily or weekly hire?	Ce film est à louer pour la journée ou pour la semaine?

CROSSWORD – ACTIVITIES

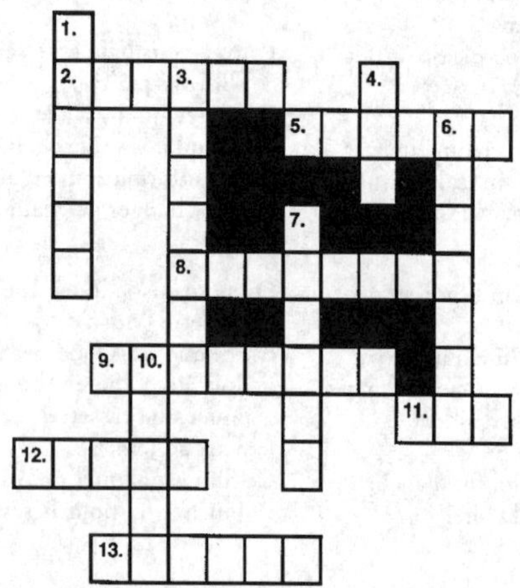

Across

2. Used in poker
5. Players on same side
8. Pastime at swimming pools
9. Broadcast
11. "——, set and match"
12. Yacht sport
13. Common use for a chalet

Down

1. Game where the Queen is most powerful
3. French Open is one
4. Goes on the score
6. Acrobatic water sport
7. To wager
10. Pack of rugby players

Answers on page 310.

FESTIVALS & HOLIDAYS

Most museums and shops are closed on public holidays. If a holiday falls on a Tuesday or Thursday, the French usually take off the Friday or Monday as well. This is what is called faire le pont.

PUBLIC HOLIDAYS IN FRANCE

Le jour de l'An	New Year's Day	1 January
Pâques	Easter	
Le lundi de Pâques	Easter Monday	
La fête du Travail	May Day	1 May
Victoire de 1945	Victory in WWII	8 May
L'Ascension	Ascension Day	
La Pentecôte	Whit Sunday	
Le lundi de Pentecôte	Whit Monday	
Le 14 juillet	Bastille Day	14 July
L'Assomption	Assumption	15 August
La Toussaint	All Saints' Day	1 November
L'Armistice de 1918	Armistice Day	11 November
Le jour de Noël	Christmas Day	25 December

Some French villages hold festivals to honour anything from a local saint to the year's garlic crop.

FESTIVALS IN FRANCE

Printemps de Bourges	Springtime song festival
Fête de la Musique	21 June, all over the country
Chorégies d'Orange	opera festival; July
Festival d'Avignon	theatre festival; July
Festival de Cannes	international film festival; May
Festival de Deauville	American cinema festival; September
Festival d'Angoulême	comics festival; spring

BIRTHDAYS & SAINTS' DAYS

When is your ...?	C'est quand ...?
birthday	ton anniversaire
saint's day	ta fête
My ... is on 18 October.	Mon/Ma ... est le 18 octobre.
Happy Birthday!	Joyeux/Bon anniversaire!
Happy Saint's Day!	Bonne fête!
birthday cake	un gâteau d'anniversaire
candles	les bougies
presents	les cadeaux
to blow out the candles	souffler les bougies
to make a wish	faire un vœu

CHRISTMAS & NEW YEAR

Christmas is celebrated traditionally in France, with a Christmas tree, presents and turkey. In Alsace, the Bogeyman (le Père Fouettard) comes to see if the children are well behaved.

At Epiphany people eat la galette des Rois, a round, flat cake made of puff pastry. The one who finds the charm (la fève) hidden in the cake is crowned king or queen. Everybody says Vive le Roi or Vive la Reine! (God save the King or Queen!).

On Saint Nicholas Day (6 December), Saint Nicholas comes and gives gingerbread to the children. In Alsace le Père Fouettard (or Hans Trapp) accompanies Saint Nicholas and threatens to take the naughty children away in his sack. In the north of France, people play practical jokes on their friends.

THEY MAY SAY ...

Joyeux Noël!
Happy Christmas!

Bonne année (et Bonne santé)!
Happy New Year!

Noël au balcon, Pâques au tison.
A warm Christmas means a cold Easter.

Christmas Day	le jour de Noël
Christmas cake	la bûche de Noël
Christmas Eve	la veille de Noël
Christmas tree	un sapin de Noël
Santa Claus	le père Noël
Candlemas	la Chandeleur
New Year's Day	Le jour de l'An; Le premier de l'An
New Year's Eve	La Saint-Sylvestre

EASTER

Easter egg	un œuf de Pâques
Happy Easter!	Joyeuses (fêtes de) Pâques!

CHRISTENINGS & WEDDINGS

baptism	un baptême
best man	le garçon d'honneur
bride	une (jeune) mariée
bridesmaids	les demoiselles d'honneur
Congratulations!	Félicitations!
engagement	les fiançailles
groom	un (jeune) marié
honeymoon	une lune de miel
wedding	un mariage
wedding anniversary	un anniversaire de mariage
wedding cake	une pièce montée
wedding present	un cadeau de mariage
wedding list	une liste de mariage

TOASTS & CONDOLENCES

Cheers!	À ta santé!; À la tienne! (inf) À votre santé!; À la vôtre! (pol)
Enjoy your meal!	Bon appétit!
Bless you!	À tes souhaits!
To absent friends!	Aux absents!

Sickness & Death

Get well soon!	Bon rétablissement!
My condolences.	Toutes mes condoléances; Sincères condoléances.
My deepest sympathy.	Ma très profonde sympathie
My thoughts are with you.	Je pense bien à toi (inf)/ vous (pol).

Goodbye & Good Luck

Good luck!	Bonne chance!; Bon courage!
I hope all goes well.	J'espère que tout ira bien.
Goodbye and all the best!	Au revoir et bonne continuation!

Useful Expressions

Hip hip hurray!	Hip hip hip hourra!
Yay for the holidays!	Vive les vacances!
Long live France!	Vive la France!
April fool!	Poisson d'avril!

CROSSWORD – FESTIVALS & HOLIDAYS

Across

3. Illuminates birthday cakes
7. Christian rite for infants
8. Candlemas

Down

1. Hope, dream
2. Celebration for fiancees
4. Solid sign of good wishes
5. Chocolate variety all too rare at weddings
6. Luck

Answers on page 310.

HEALTH

PLACES

Where is ...?	Où est ...?
the doctor	le médecin
the hospital	l'hôpital
the chemist	le pharmacien
the dentist	le dentiste

AT THE DOCTOR

I am sick.	Je suis malade.
My friend is sick.	Mon ami/e est malade.
I need a doctor.	J'ai besoin d'un docteur.
I've been vomiting.	J'ai vomi.
I feel dizzy/shivery.	J'ai des vertiges/des frissons.
I feel weak.	Je me sens faible.
I feel nauseous.	J'ai des nausées.
I can't sleep.	Je n'arrive pas à dormir.
I am constipated.	Je suis constipé/e.
I feel better.	Je me sens mieux.
I feel worse	Je me sens plus mal.
It hurts here.	J'ai une douleur ici.

I've been bitten by a dog	J'ai été mordu par un chien.
I've been bitten by an insect	J'ai été piqué par un insecte.

I've been vaccinated.	Je me suis fait vacciner.
I have my own syringe.	J'ai ma propre seringue.
I don't want a blood transfusion.	Je ne veux pas de transfusion sanguine.
I'd like to have my eyes tested.	Je voudrais me faire examiner les yeux.
I'm under the weather today.	Je suis un peu patraque aujourd'hui.

THE DOCTOR MAY ASK

What's the matter?	**Qu'est-ce qui ne va pas?**
Where does it hurt?	**Où est-ce que vous avez mal?**
Do you feel any pain?	**Vous ressentez une douleur?**
I'd like to take your temperature.	**Je voudrais prendre votre température.**
I'd like to take your blood pressure.	**Je voudrais prendre votre tension artérielle.**
How long have you been like this?	**Depuis quand êtes-vous dans cet état?**
Have you had this before?	**Cela vous est déjà arrivé?**
Do you smoke?	**Est-ce que vous fumez?**
How many cigarettes do you have a day?	**Combien de cigarettes fumez-vous par jour?**
Do you drink?	**Est-ce que vous buvez?**
How much do you drink?	**Combien buvez-vous?**
Do you take drugs?	**Est-ce que vous vous droguez?**
What do you take?	**Qu'est-ce que vous prenez?**
Are you on medication?	**Est-ce que vous prenez des médicaments?**
Are you allergic to anything?	**Êtes-vous allergique à quelque chose?**
Are you pregnant?	**Êtes-vous enceinte?**
Have you ever been pregnant?	**Avez-vous déjà été enceinte?**
Have you ever had an abortion?	**Avez-vous déjà subi un avortement?**
Is there a family history (of ...)?	**Est-ce qu'il y a des précédents familiaux (de ...)?**
Are you sexually active?	**Vous avez une vie sexuelle active?**

AILMENTS

I have ...	J'ai ...
an allergy	une allergie
a blister	une ampoule
bronchitis	une bronchite
a bruise	une ecchymose; un bleu
a burn	une brûlure
a cough	une toux
diarrhoea	la diarrhée
dry skin	la peau sèche
an earache	mal aux oreilles
fever	de la fièvre
glandular fever	la mononucléose infectieuse
a headache	mal à la tête
hayfever	le rhume des foins
hepatitis	l'hépatite
indigestion	une indigestion
an infection	une infection
inflammation	une inflammation
influenza	la grippe
itch	une démangeaison
lice	des poux
lump	une grosseur
migraine	la migraine
a pain	une douleur
rash	une rougeur; de l'urticaire
sore throat	mal à la gorge
a stomachache	mal au ventre
travel/motion sickness	le mal des transports
a venereal disease	une maladie vénérienne
worms	des vers

I'm anaemic.	Je suis anémique.
I have asthma.	J'ai de l'asthme.
I have eczema.	J'ai de l'eczéma.

I have a cold.	Je suis enrhumé/e.
I have a sprain.	Je me suis fait une entorse.
I have sunburn.	J'ai pris un coup de soleil.
I have high/low blood pressure.	Je fais de l'hypertension/ l'hypotension.

WOMEN'S HEALTH

I'm pregnant.	Je suis enceinte.
I think I'm pregnant.	Je pense que je suis enceinte.
I haven't had my period for ... weeks.	Je n'ai pas eu mes règles depuis ... semaines.
I'm on the pill.	Je prends la pilule.
I'd like to see a female doctor.	Est-ce que je peux voir une femme médecin?
I have a vaginal infection.	J'ai une infection vaginale.

DID YOU KNOW ...

Surprisingly, some words only have a masculine form, eg:

un amateur	amateur
un auteur	author
un écrivain	writer
un médecin	doctor
un sculpteur	sculptor
un mannequin	model
un témoin	witness

And some words only have a feminine form, eg:

une canaille	rogue/rascal
une crapule	villain
une sentinelle	sentry

I'd like something for period pain.	J'aimerais quelque chose contre les règles douloureuses.
I'm on hormone replacement therapy.	Je suis un traitement hormonal.
I'd like the morning after pill.	Je voudrais la pilule du lendemain.
I'd like to have a pregnancy test.	Je voudrais faire un test de grossesse.
I'd like to terminate my pregnancy.	Je voudrais interrompre ma grossesse.
I'd like ...	Je voudrais ...
a diaphragm	un diaphragme
an IUD	un stérilet; un DIU
the pill	la pilule
abortion	un avortement

cramps	des crampes
cystitis	une cystite
endometriosis	un endomètre
mamogram	une mammographie
menstruation	les règles
minipill	une minipilule
miscarriage	une fausse couche
pap smear	un frottis
period pain	des règles douloureuses
thrush	une mycose vaginale

SPECIAL HEALTH NEEDS

I'm on a special diet.	Je suis un régime particulier.
I'm on regular medication (for ...).	Je prends régulièrement des médicaments (pour ...).
This is my usual medicine.	Voici mes médicaments habituels.

I'm allergic to ...	Je suis allergique ...
antibiotics	aux antibiotiques
penicillin	à la pénicilline
dairy products	aux produits laitiers
bees	aux abeilles
acarids	aux acariens
Ventolin	à la Ventoline
wasps	aux guêpes
I'm ...	Je suis ...
diabetic	diabétique
epileptic	épileptique
asthmatic	asthmatique
anaemic	anémique
HIV positive	séropositif/séropositive
I need Ventolin.	J'ai besoin de Ventoline.
I have a hearing aid.	J'ai un appareil acoustique.
I have a pacemaker.	J'ai un pacemaker/un stimulateur cardiaque.

See also Disabled Travellers in Specific Needs, page 219.

ALTERNATIVE TREATMENTS

acupuncture	l'acupuncture
aromatherapy	l'aromathérapie
herbalist	un/e herboriste
iridology	l'iridologie
massage therapist	un masseur/une masseuse
massage	un massage
meditation	la méditation
naturopath	un naturopathe
physiotherapist	un kinésithérapeute
physiotherapy	la kinésithérapie
reflexology	la réflexologie
therapy	une thérapie
tonic	un fortifiant
yoga	le yoga

PARTS OF THE BODY

ankle	la cheville	knee	le genou
appendix	l'appendice	leg	la jambe
arm	le bras	mouth	la bouche
back	le dos	muscle	le muscle
breast	le sein	nose	le nez
chest	la poitrine	ribs	les côtes
ear	l'oreille	shoulder	l'épaule
eye	l'œil	skin	la peau
finger	le doigt	spine	la colonne vertébrale
foot	le pied		
hand	la main	stomach	l'estomac
head	la tête	teeth	les dents
heart	le cœur	testicles	les testicules
jaw	la mâchoire	throat	la gorge

I can't move my ...	Je ne peux pas bouger ...
My ... hurts.	J'ai de la douleur dans ...

BODY TALK

Here are a few colloquial expressions containing the names of body parts:

J'ai l'estomac dans les talons.
I'm starving. (*I have my stomach in my heels*)

Il a un verre dans le nez.
He is drunk. (*he has a glass in his nose*)

Je n'ai plus de jambes.
I'm exhausted. (*I don't have any more legs*)

Elle a la langue bien pendue.
She's a chatterbox. (*she has a well-fixed tongue*)

Il n'a pas ses yeux dans sa poche.
He's nosy. (*he doesn't have his eyes in his pocket*)

AT THE CHEMIST

I need medication for ...	J'ai besoin d'un médicament pour ...
I have a prescription.	J'ai une ordonnance.
Where is the nearest all-night chemist?	Où est la pharmacie de nuit la plus proche?
Do I need a prescription for ...?	J'ai besoin d'une ordonnance pour ...?
How many times a day?	Combien de fois par jour?
Take (two) tablets ... times a day.	Prenez (deux) cachets ... fois par jour.
before/after meals	avant/après les repas

antibiotics	des antibiotiques
antiseptic	de l'antiseptique
aspirin	de l'aspirine
bandage	un bandage
Band-Aid	un pansement (adhésif)
contraceptive	un contraceptif
cough medicine	une pastille pour la toux
laxatives	des laxatifs
painkillers	des calmants; des analgésiques
sleeping pills	des somnifères
vitamins	des vitamines

AT THE DENTIST

I have a toothache.	J'ai mal aux dents.
I have a cavity.	J'ai une cavité.
I've lost a filling.	J'ai perdu un plombage.
I've broken a tooth.	Je me suis cassé une dent.
My gums hurt.	Mes gencives me font mal.
I don't want it extracted.	Je ne veux pas que vous l'arrachiez.
Please give me an anaesthetic.	Sous anesthésie, s'il vous plaît.

USEFUL WORDS

accident	un accident
addiction	la dépendance; la toxicomanie
antibiotics	des antibiotiques
antiseptic	de l'antiseptique
aspirin	de l'aspirine
bandage	un pansement; un bandage
bite	
(dog)	une morsure
(insect)	une piqûre
blood group	un groupe sanguin
blood pressure	la tension (artérielle)
blood test	une analyse de sang
contact lenses	des verres de contact; des lentilles de contact
contraceptive	un contraceptif
disease	une maladie
drug	une drogue
injection	une injection; une piqûre
injury	une blessure
overdose	une overdose
oxygen	l'oxygène
psychotherapy	la psychothérapie
virus	un virus
vitamins	des vitamines

CROSSWORD – HEALTH

Across
2. Eruption under skin
4. The flu
7. From discomfort to agony
8. Vital human organ
10. Medicine
13. Uppermost part of body
14. Damage to body

Down
1. Can lose or gain depending on this
3. Features arches and nails
5. Can stop minor bleeding
6. Required from doctor for certain medications
9. Fertilised
11. Part of your body you can't see
12. Unwell

Answers on page 310.

SPECIFIC NEEDS

DISABLED TRAVELLERS

SIGN

RÉSERVÉ AUX HANDICAPÉS	RESERVED FOR DISABLED

I'm disabled/handicapped.	**Je suis handicapé/e.**
I need assistance.	**J'ai besoin d'aide.**
What services do you have for disabled people?	**Quels services avez-vous pour les handicapés?**
Is there wheelchair access?	**Y a-t-il un accès pour fauteuil roulant?**
I'm deaf. Speak more loudly.	**Je suis sourd/e. Parlez plus fort.**
I can lipread.	**Je peux lire sur les lèvres.**
I have a hearing aid.	**J'ai un audiophone.**
Does anyone here know sign language?	**Quelqu'un connaît le langage par signes?**
I am blind.	**Je suis aveugle.**
Are guide dogs permitted?	**Est-ce que les chiens d'aveugle sont permis?**
Is there information in braille?	**Est-ce qu'il y a des renseignements en braille?**

disabled person	**un/e handicapé/e; un/e invalide**
disabled ex-servicemen	**GIG (grands invalides de guerre)**
disabled civilians	**GIC (grands invalides civils)**
wheelchair	**un fauteuil roulant**
paraplegic/quadriplegic	**paraplégique/tétraplégique**
braille library	**une bibliothèque de braille**

For more phrases on special health needs, see page 213.

GAY TRAVELLERS

Some gay magazines are *Illico*, *Double Face* and *Exit*. Specifically for women there is *Lesbia*. The *Guide Gay Paris* is a French-English guide to Paris

Is there a gay club here?	Y a-t-il une boîte gay ici?
Could you tell me where the gay hangouts are?	Pourriez-vous m'indiquer les endroits gay?
Am I likely to be harassed?	Est-ce que je risque d'être embêté/e?
Is there a gay bookshop?	Est-ce qu'il y a une librairie gay?
Is there a local gay guide?	Est-ce qu'il y a un guide local pour les gays?
Where can I buy some gay magazines?	Où pourrais-je acheter des magazines gay?

homosexual; gay	un homo(sexuel)/ une homo(sexuelle)
lesbian	une lesbienne
bisexual	bisexuel/bisexuelle
transexual	un transexuel
transvestite	un travesti

to swing both ways;
to be AC-DC
être à voile et à vapeur
('to be both sail and wind')

gay bar
un bar gay
gay restaurant
un resto gay
gay club
une boîte gay
my boyfriend/girlfriend
mon ami/e

THEY MAY SAY ...

Pejorative names we hope you don't hear for men are **tante, pédale, pédé**; and for women, **gouine, gazon maudit**. Some words are the same as in English, for example, **drag-queen, drag-show, gay-pride**.

TRAVELLING WITH THE FAMILY

I'm travelling with my family.	Je voyage avec ma famille.
Are there facilities for babies?	Est-ce que vous avez ce qu'il faut pour un bébé?
Are there other families in the hotel/group?	Est-ce qu'il y a d'autres familles dans cet hôtel/ ce groupe?
Do you have a child-minding service?	Avez-vous un service de garde d'enfants?
Where can I find a (English-speaking) babysitter?	Où est-ce que je peux trouver une baby-sitter (qui parle anglais)?
Can you put an extra bed/ cot in the room?	Pouvez-vous mettre un lit/ un lit d'enfant supplémentaire?
I need a car with a child seat.	J'ai besoin d'une voiture avec un siège-enfant.
Is it safe for babies/children?	C'est sans danger pour les bébés/les enfants?
Is it suitable for children?	Ça convient aux enfants?
Are there any activities for children?	Il y a des activités pour les enfants?
Is there a family discount?	Il y a un tarif réduit pour les enfants?
Are children allowed?	Les enfants sont permis?

Do you have a children's menu?
Vous avez un menu pour enfants?

Is there a playground around here?
Est-ce qu'il y a un terrain de jeux près d'ici?

For phrases on shopping for the baby, see page 150.

Ç

The letter ç is a soft sound, as the 's' in 'sun'. So the word garçon is pronounced 'gahr-sson'.

LOOKING FOR A JOB

Where can I find local job advertisements?	Où pourrais-je trouver des annonces d'emploi locales?
I'm looking for a temping agency.	Je cherche une agence d'intérim.
I'd like to temp.	Je voudrais faire de l'intérim/ être intérimaire.
By what date do I have to apply?	Quand dois-je poser ma candidature?
What sort of work could I find around here?	Quel genre de travail pourrais-je trouver par ici?
Do I need a work permit?	J'ai besoin d'un permis de travail?
Where can I apply for a work permit?	Où dois-je m'adresser pour obtenir un permis de travail?
What qualifications do I need?	Quelles conditions dois-je remplir?
What experience do I need?	Je dois faire preuve de quelle expérience?
I've had experience.	J'ai de l'expérience.
I haven't had experience.	Je n'ai pas d'expérience.
I've come about the position advertised.	Je suis venu/e pour l'emploi proposé.
I'm ringing about the position advertised.	Je téléphone au sujet de la petite annonce.
What are the job requirements?	Quelles sont les conditions/ les responsabilités de ce travail?
What sort of training do you offer?	Quelle formation offrez-vous?
What is the wage?	Vous payez combien?
How often will I be paid?	Vous payez quand?
Do I have to pay tax?	Je dois payer des impôts?

manager	un directeur
mobile phone	un portable
pager phone	un alphapage
profit	un bénéfice
salary	un salaire
seminar	un séminaire; un colloque
trade fair	une foire-exposition; un salon professionnel
work experience	l'expérience professionnelle
work permit	un permis de travail

For phrases about occupations see page 53.

ON TOUR

We're part of a group.	Nous faisons partie d'un groupe.
We're on tour.	Nous sommes en tournée.
I'm with the band/team.	Je suis avec l'orchestre/l'équipe.
Please speak to our manager.	Adressez-vous à notre imprésario/manager, s'il vous plaît.
We've lost our equipment.	Nous avons perdu notre équipement.
We sent equipment on this flight/train.	Nous avons envoyé notre équipement par ce vol/train.
I'm staying with a host family.	Je suis dans une famille d'accueil.
I'm still a groupie after all these years.	Je suis toujours une groupie après toutes ces années.
We're playing on ...	Nous jouons ...
Friday	vendredi
the 15 June	le quinze juin

When can I start?	Quand pourrais-je commencer?
I can start ...	Je peux commencer ...
today	aujourd'hui
tomorrow	demain
next week	la semaine prochaine
next Monday	lundi prochain

Useful Words

application	une demande d'emploi; une candidature à un poste
career	une carrière
casual	temporaire
certificate	un certificat
degree; diploma	un diplôme
employee	un/e employé/e
employer	un employeur
full-time	à plein temps
holiday/summer job	un petit boulot de vacances/d'été
interview	une entrevue
job; occupation	un travail; un métier (trade)
job opportunity	un débouché
paid holidays	congés payés
part-time (half-time)	à temps partiel; à mi-temps
position	un poste; un emploi; une situation
qualifications	des qualifications
references	des références
cv; resume	un cv ('say-vay')
skills	des compétences
trainee	un/e stagiaire
traineeship	un stage
training	une formation
union	un syndicat
voluntary	volontaire
volunteer	un bénévole

ON BUSINESS

I'm on a course.	Je suis en stage.
I'm on a business trip.	Je suis en voyage d'affaires.
Here's my business card.	Voici ma carte.
I have an appointement with ...	J'ai rendez-vous avec ...
I need an interpreter.	J'ai besoin d'un interprète.
We're attending a conference.	Nous assistons à un congrès.
Where can I make photocopies?	Où puis-je faire des photocopies?
May I use your phone?	Puis-je utiliser votre téléphone?
Could you provide me with an overhead projector?	Pourriez-vous me procurer un rétroprojecteur?
Can you give me an estimate of the cost?	Pouvez-vous me donner un devis?
I need to use a computer.	J'ai besoin d'un ordinateur.
I need to send an email.	Je dois envoyer un e-mail.

Technology

Bulletin Board Service	le babillard; les services télématiques
computer	un ordinateur
email	le courrier électronique; un e-mail
Internet	Internet; le Net
keyboard	un clavier
laptop	un (ordinateur) portable
mouse	une souris
network	un réseau
newsgroups	des forums de discussions
Web pages	des pages Web
printer	une imprimante
site (Web)	un site
software	un logiciel
Web browser	un fureteur; un navigateur
word processor	un traitement de texte

Useful Words

ballpark figure	un chiffre approximatif
branch office	une succursale
colleague	un/e collègue; un confrère
company	une entreprise; une société
conference	une conférence
(big)	un congrès
(small)	un colloque
contract	un contrat
distributor	un concessionnaire; un distributeur
enclosed (document)	ci-joint; ci-inclus
executive	un cadre
expenses	des frais
factory	une usine
fax machine	un télécopieur; un fax
industry	une industrie
interest rate	un taux d'intérêt
invoice	une facture
loss	une perte

DID YOU KNOW ...

The French on-line service is called **minitel**

If you're using Windows software in French, you open a **fenêtre** rather than a 'window'. Some letters and most symbols are in different positions on a French keyboard but with most computers you can easily switch to an English/American keyboard by hitting alt-shift.

FILM & TV

We're filming.	Nous tournons.
We're filming here for (four) days/weeks.	Nous tournons ici pour (quatre) jours/semaines.
Can we film here?	On peut tourner ici?
We're making a ...	Nous faisons un ...
documentary	documentaire
film	film
TV program	programme télé

actor	un acteur/une actrice
camera operator	le/la cadreur/e
cast	la distribution
crew	une équipe (de tournage)
director	un réalisateur/une réalisatrice
editor	un monteur/une monteuse
producer	un producteur/une productrice
scriptwriter	un/e scénariste
stuntperson	un cascadeur/une cascadeuse

camera	la caméra
catering	l'intendance
continuity person	un/e scripte
editing	le montage
lighting	l'éclairage
location	les extérieurs
makeup	le maquillage
rushes	les projections d'essai; les rushes
script	un scénario
sound	le son
stunt	la cascade
wardrobe	les costumes

THEY MAY SAY ...

On tourne!
Rolling!

Moteur!
Action!

Coupez!
Cut!

PILGRIMAGE & RELIGION

Where can I pray?	Où pourrais-je prier?
Can I receive communion here?	Je peux recevoir la communion?
Where can I make confession (in English)?	Où pourrais-je me confesser (en anglais)?
Can I attend this service?	
(catholic)	Je peux assister à cette messe?
(protestant)	Je peux assister à ce culte?

SIGN

OFFICE/MESSE EN COURS	SERVICE IN PROGRESS

christening	un baptême
church	une église
communion	la communion
confession	la confession
funeral	un enterrement
prayer	une prière
priest	un prêtre
religious procession	une procession religieuse
sabbath	le sabbat
sacraments	des sacrements
shrine	un lieu saint; un lieu de pèlerinage
wedding	un mariage

Tracing Roots & History

In which cemetery would I find (Jim Morrison's) grave?	Dans quel cimetière pourrais-je trouver la tombe de (Jim Morrison)?
Is there anyone here by the name of ...?	Est-ce qu'il y a quelqu'un ici qui s'appelle ...?

(I think) my ancestors came from this area.	(Je crois que) mes ancêtres venaient de cette région.
I'm looking for my relatives.	Je cherche des personnes de ma famille/des parents.

I think he fought/died near here.	Je crois qu'il a combattu/est mort près d'ici.
My ... fought/died here in WWI/II.	Mon ... a combattu/est mort ici pendant la Première/ Seconde Guerre?
My ... nursed here in WWI/II.	Ma ... a été infirmière ici pendant la Première/ Seconde Guerre.

See page 106, for names of family members.

CROSSWORD – SPECIFIC NEEDS

Across
1. Clerical workplace
3. Formal meeting, often profession-related
7. One's immediate relations
10. Bill, IOU
11. To talk to God
12. Industrial workplace

Down
2. Unable to hear
4. Microchip-driven device
5. Why you work
6. Tiny bed
8. Offspring
9. Be this, read braille

Answers on page 310.

TELLING THE TIME

The French usually use the 24-hour clock.

What time is it?	Quelle heure est-il?
It is ... o'clock.	Il est ... heure(s).
It's one o'clock	Il est une heure.
It's two o'clock	Il est deux heures.
It's five past six.	Il est six heures cinq.
It's quarter past six.	Il est six heures et quart.
It's half past six.	Il est six heures et demie.
	Il est six heures trente.
It's quarter to seven.	Il est sept heures moins le quart.
It's about eleven.	Il est environ onze heures.
It's 10 am.	Il est dix heures.
It's 10 pm.	Il est vingt-deux heures.
	Il est dix heures du soir.
It's early/late.	Il est tôt/tard.
We're early/late.	Nous sommes en avance/en retard.
in the morning	du matin
in the afternoon	de l'après-midi
in the evening	du soir

DAYS

Monday	lundi
Tuesday	mardi
Wednesday	mercredi
Thursday	jeudi
Friday	vendredi
Saturday	samedi
Sunday	dimanche

MONTHS

January	janvier	July	juillet
February	février	August	août
March	mars	September	septembre
April	avril	October	octobre
May	mai	November	novembre
June	juin	December	décembre

DATES

What date is it today?	C'est quel jour aujourd'hui?
It's 18 October.	C'est le 18 octobre.
It's 1 October.	C'est le premier octobre.
1998	mille neuf cent quatre-vingt-dix-huit
2000	deux mille

PRESENT

today	aujourd'hui
this morning	ce matin
this afternoon	cet/cette après-midi
tonight	ce soir
this week	cette semaine
this month	ce mois
this year	cette année
right now	tout de suite
immediately	immédiatement
now	maintenant

PAST

yesterday	hier
day before yesterday	avant-hier
yesterday morning	hier matin
yesterday afternoon	hier après-midi

last night/evening	hier soir
last week	la semaine dernière
last month	le mois dernier
last year	l'année dernière
half an hour ago	il y a une demi-heure
five days ago	il y a cinq jours
since ... o'clock	depuis ... heure(s)

FUTURE

tomorrow	demain
the day after tomorrow	après-demain
tomorrow morning	demain matin
tomorrow afternoon	demain après-midi
tomorrow evening	demain soir
next week	la semaine prochaine
next year	l'année prochaine
next month	le mois prochain
soon	bientôt
in ... minutes/hours/days	dans ... minute(s)/heure(s)/ jour(s)
within an hour/day	d'ici une heure/un jour

DURING THE DAY

day	le jour
dawn	l'aube; l'aurore
sunrise	l'aube; le lever du soleil
early	tôt
morning	le matin
midday/noon	midi
afternoon	l'après-midi
sundown	le coucher du soleil
evening	le soir
night	la nuit
midnight	minuit

USEFUL WORDS

calendar	un calendrier	future	l'avenir
clock	une horloge; une pendule	later	plus tard
		minute	une minute
diary	un agenda	never	jamais
watch	une montre	not yet	pas encore
always	toujours	often	souvent
annual	annuel/le	on time	à l'heure
before	avant	past	le passé
every day	quotidien/ne	present	le présent
forever	toujours; très longtemps	recently	récemment
		second	une seconde
fortnight	une quinzaine; quinze jours	seldom	rarement
		sometime	un de ces jours
from time to time	de temps en temps	sometimes	quelquefois
		soon	bientôt

CROSSWORD – TIME & DATES

Across

3. Ten of these a decade
5. Day two days before tomorrow
7. On average, 4.3. of these a month
9. Literally translated as 'all days'
12. The witching hour
14. One of these named after Augustus Caesar

Down

1. Before midday
2. Consists of 60 minutes
4. Moment you are living in
6. A day that never comes
7. Regularly
8. Time it takes Earth to spin full circle
10. At no time, not ever
11. The fourth dimension?
13. Worst time to get out of bed

Answers on page 310.

NUMBERS & AMOUNTS

CARDINAL NUMBERS

0	zéro	17	dix-sept
1	un	18	dix-huit
2	deux	19	dix-neuf
3	trois	20	vingt
4	quatre	21	vingt et un
5	cinq	22	vingt-deux
6	six	30	trente
7	sept	40	quarante
8	huit	50	cinquante
9	neuf	60	soixante
10	dix	70	soixante-dix
11	onze	80	quatre-vingts
12	douze	90	quatre-vingt-dix
13	treize	100	cent
14	quatorze	1000	mille
15	quinze	one million	un million
16	seize		

ORDINAL NUMBERS

first	premier (1er)/première (1ère)
second	second/deuxième (2e)
third	troisième (3e)
fourth	quatrième (4e)
fifth	cinquième (5e)
sixth	sixième (6e)
seventh	septième (7e)
eighth	huitième (8e)
ninth	neuvième (9e)
tenth	dixième (10e)
twentieth	vingtième (20e)
hundredth	centième (100e)
thousandth	millième (1000e)

FRACTIONS

1/4	un quart	1/2	un demi
1/3	un tiers	3/4	trois-quarts

USEFUL WORDS

a little	un peu	many	beaucoup de
double	double	more	plus
a dozen	une douzaine	once	une fois
Enough!	Assez!; Ça suffit!	a pair	une paire
few	peu de	percent	pour cent
a few	quelques	some	du (m)/de la (f)/ des (pl)
(about) a hundred	une centaine	too much	trop
less	moins	twice	deux fois

CROSSWORD – NUMBERS & AMOUNTS

Across
5. Four times 7.5
7. Not all, a few
9. Twelve
10. In excess
11. Less
12. Number invented by Arab civilisation
13. One spot below ninth

Down
1. Years in a century
2. Number of sides to an octagon
3. Millennium of years
4. A great deal, many
6. One-fourth
8. Four times 3.5

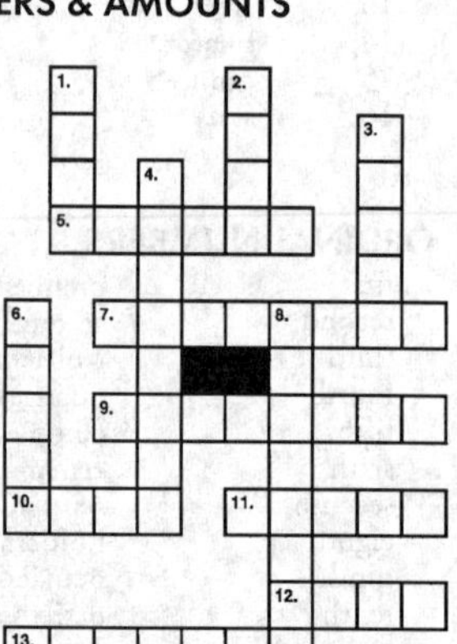

Answers on page 310.

Since the French Revolution, linguistic unification has been imposed in France through the use of the Paris dialect in media, politics and education. Because of the privileged status of its speakers, this variety came to be known as standard French. However, there are many other dialects spoken throughout the country which are often perjoratively termed **patois**. They vary in vocabulary, grammar and especially pronunciation. For example, southern French is more nasal and sounds twangy, with words such as **pain** (bread) and **vin** (wine) becoming 'paing' and 'ving' respectively. In addition, a number of other separate languages or dialects are spoken in France: Alsatian, Franconian, Basque, Breton, Catalan, Corsican and Occitan.

ALSATIAN & FRANCONIAN

Throughout history, the people of the regions of Alsace and Lorraine in the north-east of France have moved back and forth under the respective control of the Germans and the French and this has markedly influenced their language. While French is the language of public life and education, the people of Alsace and Lorraine are exposed to standard German *(Hochdeutsch)* through the media of their German neighbours. Like Franconian, which is spoken in Luxembourg and the north of Lorraine, Alsatian is a Germanic dialect which is used mainly at home, amongst friends or in specialised domains (eg winemaking terminology).

river	**bach**
mountain/hill	**berg; hübel**
fountain	**brunnen; burn**
farm	**hof**
rock	**stein; fels**
valley	**thal; tal**
forest	**wald**

Due to the German influence Alsatian cuisine is very different from typical French cuisine:

bibeleskäs	soft, white cheese with potatoes
bretzel	pretzel
flammekueche	salty tart with soft, white cheese and onions
kassler	smoked pork
raifort	horseradish
spaetzle	pasta
winstub	an Alsatian café

BASQUE

The origins of the Basque language (Euskara) are shrouded in mystery. Some scholars believe it is related to languages from the Caucasus, others link it to languages from Africa, and still others highlight similarities with languages from Asia (Japanese for example). Despite the successive invasions of the Gauls and the Romans, Basque has managed to survive to the present day. Although Basque is not related to neighbouring languages (it is not an Indo-European language) it has been influenced by the languages of its invaders and neighbours: Latin, Castilian, French and Celtic languages. On the other hand, French and English have taken words from Basque. The word 'bizarre', for example, is of Basque origin.

Basque is spoken by about 1,000,000 people in France and Spain. The French Basque Country *(Pays Basque)* is north of the Pyrénées in France's far south-western corner. Centuries of neglect and marginalisation, combined with two centuries of French republicanism and 40 years of Spanish fascism, pushed Basque to the brink of extinction but pride in the language has resulted in its preservation. (There is now a television station in France that broadcasts in Basque.)

Note that in Basque, z is pronounced as the 's' in 'sun' and tx is pronounced as the 'ch' in 'church'.

Greetings & Civilities

Hi!	Kaixo!
How are you?	Zer moduz?
What's up?	Zer berri?
Fine and you?	Ongi eta zu?
Goodbye.	Agur.
See you later.	Gero arte.
Please.	Mesedez.
Thank you.	Eskerrik asko.
Excuse me	Barkatu
You're welcome.	Ez horregatik.
How do you say that in Basque?	Nola esaten da hori euskaraz?

BASQUE SIGNS

IREKITA	OPEN
ITXITA	CLOSED
IRTEERA	EXIT
SARRERA	ENTRANCE
KOMUNA	TOILETS
TURISMO BULEGOA	TOURIST OFFICE

Food

The Basque Country has a reputation for having some of the best food in the world. There are a variety of places to eat; from first-class restaurants, small restaurants, bars serving food, and cider houses sagardotegi. The coast, of course, is best known for its seafood.

Waiter!	Aizu!
I'd like ...	... nahi nuke.

salad	entsalada
vegetables	barazkiak
chips (French Fries)	patata frijituak
sheep's curds	mamia
beer	garagardoa
beer (draught)	kaina bat
wine	ardo
coffee	kafe
water	aura

BRETON

Breton (Brezhoneg) is a Celtic language which is spoken in the extreme west part of Brittany. It originated in the 5th and 6th centuries when Anglo-Saxon invaders forced Britons to flee Wales and Cornwall. Estimates of the number of Breton speakers range from 300,00 to 600,000, which makes it the most spoken Celtic language apart from Irish. But it is important to distinguish native speakers who use Breton in everyday life (farmers, fishermen, etc) from the growing number of néobretonnants who have learnt the language of their parents and grandparents and who send their children to Breton-speaking schools *(Diwan)*. As with all Celtic languages, it is unlikely that Breton will fully recover from nearly two centuries of neglect and marginalisation as a result of French unification and centralisation policies.

Brittany	Breiz
Yes.	Ya.
No.	N'on ket.
Pardon.	Fez noz.
Goodbye.	Kenavo.
What's your name?	Pe anv bihan a vez graet ac' hanoc' h?
My name is ...	Graet a vez ... ac'hanon.
parish	ploe; plou; plo; pleu
holy place	loc
church	lann

village; house	ker
valley	traon; trou; tro
wood	coat; goat; goët; hoët

un far breton	batter pudding with prunes
un kouign amann	a rich buttery brioche
du chouchenn	Breton mead

CATALAN

Catalan is a Romance language, closely related to Occitan, with around 200,000 speakers in France. These people are based around the city of Perpignan in the Department of Pyrénées Orientales.

Like the Basque speakers in France in relation to their Spanish counterparts, the Catalan speakers in France are markedly worse off than those in Andorra, Catalonia and the Balearic Islands, where it is one of the official languages. Nevertheless, they too benefit from the cultural achievements of their southern neighbours, who produced painters such as Dalí, architects like Gaudí and great writers like Mercè Rodoreda. Catalan militants in France are divided between the creation of a greater Catalunya with the centre in Barcelona, and the prospect of extended autonomy within France.

Greetings & Civilities

Hello.	Hola!
Goodbye.	Adéu; Adéu-siau.
Yes/No.	Sì/No.
Excuse me.	Perdoni.
May I/Do you mind?	Puc/Em permet?
Sorry. (forgive me)	Ho sento; Perdoni.
Please.	Sisplau; Si us plau.
Thank you (very much).	(Moltes) Gràcies.
You're welcome; Fine.	De res.
See you.	A reveure.

How are you?	Com estàs?
(Very) well.	(Molt) bé.
Not too bad	Anar fent.
Awful.	Malament.
No problem.	Això rai.
What is your name?	Com et dius? (inf)
	Com es diu? (pol)
My name's ...	Em dic ...
What a laugh!	Quin tip de riure!
Where are you from?	D'on ets?
What is this called in Catalan?	Com es diu això en català?

Getting Around

Excuse me, where is ...?	Perdoni, on és ...?
the bus station	l'estació d'autobús/autocar
the post office	Correus
the train station	l'estació de tren

CATALAN SIGNS

OBERT	OPEN
TANCAT	CLOSED
ENTRADA	ENTRANCE
INFORMACIO	INFORMATION
NO TOCAR	DO NOT TOUCH
SORTIDA	EXIT
SERVEIS	TOILETS

Typical Catalan Dishes

allioli	garlic sauce
calçots	shallots, usually served braised with an almond dipping sauce. A seasonal delicacy.
escalivada	roasted red peppers in olive oil

escudella I carn d'olla	a Christmas dish of soup and meatballs
mel i mató	a dessert of curd cheese with honey
mongetes seques i butifarra	haricot beans with thick pork sausage
pa amb tomàquet i pernil	crusty bread rubbed with ripe tomatoes, garlic and olive oil, often topped with cured ham

CORSICAN

Corsica became French territory in 1769 (the year Napoleon Bonaparte was born). French, therefore, is the official language of the island. Corsican (Corsu) is a dialect of Italian and has several sub-varieties. Unlike most other regional languages and dialects spoken in France, Corsican has resisted 'francisation' and is today an important element of pride and identity. It is used in the campaign literature of Corsican nationalists, in folk songs and on some radio programs. For the 150,000 or so speakers, Corsican is a language mainly used at home and with friends. Before the mid-seventies, however, Corsican was just an oral language but now it is a compulsory subject in schools and universities.

Yes.	Yé.
No.	No; Inno.
Good morning.	Bondiornu.
Good evening.	Bona sera.
Good evening.	A vedeci.
How are you?	Cumu state?
I understand.	Capiscu.
I don't understand.	Un capiscu micca.
What time is it?	Chi ora e?
today	hoddie
tomorrow	dumane

breakfast	u spuntinu	wine	vinu
lunch	a cullazio	red	rossu
dinner	a cena	white	biancu
oil	l'oliu	rose	russulatu

OCCITAN

The generic term Occitan refers to the dialects spoken over a large territory in the south of France, spreading from the area north of Bordeaux to the region south of Grenoble, and even extending partially into northern Italy. As the language of the troubadours, Occitan enjoyed great literary prestige during the Middle Ages. However, economic and religious imperialism from the north resulted in the Parisian dialect being imposed in administrative spheres.

Amongst the characteristics which separate Occitan from standard French and which justify its claim to be an independent language is the absence of nasal vowels and the omission of personal pronouns (eg, I, we, him, they, etc.).

Unlike Catalan, Occitan has no standard and so reference is often made to the individual varieties: Provençal, Gascon, Limousin, Languedocien, etc. Recent estimates suggest around eight million speakers, of which two million use the language every day.

The most important of the Occitan languages is Provençal. It was the standard and literary language from the 12th to 14th centuries but due to growing political and religious pressure from the North it deteriorated into a collection of divergent dialects. It is closely related to Catalan and, although influenced by French, its spelling and grammar are closer to Spanish.

See!	Vé!	farm	mas
Well! well!	Peuchère!	granny	mamet
Bloody hell!	Putain(g)!	grandad	papet
My goodness!	Boudiou!	tired	escagassé
child	pitchoun	to gossip	cascayer
sun	cagnard		

EMERGENCIES

Dial 15 anywhere in France in case of an emergency.

Help!	Au secours!
Go away!	Allez-vous-en!
Careful/Look out!	Attention!
Fire!	Au feu!
Leave me alone!	Laissez-moi tranquille!
Thief!	Au voleur!
It's an emergency!	C'est urgent!
There's been an accident!	Il y a eu un accident!
Call a doctor!	Appelez un médecin!
Call an ambulance!	Appelez une ambulance!
Call the police!	Appelez la police!
Where is the police station?	Où est le commissariat de police?
Could you help me, please?	Est-ce que vous pourriez m'aider, s'il vous plaît?
I've been raped.	J'ai été violé/e.
I've been robbed.	J'ai été volé/e.
I'm ill.	Je suis malade.
My friend is ill.	Mon ami/e est malade.
I'm lost.	Je me suis perdu/e.
I've lost my friend.	J'ai perdu mon ami/e.
Where are the toilets?	Où sont les toilettes?
I speak English.	Je parle anglais.
Could I please use the telephone?	Est-ce que je pourrais utiliser le téléphone?
I have medical insurance.	J'ai une assurance maladie.
My possessions are insured.	Mes biens sont assurés.

... was stolen.	On m'a volé ...
I've lost ...	J'ai perdu ...
my bags	mes bagages
my handbag	mon sac à main
my money	mon argent
my travellers cheques	mes chèques de voyage
my passport	mon passeport

DEALING WITH THE POLICE

SIGNS

POLICE	POLICE
COMMISSARIAT DE POLICE	POLICE STATION

I want to report an offence.	Je veux signaler un délit.
I'm sorry. I apologise.	Je suis désolé/e. Je m'excuse.
I didn't realise I was doing anything wrong.	Je ne savais pas que je n'avais pas le droit de le faire.
I'm innocent.	Je suis innocent/e.
I didn't do it.	Ce n'est pas moi qui l'ai fait.
What am I accused of?	De quoi suis-je accusé/e?
Do I have the right to make a call?	J'ai le droit de donner un coup de fil?
Can I call someone?	Je peux appeler quelqu'un?
I wish to contact my embassy/consulate.	Je veux contacter mon ambassade/mon consulat.
Can I have a lawyer?	Je peux avoir un avocat?
I will only make a statement in the presence of my lawyer.	Je ne parlerai qu'en présence de mon avocat.
I refuse to be searched unless my lawyer is here.	Je refuse d'être fouillé/e avant l'arrivée de mon avocat.

I want to see a female officer.	Je veux voir un agent de police féminin.
Is there someone here who speaks English?	Y a-t-il quelqu'un qui parle anglais ?
I'm sorry, I don't speak French.	Je suis désolé/e, je ne parle pas français.
Can I pay an on-the-spot fine?	Je peux payer l'amende tout de suite?
Is there a fine?	Je vais avoir une amende?
That's just where I keep spare change.	C'est là que je garde ma monnaie.
This is just for personal use.	C'est uniquement pour mon usage personnel.

THEY MAY SAY ...

Quels sont vos nom et adresse?
What is your name and address?

Montrez-moi ...	Show me ...
votre passeport	your passport
vos papiers (d'identité)	your identity papers
votre permis de conduire	your driving licence

Montrez-moi votre permis de travail.
Show me your work permit.
Je vous arrête.
You are under arrest.
Vous allez avoir une contravention.
We are giving you a traffic fine.
Il faut nous accompagner au commissariat.
You must come with us to the police station.
Vous avez le droit de ne parler qu'en présence de votre avocat.
You don't have to say anything until you are in the presence of a lawyer.

Charges

theft	un vol
to be in possession (of drugs/weapons)	être en possession (de drogue/d'armes)
rape	un viol
murder	un meurtre
aiding & abetting	une complicité
disturbing the peace	un tapage (nocturne)
drunk & disorderly	en état d'ébriété

Useful Words

to arrest	arrêter
cell	une cellule
cop	un flic; un poulet
court	un tribunal
identity papers	des papiers d'identité
judge	un juge
lawyer	un/e avocat/e
police car	une voiture de police
police officer	un gendarme (country) un policier; un agent de police (city)
prison	une prison
to be put in police custody	être placé en garde à vue
to be released through lack of evidence	être relâché par manque de preuves

ENGLISH – FRENCH

A

In this dictionary, as in the rest of the book, the masculine version of a word appears first, separated from the feminine by a slash. Synonyms and alternative meanings are separated by a semicolon. The article has been included, either definite ('the') or indefinite ('a/an'), depending on how the word is most likely to be used. Where the gender of a word is not obvious from the article, we have used the abbreviations (m) or (f). The past participles of verbs (see page 33) have been included in brackets.

A

a/an		un/e
to be able		pouvoir
I can.		Je peux.
I can't.		Je ne peux pas.
abortion	un	avortement
about/ approximately		environ; à peu près
above		au-dessus
abroad		à l'étranger
absolutely		absolument
to accept		accepter (accepté)
accident	un	accident
accommodation	le	logement
to accompany		accompagner (accompagné)
account	un	compte
ache	une	douleur
achievement	un	exploit;
	une	réussite
acid (drug)	l'	acide (m)
to act		jouer (joué)
actor	un	acteur/
	une	actrice
acupuncture	l'	acupuncture (f)
adaptor	un	adaptateur
addict	un	intoxiqué/
	une	intoxiquée
addiction	la	dépendance;
	la	toxicomanie
additional		supplémentaire
address	une	adresse
administration	l'	administration (f)
to admire		admirer
admission	une	admission;
	une	entrée
adventure	un	aventure
advertisement	une	réclame;
	une	publicité
advice	un	un conseil
to advise		conseiller (conseillé)
aerogram	un	aérogramme
aeroplane	un	avion
affair	une	liaison
to be afraid		avoir peur
after		après
afternoon	un	après-midi
aftershave	un	après-rasage
again		encore
against		contre
age	l'	âge (m)
aggressive		agressif/ agressive

D I C T I O N A R Y

to agree		être d'accord
I agree.		
Je suis d'accord.		
I don't agree.		
Je ne suis pas d'accord.		
Do you agree?		
Vous êtes d'accord?		
agriculture	l'	agriculture (f)
ahead		en avant
AIDS	le	SIDA
air	l'	air (m)
air (for tyres)	le	compresseur
air mail		par avion
air-conditioned		climatisé
alarm clock	un	réveil
alcohol	l'	alcool (m)
alive		vivant/e
all		tout
allergic to		allergique à
allergy	une	allergie
to allow		permettre (permis)
almost		presque
alone		tout/e seul/e
aloud		à haute voix
already		déjà
also		aussi
alternative	une	alternative
always		toujours
amateur	un	amateur
amazing		stupéfiant/e
ambassador	un / une	ambassadeur/ ambassadrice
ambulance	une	ambulance
among		parmi
amount (money)	la	somme
anaemic		anémique
anarchy	l'	anarchie (f)
ancient		antique
and		et
angle	un	angle
angry		fâché/e

animal	un	animal
ankle	la	cheville
annual		annuel/le
another	un/e	autre
to answer		répondre (répondu)
answer	une	réponse
ant	une	fourmi
antibiotics	les	antibiotiques
antiseptic	un	antiseptique
anyone		n'importe qui
anything		n'importe quoi
anywhere		n'importe où
appendix	les	appendices
appointment	un	rendez-vous
approval	l'	approbation (f)
approximately		environ; à peu près
April		avril
archaeology	l'	archéologie (f)
architecture	l'	architecture
to argue		se disputer (disputé)
argument	un	débat
arm	le	bras
armchair	un	fauteuil
around		autour
to arrest		arrêter (arrêté)
to arrive		arriver (arrivé)
art	l'	art (m)
art gallery	un / une	musée (state); galerie (private)
artist	un/e	artiste
as		comme
ashtray	un	cendrier
to ask		demander (demandé)
aspirin	une	aspirine
associate	un / une	associé/ associée
asthmatic		asthmatique
at		à

athletics	l'	athlétisme (m)
atmosphere	une	atmosphère
attached		attaché/e
auction	la	vente aux enchères
August		août
automatic		automatique
automatic teller machine (ATM)	le	guichet automatique de banque (GAB)
autumn	l'	automne (m)
avenue	une	avenue
away		absent; hors d'ici; au loin
awful		affreux; terrible

B

B&W (film)		noir et blanc
baby	le	bébé
babysitter	un/e	baby-sitter
back	le	dos
backpack	un	sac-à-dos
bad		mauvais/e
bag	le	sac
baggage	les	bagages
bakery	la	boulangerie
balcony	le	balcon
ball	une	balle (de tennis);
	un	ballon (de football)
ballet	le	ballet
band	une	bande;
	un	orchestre
bandage	un	pansement
bank	la	banque
bank draft	une	traite bancaire
bank notes	les	billets de banque
baptism	un	baptême
barley	l'	orge (f)
baseball	le	baseball
basic		fondamental
basketball	le	basket(ball)
bastard	un	salaud;
	un	connard
bat	une	batte
bathroom	la	salle de bain
battery	une	pile
battery (car)	une	batterie
to be		être
I am ...		
Je suis ...		
You are ...		
Vous êtes ...		
beach	la	plage
beautiful		beau/belle
because		parce que
to become		devenir (devenu)
bed	un	lit
to go to bed		se coucher (couché)
bed linen	les	draps
bee	une	abeille
before		avant
beggar	un	mendiant
to begin		commencer (commencé)
beginner	un	débutant/
	une	débutante
behind		derrière
belief	la	croyance
to believe		croire
to belong		appartenir (appartenu)
belongings	les	affaires
below		sous
beside		à côté de
best	le/la	meilleur/e
best man	le	garçon d'honneur
bet	un	pari
to bet		parier (parié); miser (misé)
between		entre

beyond (space)		au-delà de
bib	un	bavoir
bicycle; bike	une	bicyclette;
	un	vélo
big		grand/e
bigger		plus grand/e
biggest	le/la	plus grand/e
bill	la	note
bill (restaurant)	une	addition
bird	un	oiseau
birthday	un	anniversaire
Happy birthday!		Bon anniversaire!
bitch	une	salope
bite	une	morsure
to bite		mordre (mordu)
bitter		amer/amère
black		noir/e
blame	la	faute
blanket	la	couverture
blessing	la	grâce; la faveur
blind		aveugle
blister	une	ampoule
blood	le	sang
blood test	une	analyse de sang
to blow		souffler (soufflé)
blue		bleu/e
boat	un	bateau
body	le	corps
bomb	une	bombe
to book		réserver (réservé)
book	un	livre
bookshop	la	librairie
boring		ennuyeux/ ennuyeuse
born		né/e
to borrow		emprunter (emprunté)
Can I borrow this?		
Je peux l'emprunter?		
boss	le	chef
both		tous les deux
bottle	une	bouteille
bottle opener	un	ouvre-bouteille
boulevard	le	boulevard
boxing	la	boxe
boy	le	garçon
boyfriend	un	petit ami;
	un	copain
brakes	les	freins
brass	le	cuivre jaune
brave		courageux/ courageuse
to break		casser (cassé)
breakfast	le	petit déjeuner
breast	un	sein
to bribe		suborner (suborné)
bribe	un	pot-de-vin
bride	une	mariée
bridesmaid	une	demoiselle d'honneur
bridge	un	pont
brief		bref/brève
bright (shining)		brillant/e
to bring (a thing)		apporter (apporté)
(a person)		amener (amené)
broadcast	une	émission
broken		cassé/e
broken down		(tombé) en panne
bronchitis	une	bronchite
brother	le	frère
brown		brun/brune; marron
bruise	une	ecchymose;
	un	bleu
brush	la	brosse
Buddhist		bouddhiste
budget	le	budget
building	un	bâtiment

bum/ass le derrière; le cul
bump la bosse
to burn brûler (brûlé)
burn une brûlure
bus un (auto)bus
bus (intercity) un (auto)car
bus station la gare routière
bus stop un arrêt d'autobus
business les affaires
business person un homme/ une femme d'affaires
busker un/e musicien/ne des rues
busy occupé/e
but mais
butcher (shop) la boucherie
butterfly le papillon
to buy acheter (acheté)
  I'd like to buy ...
  Je voudrais acheter ...
by par

C

café le café; le troquet; le bistrot
cake un gâteau
calendar le calendrier
calf le veau
to call appeler (appelé)
camera un appareil photo
camping ground un camping
can une boîte
can (to be able to) pouvoir (pu)
  Can I ...?
  Puis-je ...?
can opener un ouvre-boîte
to cancel annuler (annulé)
candle la bougie
capitalism le capitalisme
car la voiture
card une carte
care le soin
  I don't care.
  Ça m'est égal.
career une carrière
careful soigneux/ soigneuse
Careful! Attention!
to carry porter (porté)
carton une barquette; une boîte
cartoon un dessin animé
cash l' argent (m)
cashier un caissier/ une caissière
cassette la cassette
cast la distribution
castle un château
casual (work) intermittent
cat un chat
to catch attraper (attrapé)
cathedral une cathédrale
Catholic catholique
cause la cause; la raison
caution la prudence
cave une grotte
ceiling le plafond
celebration la fête
cell une cellule
cemetary le cimetière
centre le centre
ceramic une céramique
certificate un certificat
certain certain
chain une chaîne
chair la chaise
chairlift un télésiège
champagne le champagne
championship un championnat
chance le hasard
to change échanger (échangé)

change (coins)	la	monnaie
channel	la	chaîne
charity	la	charité
to chat		bavarder (bavardé)
to chat up		draguer (dragué)
cheap		bon marché/e
check		vérifier
check-in	l'	enregistrement
cheese	le	fromage
chef	un	chef de cuisine
chemist (shop)	la	pharmacie
chemist (person)	le/la	pharmacien/ne
chess	les	échecs
chest (anatomy)	la	poitrine
chicken	le	poulet
child	un/e	enfant
children	les	enfants
chocolate	le	chocolat
choice	un	choix
choir	une	chorale
to choose		choisir (choisi)
Christian		chrétien/ne
Christmas		Noël
Merry Christmas!		Joyeux Noël!
church	une	église
cigarette	une	cigarette
cigarette machine	un	distributeur de cigarettes
cigarette papers	les	papiers à cigarettes
cinema/movies	le	cinéma; le ciné
circle	le	cercle
citizen	un/e	citoyen/ne
city	la	ville
city centre	le	centre-ville
city hall	la	mairie
city walls	les	remparts
clean		propre
to clean		nettoyer (nettoyé)

clear		clair/e
cliff	une	falaise
clock	une	horloge;
	une	pendule
to close		fermer (fermé)
close		proche
clothes	les	vêtements
cloud	le	nuage
clown	un	clown
clutch	l'	embrayage
coach (person)	un	entraîneur
coast	la	côte
coat	un	manteau
cocaine	la	cocaïne
cocktail	un	cocktail
coffee	le	café
coins	la	monnaie;
		les pièces
cold		froid/e
colleague	un/e	collègue;
	un	confrère
to collect		collectionner (collectionné)
collection	une	accumulation
college	une	école professionnelle;
	un	institut universitaire
colloquial		familier
colour	la	couleur
comb	un	peigne
combination	la	combinaison
to come		venir (venu)
Come here!		Venez ici!
comfortable		confortable
comic (person)	le/la	comique
comic (magazine)	un	comic;
	une	bande dessinée
commence		commencer (commencé)
commission	la	commission
common		commun/e
to communicate		communiquer (communiqué)

to drop		laisser tomber (laissé tomber)
dropout	un	zonard
drugs	la la	drogue; dope
drunk		ivre
dry		sec/sèche
duck	un	canard
dummy (for baby)	une	tétine
during		pendant
dust	la	poussière
duty	le	devoir

E

each		chaque
ear	une	oreille
early		tôt
to earn		gagner (gagné)
earnings	un	salaire
earring	une	boucle d'oreille
Earth		La Terre
earth/ground	la	terre
earthquake	un	tremblement de terre
at ease		à l'aise
east	l'	est (m)
Easter		Pâques
Happy Easter!		Joyeuses Pâques!
easy		facile
to eat		manger (mangé)
economical		économique
economy	l'	économie (f)
ecstasy	l' l'	extase (f); ecstasy (drug)
edge	le	bord
education	une	éducation
effect	un	effet
eight		huit
elderly		assez âgé/e
election	une	élection
electricity	l'	électricité (f)
elevator	un	ascenseur
eligible		éligible; admissible
else		d'autre
email	un	e-mail
to embarrass		gêner (gêné)
embarrassing		gênant
embassy	une	ambassade
embroidery	la	broderie
emergency	un	cas urgent
employee	un une	employé employée
employer	un	employeur
empty		vide
to end		finir (fini)
end	le	bout
endless		sans fin; interminable
energy	une	énergie
engaged		fiancé/e
engagement	les	fiançailles
engine	le	moteur
engineer	l'	ingénieur (m)
to enjoy (oneself)		s'amuser (amusé)
enough		assez
That's enough!		Ça suffit!
to enter		entrer (entré)
entertainment	le	divertissement
enthusiastic		enthousiaste
entire		entier/entière
entry	une	entrée
envelope	une	enveloppe
environment	un	environnement
epileptic		épileptique
equal		égale
equality		égalité
equipment	l'	équipement (m)
erratic (person)		fantasque

communion	la	communion
communism	le	communisme
communist		communiste
community	la	communauté
company	une	entreprise
compass	la	boussole
competition	une	compétition
complaint	la	plainte
complete		complet/complète
complex		complexe
complimentary (free)		gracieux
computer	un	ordinateur
concerning		au sujet de; à propos de
concert	un	concert
concert hall	une	salle de concert
concussion	la	commotion cérébrale
condition	la un	condition; état
condom	un	préservatif
conductor (bus)	un	receveur
confectionary	la	confiserie
conference	un un	congrès (big); colloque (small)
confession	la	confession
confident		assuré/e
to confirm		confirmer
Congratulations!		Félicitations!
conscious		conscient/e
conservative		conservateur/conservatrice
contact lenses	les les	verres de contact; lentilles de contact
contagious		contagieux/contagieuse
contraceptive	un	contraceptif
contract	un	contrat
convent	un	couvent
conversation	une	conversation
to cook		cuire (cuit); cuisiner (cuisiné)
cook	un une	cuisinier/ cuisinière
cool		frais/fraîche
to cooperate		coopérer (coopéré)
cop	un	flic; un poulet
copper	le	cuivre
cops/fuzz	les	volailles
corn	le	maïs
corner	le	coin
on the corner		au coin
correct		correct/e; exact/e
corridor	le	couloir
corruption	la	corruption
to cost		coûter (coûté)
How much is it? C'est combien?		
cotton	le	coton
couch/sofa	un	divan; sofa
cough	une	toux
cough medicine	un	syrop contre la toux
council	le	conseil
to count		compter (compté)
counter	le	comptoir; le zinc (inf)
country	le	pays
court	un	tribunal
cow	une	vache
crazy		fou/folle
credit	le	crédit
credit card	la la	carte de crédit; carte bleue
creek	une	crique
cricket	le	cricket
crime	un	délit
crop	une	récolte;
to cross		traverser (traveré)

crowd	la	foule
crowded		bondé/e; plein/e
cruise	la	croisière
cry		pleurer (pleuré)
cup	la	tasse
cupboard	le	placard
curb	le	bord du trottoir
current		courant/e
current affairs	les	magazines d'actualité
curtain	le	rideau
custom	une	coutume
customer	le/la	client/e
customs	la	douane
to cut		couper (coupé)
cute		mignon/ mignonne
cycling	le	cyclisme

D

daily		quotidien/ne
damage	les	dégats
Damn!		Bon sang!; Merde!
damp		humide
to dance		danser (dansé)
dangerous		dangereux/ dangereuse
dark		obscur/e; sombre
dark (of colour)		foncé/e
date	un	rendez-vous
date (time)	la	date
daughter	la	fille
dawn	l'	aurore/aube
day	le	jour
dead		mort/e
deaf		sourd/e
death	la	mort

debit	le	débit
December		décembre
to decide		se décider (décidé)
decision	une	décision
deduct		déduire (déduit)
deep		profond/e
definite		bien déterminé
deforestation	le	déboisement
degree/diploma	un	diplôme
delay	le	rétard/délai
delicatessen	la	charcuterie
delirious		délirant/e
to demand		exiger (exigé)
democracy	la	démocratie
demonstration (protest)	une	manifestation
dental floss	le	fil dentaire
dentist	le	dentiste
to deny		nier (nié)
deodorant	le	déodorant
to depart		partir (parti)

What time does the bus leave?
Le bus part à quelle heure?

department store	le	grand magasin
departure	le	départ
deposit	le	dépôt
description	la	description
desert	le	désert
desperate		désespéré/e
dessert	le	dessert
to destroy		détruire (détruit)
detail	le	détail
development	le	développement
diabetic		diabétique
diagram	une	diagramme
dialect	un	dialecte
diarrhoea	la	diarrhée
diary	un	agenda
dictator	un	dictateur
dictatorship	la	dictature

dictionary	un	dictionnaire
to die		mourir (mort)
diesel	le	gasoil
diet	un	régime
different		différent/e
difficult		difficile
dining car	le	wagon-restaurant
dinner	le	dîner
diploma	un	diplôme
direct		direct/e
to direct (a film)		réaliser
direction	la	direction;
	le	sens
director (film)	un	réalisateur/
	une	réalisatrice
dirty		sale
disabled		handicapé/e
disadvantage	un	désavantage
disappointed		déçu/e
disaster	un	désastre
disc jockey	un	disc-jockey
discount	une	remise
to discover		découvrir (découvert)
discrimination	la	discrimination
to discuss		discuter (discuté)
disease	une	maladie
dish	un	plat
dishonest		malhonnête
disinfectant	le	désinfectant
distance	la	distance
distant		lointain/e
distributor	un	concessionnaire
to disturb		déranger (dérangé)
to dive		plonger (plongé)
diving	la	plongée (sous-marine)
divorced		divorcé/e
to do		faire

I'll do it.
Je le fais.
Can you do it?
Pouvez-vous le faire?

doctor	un	médecin
documentary	un	documentaire
dog	un	chien
dog bite	une	morsure de chien
dole	l'	allocation;
	l'	indemnité de chômage
donkey	un	âne
dope (drugs)	la	dope
dose	la	dose
double		double
double bed	un	grand lit;
	un	lit double
down/downstairs		en bas
dozen	une	douzaine
draw	un	tiroir
to draw (picture)		dessiner (dessiné)
drawing	un	dessin
dream	un	rêve
dress	une	robe
to get dressed		s'habiller (habillé)
drink	la	boisson
drink (alcoholic)	un	verre
to drink		boire (bu)

Let's have a drink.
On boit un coup.
I don't drink.
Je ne bois pas.

to drive		conduire (conduit)

Can you drive?
Vous pouvez conduire?
May I drive?
Je peux conduire?

driver's/driving licence	le	permis d[illegible] condu[illegible]

to escape		échapper (échappé)
estate agency	une	agence immobilière
even (adv)		même
evening	un	soir
event	un	événement
every		chaque
everything		tout
every day		tous les jours
everyone		tout le monde
exactly		exactement
exam	un	examen
excellent		excellent/e
except		sauf; à l'exception de
to exchange		échanger (échangé)
excluded		pas compris
excuse	une	excuse
to excuse		excuser (excusé)
Excuse me. Excusez-moi.		
executive	un	cadre
exercise	l'	exercice (m)
exhausted		épuisé/e
exhibition	une	exposition
exile	un / une	exilé/ exilée
exit	la	sortie
exotic		exotique
expenses	les	frais
expensive		cher/chère
experience	une	expérience
to explain		expliquer (expliqué)
export		exporter (exporté)
extra		supplémentaire; de plus
extraordinary		extraordinaire
eye	un	œil
eyes	les	yeux

F

face	le / la	visage; figure
fact	le	fait
in fact		en effet
factory	une	usine
fag; smoke	une	clope
failure	un	échec
faith	la	foi; la confiance
to fall		tomber (tombé)
false/fake		faux/fausse
family	la	famille
famous		célèbre
fan	le	ventilateur
far		lointain/e
fare	le	tarif
farm	la	ferme
farmer	un / une	agriculteur/ agricultrice
fascist		fasciste
fashion	la	mode
to fast (not eat)		jeûner (jeûné)
fast (quick)		rapide
fat		gras/grasse
fate	le	destin
father	le	père
favour	un	service
fax machine	un / un	télécopieur; fax
fear	la	peur
February		février
to feed		nourrir (nourri)
to feel		toucher (touché)
feeling (something)	une / une	sensation; émotion
female		femelle

fence	une	barrière
fencing (sport)	l'	escrime (f)
ferry	un	bac
festival	la	fête
fever	une	fièvre
few		peu
fiction	la	fiction
field	un	champ
fight	une	bagarre
film	un	film
filter	un	filtre
find		trouver (trouvé)
fine (penalty)	une	amende
finger	un	doigt
finish		finir (fini)
fire	le	feu
firewood	le	bois de chauffage
first		premier/ première
first class	la	première classe
first of all		d'abord
fish	un	poisson
fishing	la	pêche
five		cinq
fizzy (water)		gazeuse
flag	un	drapeau
flash (camera)	un	flash
flashlight	une	lampe de poche
flat (surface)		plat
flavour	le	goût
fleamarket	le	marché aux puces
flight	un	vol
flood	une	inondation
floor	le	plancher
floor (of a building)	un	étage
florist	le/la	fleuriste
flower	la	fleur
flu	la	grippe
fly	une	mouche
to fly		voler (volé)
to follow		suivre (suivi)
Follow me!		
Suivez-moi!		
food	la	nourriture
foolish		bête
foot	le	pied
football	le	foot(ball)
for		pour
forecast	la	prévision
to forecast		prévoir (prévu)
foreign		étranger/ étrangère
forest	la	forêt
forever		toujours; très longtemps
to forget		oublier (oublié)
I forgot.		
J'ai oublié.		
Did you forget?		
Vouz avez oublié?		
forgive		pardonner (pardonné)
fork	une	fourchette
formal		soigné/e
fortnight	une	quinzaine; quinze jours
fortune	la	fortune;
	la	chance
forwards		en avant
fountain	la	fontaine
four		quatre
fox	un	renard
fragile		fragile
frame	un	cadre
fraud	la	supercherie
free (not bound)		libre
free (object)		gratuit/e
freedom	la	liberté
to freeze		geler (gelé)

frequent		fréquent/e
fresh		frais/fraîche
Friday		vendredi
fridge	le	frigidaire
friend	un	ami/
	une	amie
friendship	l'	amitié (f)
friendly		amical/e
frighten		effrayer (effrayé)
frog	une	grenouille
from		de
frozen		gelé/e
fruit	le	fruit
to fuck		baiser (baisé)
full		plein/e; rempli/e
full board	la	pension complète
full-time		à plein temps
funeral	un	enterrement
funny		drôle; amusant/e
furniture	les	meubles
further		plus
future	l'	avenir

G

game	un	jeu
game (food)	le	gibier
garage	un	garage
garbage	les	ordures
garbage can	la	poubelle
garden	le	jardin
gardening	le	jardinage
gas	le	gaz
		l'essence (f)
gas cartridge	la	cartouche de gaz
gate	une	barrière
gay		homosexuel/le
gem	une	pierre précieuse
general		général/e
generous		généreux/ généreuse
get off (a train, etc)		descendre (descendu)
ghost	le	fantôme
gift	un	cadeau
gipsy	le	bohémien
	la	bohémienne
girl	la	fille
girlfriend	une	petite amie;
	une	copine
to give		donner (donné)

Give it to me.
Donnez-le-moi.
I'll give you ...
Je vous donne ...

glandular fever	la	mononucléose infectieuse
glass	le	verre
glass of water	un	verre d'eau
gloves	les	gants
glue	la	colle
to go		aller (allé)

I'm going to (place).
Je vais à ...
I'm going to (do s'thing)
Je vais ...
Where are you going?
Où allez-vous?

to go out		sortir (sorti)
to go down (stairs, etc)		descendre (descendu)
goal	le	but
goat	une	chèvre
god	un	dieu
gold	l'	or (m)
goldfish	un	poisson rouge
good		bon/ne
Good luck!		Bonne chance!

Goodbye.		Au revoir
government	le	gouvernement
gradually		peu à peu
grandfather	le	grand-père
grandmother	la	grand-mère
grandparents	les	grands-parents
grape	un	raisin
grass (lawn)	le	gazon
grass (marijuana)	l'	herbe (f)
grateful		reconnaissant/e
great (fantastic)		génial/e
greedy		avide; rapace
green		vert/e
greengrocer	le	marchand de légumes
greeting	une	salutation
grief	le	chagrin
grocery	une	épicerie
groom	le	marié
to grow		pousser (poussé)
guaranteed		garanti/e
to guess		deviner (deviné)
guesthouse	une	pension (de famille)
guide	un	guide
guidebook	un	guide
guilty		coupable
guitar	la	guitare
gun	un	pistolet
gutter (road)	le	caniveau
gymnastics	la	gym(nastique)

H

habit	une	habitude
hair	les	cheveux
hairbrush	une	brosse à cheveux
haircut	une	coupe
hairdresser/barber	le	coiffeur
half	la	moitié;
	un	demi/
	une	demie
half board	la	demi-pension
hand	la	main
handbag	un	sac à main
handball	le	hand(ball)
handicrafts	les	objets artisanaux
handkerchief	le	mouchoir
handmade		fait/e à la main
handsome		beau/belle
happy		heureux/ heureuse; content/e
hat	le	chapeau
harbour	un	port
hard (not soft)		dur/e
hard (not easy)		difficile
hare	un	lièvre
hash	le	teush
to hate		haïr (haï)
to have		avoir (eu)
I have ...		
J'ai ...		
Do you have ...?		
Vous avez ...?		
Who has ...?		
Qui a ...?		
hay	le	foin
hayfever	le	rhume des foins
he		il
head	la	tête
headache	le	mal à la tête
headlights	les	phares
health	la	santé
to hear		entendre (entendu)
I can't hear it.		
Je ne l'entends pas.		
heart	le	cœur
heat	la	chaleur

heated		chauffé/e
heater	un	appareil de chauffage
heavy		lourd/e
height	la	hauteur
Hello.		Bonjour. (m)
helmet	un	casque
help	l'	aide (f);
	le	secours
to help		aider (aidé)
Help!		
Au secours!		
Can you help me.		
Pouvez-vous m'aider?		
hen	une	poule
hepatitis	l'	hépatite (f)
herbalist	un/e	herboriste
here		ici
heroine; heroin	l'	héroïne
to hide		cacher (caché)
hierarchy	la	hiérarchie
high		haut/e
to be high		être raide;
		être défoncé/e
highway	la	grande route
hiking	la	marche;
	la	randonnée
hill	une	colline
Hindu		hindou/e
to hire		louer (loué)
I'd like to hire it.		
Je veux le louer.		
history	l'	histoire (f)
to hit		frapper (frappé)
hitching	l'	auto-stop;
	le	stop
HIV	le	VIH (virus immunodéficitaire humain)
HIV positive		séropositif/séropositive

hobby	un	hobby;
	un	passe-temps
hockey	le	hockey
hole	un	trou
holiday	les	vacances
home	la	maison; chez soi
homesick		nostalgique
homework	les	devoirs
homosexuel		homosexuel/le
honest		honnête
honeymoon	la	lune de miel
hope	l'	espoir (m)
horse	un	cheval
horseracing	une	course de chevaux
hospital	un	hôpital
hospitality	l'	hospitalité (f)
host		
(quiz shows)	un	animateur
(news)	un	présentateur
hot		chaud/e
hotel	un	hôtel
hour	une	heure
house	une	maison
housework	le	ménage
How?		Comment?
How are you?		
Comment ça va?		
How much/many?		
Combien?		
How do I get there?		
Comment y aller?		
human	un	être humain
human rights	les	droits de l'homme
humane		humain/e
humour	l'	humour (m)
hungry		avoir faim
I'm hungry.		
J'ai faim.		

Are you hungry?		
Vous avez faim?		
to be in a hurry		être pressé/e
I'm in a hurry.		
Je suis pressé/e.		
hurt		blessé/e
husband	le	mari
hypnotism	le	hypnotisme

I

I	je	
ice	la	glace
with/without ice		
avec/sans glace		
idea	une	idée
I have no idea.		
Je n'ai aucune idée.		
ideal		idéal/e
identical		identique
identification	une	pièce d'identité
idol	une	idole
if		si
ignorant		ignorant/e
ill		malade
illegal		illégal/e
image	une	image
imagination	une	imagination
imitation	une	imitation
imaginative		imaginatif/ imaginative
immediately/right now		tout de suite; immédiatement
immigration	l'	immigration (f)
immunisation	une	immunisation
impolite		impoli/e
to import		importer (importé)
important		important/e
impossible		impossible
to improve		améliorer (amélioré)
improvement	une	amélioration
in		dans; en
incident	un	incident
included		compris/e; inclus/e
income	les	revenus
inconvenient		inopportun/e
independent		indépendant/e
indigestion	une	indigestion
individual	un	individu
indoors		à l'intérieur
industrial		industriel/ industrielle
industry	une	industrie
inequality	l'	inégalité (f)
infection	une	infection
inflammation	une	inflammation
influence	une	influence
influenza	la	grippe
informal		simple; familier/ familière
information	les	renseignements
injection	une	injection;
	une	piqûre
injured		blessé/e
injury	une	blessure
innocent		innocent/e
insect	un	insecte
insect bite	une	piqûre
inside		dedans
instant	un	instant
insurance	une	assurance
to insure		assurer (assuré)
It's insured.		
C'est assuré/e.		
intelligent		intelligent/e
interest	l'	intérêt (m)
interested (bias, motive)		intéressé/e
interesting		intéressant/e
intermission	un	entracte

international		international/e
Internet	l'	Internet; le Net
intersection	un	croisement;
	un	carrefour
interview	une	entrevue
intimate		intime; proche
into		dans
to introduce (people)		présenter (présenté)
investigation	une	enquête
to invite		inviter (invité)
invoice	une	facture
iron	le	fer
island	une	île
issue	la	question; le sujet
itch	une	démangeaison
item	un	article

J

jacket	une	veste
jail	la	prison
January		janvier
jar	le	pot; le bocal
jaw	la	mâchoire
jealous		jaloux/jalouse
jeans	les	blue-jeans
jewellery	les	bijoux
jewellery shop	la	bijouterie
Jewish		juif/juive
job	un	travail;
	un	emploi; un poste
to join		joindre (joint);
		unir (uni)
joke	une	plaisanterie

I'm joking.
Je plaisante.

You're joking!
Vous voulez rire?

journalist	un/e	journaliste
joy	la	joie
judge	un	juge
jug	un	pot; un pichet
July		juillet
jumper (sweater)	un	pullover
June		juin
justice	la	justice

K

kerb	le	bord du trottoir
key	la	clé
kid (human)	un/e	gosse;
	un	gamin/
	une	gamine
to kill		tuer (tué)
kilo	un	kilo
kind (nice)		gentil/le
kind (type)	un	genre; une sorte
king	le	roi
kingdom	le	royaume
kiosk	le	kiosque
to kiss		embrasser (embrassé)
kiss	un	baiser
kitchen	la	cuisine
knee	le	genou
knife	un	couteau
knitting	le	tricot
to know (be familiar with)		connaître (connu)

I know him/her.
Je le/la connais.

to know (have knowledge of)		savoir (su)

I don't know.
Je ne sais pas.

to know how to ... savoir + verb

I know how to swim.
Je sais nager.

L

lace	la	dentelle
lake	un	lac
lamp	la	lampe
land	la	terre
lane (city)	la	ruelle
lane (country)	le	chemin
language	la	langue
last		dernier/dernière
late		en retard
later		plus tard
to laugh		rire (ri)
laundry	une	blanchisserie
law	le	droit
lawyer	un	homme de loi/
	une	femme de loi;
	un/e	avocat/e
laxative	un	laxatif
lazy		paresseux/ paresseuse
to learn		apprendre (appris)
lease	un	bail
to lease		louer à bail
least	le	moins
leather	le	cuir
to leave		partir (parti)

What time does the train leave?
Le train part à quelle heure?

to leave (something)		laisser (laissé)
left		à gauche
left-wing		de gauche
leg	la	jambe
legal		légal/e
lens	un	objectif
less		moins
letter	une	lettre
level (tier)	un	niveau
liar	un	menteur/
	une	menteuse
library	une	bibliothèque
lice	les	poux
lie	un	mensonge
life	la	vie
to lift		lever (levé)
lift (elevator)	un	ascenseur
light (not heavy)		léger/légère
light (of colour)		clair/e
light bulb	une	ampoule
light meter	un	posemètre
lighter	un	briquet
to like		aimer (aimé)

I like it.
Je l'aime.
I don't like it.
Je ne l'aime pas.
Do you like ...
Vous aimez ...?

lingerie	la	lingerie
line	la	ligne
linen	le	lin
lips	les	lèvres
to listen		écouter (écouté)

Listen to me!
coutez-moi!

little bit	un	peu
to live		vivre (vécu)
to live (in a place)		habiter (habité)

Where do you live?
Où habitez-vous?
We live in Paris.
Nous habitons à Paris.

local		local/e
lock		fermer à clef
lock (n)	la	serrure
long		long/longue
to look for		chercher (cherché)
loose		large
loose change	la	petite monnaie

lorry | le camion
to lose | perdre
I've lost it.
Je l'ai perdu/e.
loser | un/e perdant/e
loss | une perte
lost | perdu/e
loud | fort/e
love | l' amour
to love | aimer (aimé)
I love you.
Je t'aime.
Do you love me?
Tu m'aimes?
loyal | loyal/e
luck | la chance
Good luck! | Bonne chance!
luggage | les bagages
lump | une grosseur
lunch | le déjeuner

M

machine | une machine
mad (angry) | fâché/e
mad (crazy) | fou/folle
magazine | un magazine
magician | un magicien
mail | la poste; le courrier
mail box | une boîte aux lettres
main road | une grande route
main square | une place centrale
majority | la majorité
to make | faire (fait)
makeup | le maquillage
to manage (business) | diriger (dirigé)
manager
(company) | le/la directeur
(restaurant, hotel) | le/la gérant/e
manner | façon; manière
manual | manuel/manuelle
many | beaucoup
map | une carte
March | mars
market | le marché
marriage | un mariage
to marry | épouser (épousé)
to be married | être marié/e
Are you married?
Vous êtes marié/e?
I'm not married.
Je ne suis pas marié/e.
martial arts | les arts martiaux
massage | un massage
matches | les allumettes
material | le matériel
mattress | le matelas
May | mai
maybe | peut-être
me | moi
meal | le repas
mechanic | un mécanicien/ une mécanicienne
medicine
(medication) | le médicament
(science) | la médecine
meditation | la méditation
to meet | rencontrer (rencontré)
We'll meet at ...
On se retrouve à ...
memory | un souvenir
menu | la carte
message | le message
messy | en désordre
metal | le métal
midday/noon | midi
midnight | minuit
migraine | une migraine
millenium | un millénaire

mind	l'	esprit (m)
minority	la	minorité
minute	une	minute
mirror	le	miroir
miss		manquer (manqué)
mistake	une	erreur
It's a mistake.		
C'est une erreur.		
mix		mélanger (mélangé)
mobile phone	un	portable;
	un	téléphone portable
modern		moderne
moisturiser	la	crème hydratante
monarchy	la	monarchie
monastery	un	monastère
Monday		lundi
money	l'	argent (m);
	la	monnaie
monkey	un	singe
month	le	mois
monument	un	monument
more		plus
morning	le	matin
mosque	une	mosquée
mosquito	un	moustique
most	le	plus
motel	un	motel
mother	la	mère
motorcycle	une	moto
motorway	une	autoroute
mountain	la	montagne
mountain bike	un	vélo tout terrain (VTT)
mountaineering	l'	alpinisme (m)
mouse	une	souris
mouth	la	bouche
to move		bouger
movie	un	film
Mr		Monsieur
Mrs		Madame
Ms; Miss		Mademoiselle
multimedia	le	multimédia
muscle	le	muscle
museum	le	musée
music	la	musique
music shop	un	disquaire
Muslim		musulman/e

N

name	le	nom
My name is ...		
Je m'appelle ...		
What's your name?		
Comment vous appelez-vous?		
narcotic	un	stupéfiant
narrow		étroit/e
national park	un	parc (naturel) national
nationality	la	nationalité
nature	la	nature
naturopath	un	naturopathe
naughty		méchant/e
nausea	la	nausée
near		proche
necessary		nécessaire; essentiel/le
necklace	un	collier
to need		avoir besoin de; avoir envie de
We need ...		
Nous avons besoin de ...		
neither		ni
network	un	réseau
never		jamais
new		nouveau/ nouvelle
New Year's Day	le	jour de l'An

Happy New Year!
Bonne Année!

news	le	journal
newsagency	une	papeterie
newspaper	le	journal
newspaper stand	un	kiosque à journaux
next		prochain/e
next to ...		près de
nice		agréable; gentil/gentille
night	la	nuit
nightclub	une	discothèque;
	une	boîte;
	un	club
nine		neuf
no vacancy		complet
No.		Non.
noisy		bruyant/e
non-smoking		non-fumeur
none		aucun/e
noon		midi
north	le	nord
northern hemisphere	l'	hémisphère nord (m)
nose	le	nez
not bad		pas mal
not yet		pas encore
notebook	un	carnet;
	un	cahier
nothing		rien
novel	un	roman
November		novembre
now		maintenant
nuclear energy	l'	énergie nucléaire (f)
nuclear power	la	puissance nucléaire
nuclear test	un	essai nucléaire
number	un	numéro;
	une	chiffre
nurse	un	infirmier/
	une	infirmière

O

oats	l'	avoine (f)
obtain		obtenir (obtenu)
obvious		évident; manifeste
occupation	une	occupation
ocean	un	océan
offence	un	délit
offensive		offensant/e; choquant/e
office	un	bureau;
	un	service (part of organization)
officer	un	officier
officer (police)	un	agent de police
often		souvent
oil	l'	huile (f)
oil (petrol)	le	pétrole
OK.		D'accord; D'ac. (inf)
old		vieux/vieille
Olympic Games	Les	Jeux Olympiques
on		sur
on time		à l'heure
once	une	fois

Once more!
Encore une fois!

one		un/e
only		seule/e
open		ouvert/e
to open		ouvrir (ouvert)

Open the door!
Ouvrez la porte!

opera	un	opéra
opera house		(le théâtre de) l'Opéra
opinion	un	avis;
	une	opinion

opponent	un/e	adversaire
opportunity	une	occasion
opposite		en face de
or		ou
orange		orange
orchestra	un	orchestre
to order		ordonner (ordonné)
order	un	ordre
order (in restaurant)		passer une commande
ordinary		ordinaire; normal/e
organisation	une	organisation
to organise		organiser (organisé)
other		autre
out of order		en panne; hors service
outgoing (person)		ouvert/e
outside		dehors
over (above)		par-dessus
over (finished)		fini/e
overdose	une	overdose
overnight		pendant la nuit
overseas		outre-mer
owe		devoir (du)
I owe you ... Je vous dois ...		
You owe me ... Vouz me devez ...		
owner	un/e	propriétaire
ox	un	b uf
oxygen	l'	oxygène (m)

P

package/packet	un	paquet
paddock	un	enclos
padlock	un	cadenas
pain	la	douleur
painkiller	un	calmant;
	un	analgésique
painter	un	peintre
painting (a work)	un	tableau
painting (the art)	la	peinture
pair	une	paire
palace	le	palais
paper	le	papier
parade		
(procession)	le	défilé
(ceremony)	la	parade
parcel	un	colis
park	le	parc
to park		stationner (stationné)
parliament	le	parlement
part	une	partie
part-time (half-time)		à temps partiel; à mi-temps
to participate		participer (participé)
particular		particulier/ particulière
party/night out	une	soirée
passenger	un	voyageur/
	une	voyageuse
passive		passif/passive
passport	le	passeport
past	le	passé
path	le	chemin;
	le	sentier
to pay for		payer (payé)
peace	la	paix
peak	une	cime;
	un	sommet
pen (ballpoint)	un	stylo; un bic
penicillin	la	pénicilline
penknife	le	canif

people	les	gens;
	les	personnes
percent		pour cent
perfect		parfait/e
performance	un	spectacle
permanent		permanent/e
permission	la	permission
permit	le	permis
to permit		permettre (permis)
persecution	la	persécution
person	la	personne
personal		personnel/le
personality	la	personnalité
pet	un	animal familier
petrol/gas	l'	essence (f)
petrol station	une	station-service
pharmacy	une	pharmacie
pheasant	un	faisan
photo	la	photo
to take a photograph		prendre en photo

Can I take a photo?
Je peux prendre une photo?

photography	la	photographie
phrase	une	expression
phrasebook	le	recueil d'expressions
physiotherapist	un/e	kinésithérapeute
physiotherapy	la	kinésithérapie
to pick (choose)		choisir (choisi)
to pick up (something)		ramasser (ramassé)
picnic	le	pique-nique
picture	une	image
piece	le	morceau
pig	un	cochon
pile	la	pile
pillow	un	oreiller
pin	une	épingle
to pinch		pincer (pincé)
pink		rose
pipe	une	pipe
place	un	endroit; un lieu
plain	une	plaine
plane	un	avion
planet	la	planète
plate	un	plat
plateau	un	plateau
platform	le	quai
to play		jouer (joué)
play	une	pièce (de théâtre)
playground	un	terrain de jeux
Please.		S'il vous plaît.
plenty	une	abondance
poetry	la	poésie
to point		indiquer (indiqué)
point	la	pointe
police	la	police
police car	une	voiture de police
police officer		
(in country)	un	gendarme;
(in city)	un	policier
policy	la	politique
politician	un	homme politique/
	une	femme politique
pollution	la	pollution
pond	un	étang;
	une	mare
pool	la	piscine
poor		pauvre
port	le	port
position	une	position
position (job)	un	poste;
	un	emploi;
	une	situation

positive		positif/positive
post office	le	bureau de poste
postcard	une	carte postale
poster	un	poster
postman	le	facteur
potato	une	pomme de terre
pottery	la	poterie
poverty	la	pauvreté
power	le	pouvoir
practical		pratique
to practise		pratiquer (pratiqué)
prayer	une	prière
to prefer		préférer (préféré)
What do you prefer? Que préférez-vous?		
pregnant		enceinte
to prepare		préparer (préparé)
prescription	une	ordonnance
present (gift)	un	cadeau
present (time)	le	présent
president	le	président
to pretend		faire semblant
pretty		joli/e
to prevent		empêcher (empêché)
prevention	la	prévention
previous		précédent/e
price	le	prix
priest	un	prêtre
prime minister	le	premier ministre
printer	une	imprimante
prison	une	prison
prisoner	le / la	prisonnier/ prisonnière
private		privé/e
probable		probable
problem	un	problème
process/ procedure	la	procédure
to produce		produire (produit)
producer	un / une	producteur/ productrice
professional		professionnel/le
profit	un	bénéfice
promise	la	promesse
to promote		promouvoir (promu)
prostitute	la	prostituée
protect		protéger (protégé)
protection	la	protection
to protest		manifester (manifesté)
protest	une	manif(estation)
provisions/food supplies	les	provisions
psychotherapy	la	psychothérapie
pub/bar	un	bar
public	le	public
to pull		tirer (tiré)
punch	le	coup de poing
puncture	la	crevaison
pure		pur/e
purple		violet/te
purpose	le	but; l'objet
purse	le	porte-monnaie
to push		pousser (poussé)
to put		mettre (mis)
puzzle	une / un	énigme; mystère
puzzle (game)	un	casse-tête

Q

qualification	une	qualification
quality	la	qualité
quantity	la	quantité
quarantine	la	quarantaine
quarter	un	quart
queen	la	reine
question/query	la	question
queue	la	queue;
	la	file
quick		rapide
quiet		tranquille
quotation	la	citation

R

rabbit	un	lapin
race (contest)	la	course
race (people)	la	race
racism	le	racisme
racket	une	raquette
radiator	le	radiateur
radical		radical/e
radio	la	radio
rage	la	rage;
	la	fureur
rail	le	garde-fou
railway	le	chemin de fer
rain	la	pluie
to rain		pleuvoir (plu)
It's raining. Il pleut.		
to raise (lift)		soulever (soulevé)
to rape		violer (violé)
rare		rare
rash	une	rougeur
rave	une	rave
raw		cru/e
razor	un	rasoir
razor blade	une	lame de rasoir
to reach		atteindre (atteint)
react		réagir (réagi)
read		lire (lu)
ready		prêt/e
real		vrai/e
to realise		se rendre compte de
reality	la	réalité
really		vraiment
rear		arrière
reason	la	raison;
	le	motif
receipt	le	reçu
to receive		recevoir (reçu)
recently		récemment
recognise		reconnaître (reconnu)
to recommend		recommander (recommandé)
to record		enregistrer (enregistré)
record (music)	un	disque
recycling	le	recyclage
red		rouge
reduce		réduire (réduit)
referee/umpire	un	arbitre
reference	une	référence
refund	un	remboursement
region	la	région
regular		normal/e
relation	un	parent/
	une	parente
relationship	un	rapport;
	une	relation
to relax		relâcher (relâché)
relevant		ayant rapport
religion	la	religion
remember		se souvenir de;
		se rappeler

Q

DICTIONARY

remote		lointain/e; éloigné/e
to rent		louer (loué)
to repair		réparer
to reply		répondre (répondu)
represent		représenter (représenté)
republic	une	république
research	la	recherche
reservation	une	réservation
response	la	réponse
rest	le	repos
restaurant	le	restaurant
resume/cv	un	cv
retired		retraité/e
to return		revenir (revenu)
revolution	la	révolution
rich		riche
right (entitlement)	le	droit
(to the) right		(à) droite
right, to be		avoir raison
right-wing		de droite
ring	une	bague
ring road	un	(boulevard) périphérique (BP)
risk	le	risque
river	une	rivière;
	un	fleuve
road	une	route
road map	une	carte routière
robber	un	voleur
robbery	un	vol
rock	un	rocher
roof	le	toit
room	une	chambre
rooster	un	coq
rope	la	corde
round		rond/e
rowing	l'	aviron (m)
rubbish	les	ordures
rubbish bin	la	poubelle
rubbish dump	la	décharge;
	le	dépôt d'ordures
rude		impoli/e
rug	un	tapis;
	une	carpette
rugby	le	rugby
ruins	les	ruines
rule	une	règle
to run		courir (couru)
rust	la	rouille

S

sabbath	le	sabbat
sacrament	un	sacrement
sad		triste
safe		sûr/e; sans risques
safety	la	sécurité
sail	une	voile
sailing	la	voile
salary	un	salaire
sale	une	vente
same		même
sand	le	sable
sanitary napkin	une	serviette hygiénique
satisfied		satisfait/e
Saturday		samedi
to save		sauver (sauvé)
to say		dire (dit)

Can you say that again?
Vous pouvez le répéter?

scared		effrayé/e
scenery	le	paysage
sceptical		sceptique
school	une	école
science	la	science
science fiction	la	science-fiction

English		French
scientist	un/e	scientifique
scissors	les	ciseaux
score	le	score
script	un	scénario
scriptwriter	un/e	scénariste
sculpture	la	sculpture
sea	la	mer
seashell	un	coquillage
season	la	saison
seat (on cycle)	une	selle
seat (place)	une	place
seatbelt	une	ceinture de sécurité
second (adj)		second/e
second (time)	la	seconde
second class		seconde/ deuxième classe
secondhand		d'occasion
secondhand clothes dealer	un	fripier
secret	le	secret
security	la	sécurité
to see		voir (vu)
I can't see.		
Je ne vois pas.		
Can you see it?		
Vous pouvez le/la voir?		
See you (later).		bientôt.
seldom		rarement
self service		libre-service
selfish		égoïste
to sell		vendre (vendu)
Do you sell ...?		
Vous vendez ...?		
seminar	un	séminaire;
	un	colloque
to send		envoyer (envoyé)
separate		séparé/e

English		French
September		septembre
serial/soap opera	un	feuilleton
serious		sérieux/sérieuse
service	le	service
seven		sept
several		plusieurs
sewing	la	couture
sex	le	sexe
sexist		sexiste
shade	l'	ombre (f)
to shake (something)		agiter (agité)
shallow		peu profond/e
shampoo	le	shampooing
shape	la	forme
to share		partager (partagé)
sharp		tranchant/e
shaving cream	la	mousse à raser
sheep	un	mouton
sheet	le	drap
shelter	l'	abri (m)
	le	refuge
shiny		brillant/e
ship	le	navire
shirt	une	chemise
shoe	une	chaussure
shoeshop	un	magasin de chaussures
to shop		faire des courses;
		faire du shopping
shop	un	magasin;
	une	boutique
short		court/e
shortage	le	manque
shoulder	une	épaule
show	un	spectacle;
	un	show

English		French
to show		**montrer (montré)**
Show me!		
Montrez-moi!		
shower	la	**douche**
shrine	un	**lieu saint;**
	un	**lieu de pèlerinage**
shut		**fermé/e**
shy		**timide**
sick		**malade**
sickness	la	**maladie**
side	le	**côté**
sign	le	**signe**
signature	la	**signature**
silk	la	**soie**
silver	l'	**argent** (m)
similar		**semblable**
simple		**simple; facile**
since		**depuis**
singer	un	**chanteur/**
	une	**chanteuse**
single (person)		**célibataire**
sister	la	**sœur**
sit (down)		**s'asseoir**
Sit down!		
Asseyez-vous!		
situation	la	**situation**
six		**six**
size	la	**taille**
skiing	le	**ski**
skill	la	**compétence**
skin	la	**peau**
ski slope	une	**piste**
skirt	une	**jupe**
sky	le	**ciel**
to sleep		**dormir (dormi)**
sleep	le	**sommeil**
sleeping bag	le	**sac de couchage**

English		French
slice	une	**tranche**
slowly		**lentement**
small		**petit/e**
smaller		**plus petit/e**
smallest	le	**plus petit/**
	la	**plus petite**
to smoke		**fumer (fumé)**
smoke	la	**fumée**
snail	un	**escargot**
snake	un	**serpent**
snow	la	**neige**
to snow		**neiger (neigé)**
soap	le	**savon**
soccer	le	**foot(ball)**
socialism	le	**socialisme**
society	la	**societé**
soft		**doux/douce**
software	un	**logiciel**
solid		**solide**
some		**quelques**
someone		**quelqu'un**
something		**quelque chose**
sometimes		**quelquefois**
son	le	**fils**
song	une	**chanson**
soon		**bientôt**
Sorry.		**Pardon.**
I'm sorry.		
Je suis désolé/e.		
soup	la	**soupe**
south	le	**sud**
southern hemisphere	l'	**hémisphère sud** (m)
souvenir	un	**souvenir**
space	l'	**espace** (m)
specialist	un/e	**spécialiste**
speech	un	**discours**
speed	la	**vitesse**
speed limit	la	**limitation de vitesse**

to spend (time) passer (passé)
to spend (money) dépenser (dépensé)
spicy épicé/e
spider une araignée
spine la colonne vertébrale; une échine
spirit l' esprit (m)
spoon une cuillère
sport le sport
sports ground le terrain de sport
spot (place) un endroit
spring le printemps
square la place
squirrel un écureuil
stadium le stade
stage la scène
stairs; staircase un escalier
stale pas frais/fraîche
stamp (postal) un timbre
to be standing être debout
star une étoile
to start commencer (commencé)
stationer's une papeterie
statue une statue
to stay rester (resté)
We're staying two days.
Nous restons deux jours.
steal voler (volé)
stolen volé/e
It's been stolen.
On me l'a volé/e.
stomach un estomac
stomachache mal au ventre
to stop (oneslf) (s')arrêter (arrêté)
Stop! Arrêtez!
story une histoire
stove le réchaud
straight droit/e
straight ahead tout droit
strange étrange
stranger un étranger/une étrangère
stream un ruisseau
street la rue
street market une braderie
strict sévère
strike une grève
to strike se mettre en grève
stroller; pusher une poussette
strong fort/e
stubborn obstiné/e
student un/e étudiant/e
studio un atelier
to study étudier (étudié)
What are you studying?
Qu'est-ce que vous faites comme études?
stupid stupide; bête
style le style
subtitles les sous-titres
suburb la banlieue
subway le métro
suddenly soudainement
to suffer souffrir (souffert)
suitcase la valise
summer l' été (m)
sun le soleil
sunblock un écran solaire total
Sunday dimanche
sunglasses les lunettes de soleil
sunrise le lever du soleil
sunscreen un écran solaire
supermarket le supermarché
superstitious superstitieux/superstitieuse

to support		supporter (supporté); soutenir (soutenu)
sure; certain		sûr/e
Are you sure? Vous êtes sûr?		
Sure!		Bien sûr!
to surf		surfer (surfé)
surfboard	une	planche de surf
surprise	la	surprise
to survive		survivre (survécu)
sweet		sucré/e
to swim		nager (nagé)
swimming pool	la	piscine
synagogue	une	synagogue
syringe	une	seringue

T

T-shirt	un	T-shirt
table	la	table
tablecloth	une	nappe
to take		prendre (pris)
Can I take it? Je peux le/la prendre?		
to talk		parler (parlé)
tall		grand/e
tampon	un	tampon hygiénique
tax	une	taxe;
	un	impôt
taxi stand	la	station de taxi
teacher	un	professeur
team	une	équipe
teaspoon	une	petite cuillère
teeth	les	dents
to telephone		téléphoner (téléphoné)
telephone box	la	cabine téléphonique
telescope	une	lunette astronomique;
	un	télescope
television	la	télé(vision)
to tell		dire (dit)
to tell (a story)		raconter (raconté)
teller/cashier	le	caissier/
	la	caissière
temperature	la	température
temple	un	temple
ten		dix
tenant	un/e	locataire
tennis	le	tennis
tent	la	tente
terrorism	le	terrorisme
test	un	essai
to thank		remercier (remercié)
Thank you.		Merci.
that		ceci; cela
theatre	le	théâtre
then		puis; ensuite
there		là
There it is.		Voilà.
Who's there?		Qui est là?
therefore; thus		donc
thief	un	voleur
Thief!		Au voleur!
thing	une	chose;
	un	truc (inf)
to think		penser (pensé)
to be thirsty		avoir soif
this		ceci; cela
three		trois
throat	la	gorge
throw		lancer (lancé); jeter (jeté)
thunderstorm	un	orage
Thursday		jeudi
ticket	un	billet
ticket office	le	guichet
tidy		en ordre
tie/draw	un	match nul
tight		étroit/e

English		French
time (by clock)	l'	heure (f)
What time is it?		
Quelle heure est-il?		
I don't have time.		
Je n'ai pas le temps.		
time (general)	le	temps
timetable (trains, buses)	les	horaires
tip	le	pourboire
tired		fatigué/e
I'm tired.		
Je suis fatigué/e		
tissue	un	mouchoir en papier
to		à
tobacco	le	tabac
today		aujourd'hui
together		ensemble
toilet	les	toilettes; WC
toilet paper	le	papier hygiénique
tomorrow		demain
tonight		ce soir
too (much/many)		trop
toothbrush	une	brosse à dents
toothpaste	le	dentifrice
toothpick	un	cure-dent
torch (flashlight)	une	lampe de poche
to touch		toucher (touché)
tour	un	voyage
tourist	un/e	touriste
tournament	un	tournoi
tow truck	une	dépanneuse
towards		vers
towel	une	serviette
town	la	ville
toy	le	jouet
track/trail	un	chemin (de randonnée)
traffic	la	circulation
traffic jam	un	bouchon
traffic lights	les	feux
train	un	train
train station	la	gare
tram	un	tramway
transfer	le	transfert
to translate		traduire (traduit)
translation	une	traduction
transport	le	transport
to travel		voyager (voyagé)
travel agency	une	agence de voyage
treatment	un	traitement
tree	un	arbre
trek	la	randonnée;
	le	trek
trick	la	ruse
to trick		tromper (trompé)
trip/journey	un	voyage
trouble	la	peine
trousers	un	pantalon
truck	le	camion
true		vrai/e
truth	la	vérité
to try		essayer (essayé)
Tuesday		mardi
tune	un	air
TV	la	télé
twice		deux fois
twin bed	un	lit jumeau
two		deux
tyre	un	pneu

U

English		French
ugly		laid/e
umbrella	le	parapluie
uncertain		incertain/e
uncomfortable		inconfortable

under		sous; au-dessous de
to understand		comprendre (compris)
I don't understand. Je ne comprends pas.		
Do you understand? Comprenez-vous?		
underwear	les	sous-vêtements
unemployed	un / une	chômeur/ chômeuse
unemployment	le	chômage
union	une	union
union (trade)	un	syndicat
universe	l'	univers (m)
university	une	université
until		jusqu'à
unusual		peu commun/e; inhabituel/le
up/upstairs		en haut
urgent		pressant/e
us		nous
to use		utiliser (utilisé)
useful		utile
usually		habituellement

V

vacancy		une chambre libre
vacation	les	vacances (f)
vaccination	la	vaccination
valley	une	vallée
valuable		de valeur
vegetarian	un/e	végétarien/ne
vehicle	le	véhicule
venereal disease	une	maladie vénérienne
venue	un	spectacle
very		très
via		via; par
video recorder	un	magnétoscope
video tape	une	bande vidéo
view	la	vue
village	le	village
virus	un	virus
visa	le	visa
to visit		aller voir (allé voir)
visitor	un/e	invité/e
vitamin	une	vitamine
voice	la	voix
voluntary		volontaire
volunteer	un/e	bénévole
to vomit		vomir (vomi)
to vote		voter (voté)

W

to wait		attendre (attendu)
Wait!		Attendez!
waiter	un / une	serveur/ serveuse
waiting room	la	salle d'attente
to wake up		se réveiller (réveillé)
walk	la	promenade
to walk		marcher (marché)
wall	un	mur
want		vouloir (voulu)
We want ... Nous voulons		
I would like ... Je voudrais ...		
What do you want? Qu'est-ce que vous voulez?		
war	la	guerre
warning	un	avertissement
to wash (oneself)		(se) laver (lavé)
wasp	une	guêpe
to watch		regarder (regardé)

Watch out!		
Attention!		
watch	une	montre
water	l'	eau (f)
waterfall	une	cascade
watersking	le	ski nautique
wave	une	vague
way	la	direction
way (manner)	une	façon
Which way for ...?		
Pour aller à ...?		
This way.		
Par ici.		
we		nous
wealthy		riche
to wear		porter (porté)
weather	le	temps
weather forecast	la	météo
wedding	un	mariage
Wednesday		mercredi
week	la	semaine
weekend	le	week-end
weightlifting	l'	haltérophilie (f)
Welcome!		Bienvenu/e!
well (adv)		bien
west	l'	ouest (m)
wet		mouillé/e
what (adj)		quel/quelle
What?		Comment?; Quoi?
wheat	le	blé
wheel	une	roue
wheelchair	un	fauteuil roulant
when		quand
where		où
which		quel/le
weather	le	temps
to whistle		siffler (sifflé)
white		blanc/blanche
Who?		Qui?
Who are you?		
Qui êtes-vous?		
Who is it?		
Qui est-ce?		
whole		tout/e; entier/entière
Why?		Pourquoi?
wide		large
widow	une	veuve
widower	un	veuf
wife	la	femme
wild		sauvage
to win		gagner (gagné)
Who won?		
Qui a gagné?		
window	la	fenêtre
windscreen	le	pare-brise
windsurfer	une	planche à voile
wine	le	vin
winner	un/e	gagnant/e
winter	l'	hiver (m)
with		avec
withdrawal	un	retrait
without		sans
witness	un	témoin
wonderful		merveilleux/ merveilleuse
wood	le	bois
wool	la	laine
word	une	parole;
	un	mot
work	le	travail
work permit	un	permis de travail
worker	un	ouvrier/
	une	ouvrière
world	le	monde
world title	un	titre mondial
worms	les	vers
worry	une	inquiétude;
	un	souci; un ennui
worse		pire
to write		écrire (écrit)

writer	un	écrivain
wrong		faux/fausse
to be wrong		avoir tort
You're wrong.		
Vous avez tort.		

Y

year	une	année
two years ago		
il y a deux ans		
yellow		jaune
Yes.		Oui.
yesterday		hier
yet		encore
yoga	le	yoga
you		tu (sg & inf); vous (pl & pol)
young		jeune
youth hostel	une	auberge de jeunesse

Z

zero		zéro
zip	la	fermeture éclair
zone	la	zone
zoo	un	zoo

In this dictionary, as in the rest of the book, the masculine version of a word appears first, separated from the feminine by a slash. Synonyms and alternative meanings are separated by a semi-colon. The article has been included, either definite ('the') or indefinite ('a/an'), depending on how the word is most likely to be used. Where the gender of a word is not obvious from the article, we have used the abbreviations (m) or (f). The past participles of verbs (see page 33) have been included in brackets.

A

	à	at; to
une	abeille	bee
	d'abord	at first; firstly
l'	abri (m)	shade
	absolument	absolutely
	accepter (accepté)	to accept
un	accident	accident
	D'accord. (D'ac)	OK.
	être d'accord	to agree
	Je (ne) suis (pas) d'accord.	I (don't) agree.
	Vous êtes d'accord?	Do you agree?
une	accumulation	collection
	acheter (acheté)	to buy
un/e	acteur/actrice	actor
un	adaptateur	adaptor
une	addition	bill (restaurant)
	admirer (admiré)	to admire
un/e	adversaire	opponent
les	affaires	belongings; business
	affreux/affreuse	awful
une	agence de voyage	travel agency
un	agenda	diary
un	agent de police	officer (police)
	agiter (agité)	to shake (something); to wave; to stir
	agréable	nice
un / une	agriculteur/ agricultrice	farmer
l'	agriculture (f)	agriculture
	J'ai ...	I have ...
l'	aide (f)	help
	aider (aidé)	to help
	aimer (aimé)	to like; to love
	Je l'aime.	I like it.
	Je ne l'aime pas.	I don't like it.
	Je t'aime.	I love you.
	Vous aimez ...?	Do you like ...?
un	air	tune
l'	air (m)	air
	à l'aise	at ease

l'	alcool (m)	alcohol
	aller (allé)	to go
	Où allez-vous?	
	Where are you going?	
	aller voir (allé voir)	to visit
une	allergie	allergy
l'	allocation (f)	dole
les	allumettes	matches
l'	alpinisme (m)	mountaineering
une	ambassade	embassy
un	ambassadeur/	ambassador
une	ambassadrice	
une	amélioration	improvement
	améliorer (amélioré)	to improve
une	amende	fine (penalty)
	amener (amené)	to bring
	amer/amère	bitter
	amical/e	friendly
une	amitié	friendship
un/e	ami/e	friend
l'	amour (m)	love
une	ampoule	light bulb; blister
	amusant/e	funny; amusing
	s'amuser	to enjoy (oneself)
une	analyse de sang	blood test
l'	anarchie (f)	anarchy
un	âne	donkey
	anémique	anaemic
un	angle	angle
un	animal familier	pet
une	année	year
un	anniversaire	birthday
une	annonce	advertisement; announcement
	annuel/le	annual
	annuler (annulé)	to cancel
un	appareil de chauffage	heater

un	appareil photo	camera
	appartenir (appartenu)	to belong
	appeler (appelé)	to call
	Je m'appelle ...	My name is ...
les	appendices	appendix
	apprendre (appris)	to learn
l'	approbation (f)	approval
	après	after
un	après-midi	afternoon
un	après-rasage	aftershave
une	araignée	spider
un	arbitre	referee/umpire
un	arbre	tree
l'	argent (m)	money; silver
un	arrêt d'autobus	bus stop
	(s')arrêter	to stop (oneslf); to arrest
	Arrêtez!	Stop!
	arrière	rear
	arriver (arrivé)	to arrive
l'	art (m)	art
un	article	item; article
un/e	artiste	artist
les	arts martiaux	martial arts
un	ascenseur	elevator; lift
	s'asseoir (assis)	to sit down
	Asseyez-vous!	Sit down!
	assez	enough
	assez âgé/e	elderly
une	assiette	plate
une	assurance	insurance
	assuré/e	confident; insured
	assurer (assuré)	to insure
un	atelier	studio
l'	athlétisme (m)	athletics
	attaché/e	attached
	atteindre (atteint)	to reach

	French	English
	attendre (attendu)	to wait
	Attendez!	Wait!
	Attention!	Careful!
	attraper (attrapé)	to catch
	Au revoir	Goodbye.
	Au secours!	Help!
	au coin	on the corner
	au-delà de	beyond (space)
	au-dessous de; sous	under
	au-dessus (de)	above
l'	**aube** (f)	dawn; sunrise
une	**auberge de jeunesse**	youth hostel
	aucun/e	not one; none
	aujourd'hui	today
l'	**aurore** (f)	dawn
	aussi	also
un	**autocar**	bus (intercity)
l' / le	**auto-stop; stop**	hitching
l'	**automne** (m)	autumn
une	**autoroute**	motorway
	autour (de)	around
	autre	other
un/e	**autre**	another
	d'autre	else
	avant	before
	en avant	ahead; forwards
	avec	with
l'	**avenir** (m)	future
un	**aventure**	adventure
une	**avenue**	avenue
un	**avertissement**	warning
	aveugle	blind
	avide; rapace	greedy
un	**avion**	aeroplane
l'	**aviron** (m)	rowing
un	**avis**	opinion; advice
un/e	**avocat/e**	lawyer
l'	**avoine** (f)	oats
	avoir (eu)	to have
	Vous avez ...?	Do you have ...?
	avoir besoin de	to need
	avoir faim	hungry
	avoir peur	to be afraid
	avoir raison	to be right
	avoir soif	to be thirsty
	avoir tort	to be wrong
un	**avortement**	abortion
	ayant rapport	relevant

B

	French	English
un	**bac**	ferry
les	**bagages**	baggage
une	**bagarre**	fight
une	**bague**	ring
un	**baiser**	kiss
	baiser (baisé)	to fuck
le	**balcon**	balcony
une	**balle**	ball
une	**bande vidéo**	video tape
une	**bande**	band
une	**bande dessinée (BD)**	comic (magazine)
la	**banlieue**	suburb
la	**banque**	bank
un	**baptême**	baptism
une	**barrière**	fence; gate
	bas/se	low
	en bas	down; downstairs
un	**bateau**	boat
un	**bâtiment**	building
une	**batte**	bat
une	**batterie**	battery (car)
	beau	handsome
	beaucoup (de)	a lot (of); many
le	**bébé**	baby
	belle	beautiful
un	**bénéfice**	profit

un/e	bénévole	volunteer
le	besoin	need
	Nous avons besoin de ... We need ...	
	bête	foolish; stupid
une	bibliothèque	library
un	bic	pen (ballpoint)
	Bien sûr!	Sure!
	bien	well
	bien déterminé/e	definite
	bientôt	soon
	Bienvenu!	Welcome!
la	bijouterie	jewellery shop
les	bijoux	jewellery
un	billet	ticket
les	billets de banque	banknotes
le	bistrot	bistro; café
	blanc/blanche	white
une	blanchisserie	laundry
le	blé	wheat
	blessé/e	hurt; injured
une	blessure	injury
un	bleu	bruise
	bleu/e	blue
un	bocal	jar
un	b f	ox
le/la	bohémien/ne	gipsy
	boire (bu)	to drink
	Je ne bois pas. I don't drink.	
	On boit un coup. Let's have a drink.	
le	bois	wood
le	bois de chauffage	firewood
la	boisson	drink
une	boîte	can; nightclub
une	boîte aux lettres	mail box
une	bombe	bomb
	bon marché	cheap
	bon/ne	good
	bondé/e	crowded
	Bonjour.	Hello.
	Bonne chance!	Good luck!
le	bord	edge
le	bord du trottoir	curb/kerb
la	bosse	bump
la	bouche	mouth
la	boucherie	butcher shop
un	bouchon	traffic jam
une	boucle d'oreille	earring
	bouddhiste	Buddhist
	bouger (bougé)	to move
la	bougie	candle
la	boulangerie	bakery
la	boussole	compass
le	bout	end
une	bouteille	bottle
la	boxe	boxing
le	bras	arm
une	braderie	street market
	bref/brève	brief
	brillant/e	bright ; shiny
un	briquet	lighter
la	broderie	embroidery
une	bronchite	bronchitis
la	brosse	brush
une	brosse à cheveux	hairbrush
une	brosse à dents	toothbrush
	brûler	to burn
une	brûlure	burn
	brun/brune; marron	brown
	bruyant/e	noisy
le	budget	budget
le	bureau de poste	post office
un	bureau	office
le	bus	bus
	Le (bus) part à quelle heure? What (time) does the bus leave?	
le	but	goal; purpose

	debout	standing
un/e	**débutant/e**	beginner
la	**décharge**	rubbish dump
	se décider	to decide
	déçu/e	disappointed
	découvrir	to discover
	dedans	inside
	déduire (déduit)	deduct
le	**défilé**	parade
les	**dégats**	damage
	dehors	outside
le	**déjeuner**	lunch
	déjà	already
le	**délai**	delay
	délirant/e	delirious
	demain	tomorrow
	demander (demandé)	to ask
une	**démangeaison**	itch
un/e	**demi/e**	half
la	**demi-pension**	half board
la	**dentelle**	lace
le	**dentifrice**	toothpaste
les	**dents**	teeth
le	**départ**	departure
la	**dépendance**	addiction
	dépenser (dépensé)	to spend (money)
	depuis	since
le	**dépôt**	deposit
le	**dépôt d'ordures**	rubbish dump
	déranger	to disturb
	dernier/dernière	last
	derrière	behind
le	**derrière**	bottom; behind
un	**désastre**	disaster
	désespéré/e	desperate
	en désordre	messy
un	**dessin**	drawing
un	**dessin animé**	cartoon
	dessiner	to draw (picture)

le	**destin**	fate
	détruire (détruit)	to destroy
	deux fois	twice
	deuxième classe	second class
	devenir (devenu)	to become
	deviner (deviné)	to guess
le	**devoir**	duty
	devoir (dû)	to owe
la	**dictature**	dictatorship
un	**dieu**	god
	difficile	difficult
	dire (dit)	to say; to tell
	direct/e	direct
	diriger (dirigé)	to direct
un	**discours**	speech
	discuter (discuté)	to discuss
	se disputer	to argue
un	**disquaire**	music shop
un	**disque**	record (musi
le	**distributeur (de billets)**	automatic tel machine
une	**distribution**	cast
un	**divan**	couch/sofa
le	**divertissement**	entertainmer
un	**doigt**	finger
le	**dommage**	damage
	donc	therefore; the
	donner (donné)	to give
	Donnez-le-moi.	Give it to r
	dormir (dormi)	to sleep
le	**dos**	back
la	**douane**	customs
la	**douche**	shower
la	**douleur**	pain; ache
	doux/douce	soft
une	**douzaine**	dozen
le	**drap**	sheet
un	**drapeau**	flag
une	**drogue**	drug
le	**droit**	law; right (entitlement)

C

la	**cabine téléphonique**	telephone box
	cacher (caché)	to hide
le	**cadeau**	present; gift
un	**cadenas**	padlock
un	**cadre**	frame; executive
le/la	**caissier/caissière**	teller; cashier
le	**calendrier**	calendar
le	**camion**	lorry/truck
un	**camping**	camping ground
un	**canard**	duck
le	**canif**	penknife
le	**caniveau**	gutter (road)
une	**carrière**	career
un	**car**	intercity bus; coach
le	**carnet**	notebook
une	**carte**	map
la	**carte**	menu
la	**carte bleue**	credit card
la	**carte de crédit**	credit card
une	**carte postale**	postcard
une	**carte routière**	road map
la	**cartouche de gaz**	gas cartridge
un	**cas urgent**	emergency
une	**cascade**	waterfall
un	**casse-tête**	puzzle (game)
	casser (cassé)	to break
la	**cause**	cause
	ce soir	tonight
une	**ceinture de sécurité**	seatbelt
	célèbre	famous
	célibataire	single
un	**cendrier**	ashtray
le	**centre**	centre
le	**centre-ville**	city centre

un	**cercle**	circle
	certain/e	certain
une	**chaîne**	chain
le	**chagrin**	grief
la	**chaise**	chair
la	**chaleur**	heat
une	**chambre**	room
une	**chambre libre**	vacancy
un	**champ**	field
un	**championnat**	championship
la	**chance**	luck
une	**chanson**	song
un/une	**chanteur/chanteuse**	singer
le	**chapeau**	hat
	chaque	each; every
la	**charcuterie**	delicatessen
la	**charité**	charity
un	**chat**	cat
	chaud/e	hot
	chauffé/e	heated
une	**chaussure**	shoe
le	**chef**	boss
un	**chef de cuisine**	chef
le	**chemin**	path; lane (country)
un	**chemin (de randonnée)**	track/trail
le	**chemin de fer**	railway
une	**chemise**	shirt
	cher/chère	expensive
	chercher (cherché)	to look for
un	**cheval**	horse
les	**cheveux**	hair
la	**cheville**	ankle
une	**chèvre**	goat
	chez soi	at home
un	**chien**	dog
	choisir (choisi)	to choose; to pick

	French	English
un	choix	choice
une	chose	thing
	chrétien/ne	Christian
le	chômage	unemployment
un/e	chômeur/chômeuse	unemployed person
	choquant/e	shocking; appalling
le	ciel	sky
une	cime	peak
le	cimetière	cemetary
la	circulation	traffic
les	ciseaux	scissors
la	citation	quotation
un/e	citoyen/ne	citizen
	clair/e	clear; light (colour)
la	clé	key
	climatisé/e	air-conditioned
une	clope	fag/smoke
un	cochon	pig
le	cœur	heart
le	coiffeur	hairdresser/barber
le	coin	corner
un	colis	parcel
la	colle	glue
un	collier	necklace
une	colline	hill
un	colloque	small conference
une	colonne	column
une	colonne vertébrale	spinal column
	Combien?	How much/many?
la	combinaison	combination
le/la	comique	comedian
	commander	to order
	comme	as
	commencer (commencé)	to begin/start

	French	English
	Comment?	How?; Pardon?
	Comment ça va?	How are you?
	Comment vous appelez-vous?	What's your name?
	Comment y aller?	How do I get there?
une	commotion (cérébrale)	concussion
	commun/e	common
la	communauté	community
	communiquer (communiqué)	to communicate
le	compétence	skill
	complet/complète	full; complete
	comprendre (compris)	to understand
	Je ne comprends pas.	I don't understand.
	Comprenez-vous?	Do you understand?
le	compresseur	air (for tyres)
	compris/e	included; understood
un	compte	account
	compter (compté)	to count
le	comptoir	counter
un	concert	concert
un	concessionnaire	distributor
la	condition	condition
un	conducteur	driver
	conduire (conduit)	to drive
	Je peux conduire?	Can I drive?
	Vous pouvez conduire?	Can you drive?
la	confiance	confidence; trust
	confirmer (confirmé)	to confirm

	French	English
la	confiserie	confectioner's/sweetshop
	confortable	comfortable
un	congrès	conference
	connaître (connu)	to know (be familiar with)
	Je le/la connais.	I know him/her.
un	connard	bastard; fool
	conscient/e	conscious
le	conseil	advice; council
	conseiller (conseillé)	to advise
	conservateur/conservatrice	conservative
	contagieux/contagieuse	contagious
	content/e	happy; content
un	contraceptif	contraceptive
un	contrat	contract
	contre	against
	coopérer (coopéré)	to cooperate
le/la	copain/copine	friend
un	coq	rooster
la	corde	rope
le	corps	body
la	côte	coast
le	côté	side
	à côté de	beside
	se coucher	to go to bed
la	couleur	colour
le	couloir	corridor
un	coup	knock; blow; drink (alcoholic)
un	coup de poing	punch
	coupable	guilty
une	coupe	haircut
	couper (coupé)	to cut
	courageux/courageuse	brave

	French	English
	courant/e	current
	courir (couru)	to run
une	course	race (contest)
la	course de chevaux	horseracing
	court/e	short
un	couteau	knife
	coûter (coûté)	to cost
le	couvert	cover; lid
	mettre le couvert	to set the table
	couvert/e	covered (up)
la	couverture	blanket
la	crevaison	puncture
le	cricket	cricket
une	crique	creek
	croire (cru)	to believe
la	croisière	cruise
la	croyance	belief
	cru/e	raw
une	cuillère	spoon
le	cuir	leather
	cuire (cuit)	to cook
la	cuisine	kitchen
un	cuisinier/	cook
une	cuisinière	
le	cul	bum; ass
un	cure-dent	toothpick
le	cyclisme	cycling

D

	French	English
	dangereux/dangereuse	dangerous
	dans	in; into
	danser	to dance
la	date	date (time)
	de	from
le	DAB	ATM
un	débat	argument
le	débit	debit

les **droits de l'homme** human rights
droit/e straight
(à) droite (to the) right
de droite right-wing
drôle funny
dur/e hard (not soft)
durer to last

E

l' **eau** (f) water
une **ecchymose** bruise
échanger (échangé) to exchange
échapper (échappé) to escape
un **échec** failure
les **échecs** chess
une **échine** spine
une **école** school
une **école professionnelle** college
l' **économie** (f) economy
économique economical
écouter (écouté) to listen
coutez-moi! Listen to me!
un **écran solaire** sunscreen
un **écran solaire total** sunblock
écrire (écrit) to write
écrivain writer
un **effet** effect
effrayer (effrayé) to frighten; to scare
égal/e equal
Ça m'est égal. I don't care.
une **égalité** equality
une **église** church
égoïste selfish
éloigné/e distant; remote
embrasser (embrassé) to kiss
l' **embrayage** (m) clutch (car)
une **émission** broadcast
une **émotion** emotion; feeling
empêcher (empêché) to prevent
un **emploi** job
un/e **employé/e** employee
employer (employé) to employ; to use
un **employeur** employer
emprunter (emprunté) to borrow
Je peux l'emprunter?
Can I borrow this?
en in
enceinte pregnant
un **enclos** paddock
encore again; yet
Encore une fois!
Once more!
un **endroit** place
l' **énergie nucléaire** (f) nuclear energy
un/e **enfant** child
une **énigme** puzzle; enigma
ennuyeux/ennuyeuse boring
une **enquête** enquiry; investigation
enregistrer (enregistré) to record
ensemble together
ensuite next; then
entendre (entendu) to hear
Je n'entends pas.
I can't hear it.
un **enterrement** funeral; burial

	enthousiaste	enthusiastic
	entier/entière	whole; entire
un	entraîneur	coach
un	entracte	intermission
	entre	between; among
l'	entrée (f)	entry; entrance
une	entreprise	company
	entrer (entré)	to enter
une	entrevue	interview
l'	envie (f)	need; desire
	environ	about; around
	envoyer (envoyé)	to send
une	épaule	shoulder
	épicé/e	spicy
une	épicerie	grocery
une	épingle	pin
	épouser (épousé)	to marry
	épuisé/e	exhausted
une	équipe	team
une	erreur	mistake
les	escaliers	stairs
un	escargot	snail
l'	escrime (f)	fencing (sport)
un	espace	space
l'	espoir (m)	hope
l'	esprit (m)	spirit; mind
un	essai	test
un	essai nucléaire	nuclear test
	essayer (essayé)	to try
l'	essence (f)	petrol/gas
	essentiel/essentielle	essential
l'	est (m)	east
un	estomac	stomach
	et	and
	envie	to need
un	étage	storey; floor
un	étang	pond
un	état	state; condition
l'	été (m)	summer
une	étoile	star
	étrange	strange
	étranger/étrangère	foreign
un/e	étranger/étrangère	stranger
	à l'étranger	abroad
	être	to be
	Je suis ...	I am ...
	Vous êtes ...	You are ...
un	être humain	human being
	étroit/e	tight
	étudiant/e	student
un	événement	event
	évidemment	of course; obviously
	évident/e	obvious; evident
un	examen	exam
	à l'exception de	except
	exiger (exigé)	to demand
	expliquer (expliqué)	to explain
un	exploit	achievement
	exporter (exporté)	export
une	exposition	exhibition
une	expression	phrase

F

la	face	side; face
en face de		opposite
	fâché/e	angry
	facile	easy
le	facteur	postman
une	facture	invoice
la	faim	hunger

J'ai faim.
I'm hungry.
Vouz avez faim?
Are you hungry?

	faire (fait)	to do; to make
	Je le fais.	I'll do it.
	fait/e à la main	handmade
	faire des courses	to shop
	faire semblant	to pretend
un	faisan	pheasant
le	fait	fact
une	falaise	cliff
	familier/familière	familiar; colloquial
la	famille	family
	fantasque	erratic (person)
le	fantôme	ghost
	fatigué/e	tired
	Je suis fatigué/e I'm tired.	
la	faute	blame
un	fauteuil	armchair
un	fauteuil roulant	wheelchair
	faux/fausse	false; wrong
la	faveur	favour
un	fax	fax machine
	Félicitations!	Congratulations!
	femelle	female
la	femme	woman; wife
une	femme d'affaires	businesswoman
une	femme de loi	lawyer (f)
une	femme politique	politician (f)
la	fenêtre	window
le	fer	iron
la	fermeture éclair	zip
la	ferme	farm
	fermer (fermé)	to close; to shut
	fermer à clef	to lock
la	fête	celebration; festival
le	feu	fire
un	feuilleton	serial/soap opera
les	fiançailles	engagement
	fiancé/e	engaged
une	fièvre	fever
la	figure	face
le	fil dentaire	dental floss
la	fille	girl; daughter
le	fils	son
un	filtre	filter
	fini/e	over (finished)
	finir (fini)	to finish; to end
la	fleur	flower
le/la	fleuriste	florist
un	fleuve	river
un	flic	cop
la	foi	faith
le	foin	hay
une	fois	once
	foncé/e	dark (of colour)
	fondamental/e	basic
la	fontaine	fountain
la	forêt	forest
la	forme	shape
	fort/e	strong; loud
	fou/folle	crazy; mad
la	foule	crowd
une	fourchette	fork
une	fourmi	ant
les	frais	expenses
	frais/fraîche	fresh; cool
	frapper (frappé)	to hit
les	freins	brakes
le	frère	brother
	froid/e	cold
le	fromage	cheese
le	fruit	fruit
la	fumée	smoke
	fumer (fumé)	to smoke
la	fureur	fury; rage

G

le	GAB	ATM
un/e	gagnant/e	winner
	gagner (gagné)	to earn; to win

H

une	galerie	art gallery (private)
un/e	gamin/e	kid (human)
les	gants	gloves
le	garçon	boy
le	garçon d'honneur	best man
le	garde-fou	rail
la	gare	train station
la	gare routière	bus station
le	gasoil	diesel
un	gâteau	cake
	(à) gauche	(to the) left
	de gauche	left-wing
le	gaz	gas
	gazeuse	fizzy (water)
le	gazon	grass (lawn)
	geler (gelé)	to freeze
	gênant/e	embarrassing
un	gendarme	police officer (in country)
	gêner (gêné)	to embarrass
	généreux/ généreuse	generous
le	genou	knee
un	genre	kind; type
les	gens	people
	gentil/gentille	kind; nice
le/la	gérant/e	manager (restaurant, hotel)
le	gibier	game (food)
la	glace	ice

avec/sans glace
with/without ice

la	gorge	throat
un/e	gosse	kid (human)
le	goût	flavour
le	gouvernement	government
la	grâce	blessing
	gracieux	complimentary (free)
un	grand lit	double bed
le	grand magasin	department store
la	grand-mère	grandmother
le	grand-père	grandfather
	grand/e	big; tall
la	grande route	main road; highway
	gras/grasse	fat
	gratuit/e	free (object)
une	grenouille	frog
la	grippe	influenza
une	grosseur	lump
une	grotte	cave
une	guêpe	wasp
la	guerre	war
le	guichet	ticket office
le	guichet automatique de banque	automatic teller machine

H

	habiter (habité)	to live (in a place)

Où habitez-vous?
Where do you live?
Nous habitons à Paris.
We live in Paris.

une	habitude	habit
	habituellement	usually
	haïr (haï)	to hate
l'	haltérophilie (f)	weightlifting
le	hasard	chance
par hasard		by chance
	haut/e	high
en haut		up; upstairs
à haute voix		aloud
la	hauteur	height

DICTIONARY

l' **hémisphère nord (m)** northern hemisphere
l' **hémisphère sud (m)** southern hemisphere
l' **hépatite (f)** hepatitis
l' **herbe (f)** grass (lawn); marijuana (inf)
l' **heure** time (by clock)
Quelle heure est-il? What time is it?
à l'heure on time
une **heure** hour
heureux/heureuse happy
hier yesterday
hindou/e Hindu
l' **histoire (f)** history; story
l' **hiver (m)** winter
un **homme d'affaires** businessman
un **homme politique** politician (m)
un **homme de loi** lawyer (m)
honnête honest
un **hôpital** hospital
une **horloge** clock
hors d'ici away
l' **huile (f)** oil
humain/e human; humane
humide damp
l' **humour (m)** humour

I

ici here
une **idée** idea
Je n'ai aucune idée. I have no idea.
identique identical
une **idole** idol
il he
une **île** island
il y a there is/are
il y a (deux ans) (two years) ago
une **image** image; picture
impoli/e impolite; rude
important/e important
n'importe où anywhere
n'importe qui anyone
n'importe quoi anything
importer (importé) to import
un **impôt** tax
une **imprimante** printer
incertain/e uncertain
un **incident** incident
inclus/e included
inconfortable uncomfortable
l' **indemnité (f) de chômage** dole
indiquer (indiqué) to point
un **individu** individual
l' **inégalité (f)** inequality
un/e **infirmier/infirmière** nurse
un **ingénieur** engineer
inhabituel/inhabituelle unusual
une **inondation** flood
inopportun/e inconvenient
intéressant/e interesting
intéressé/e interested (bias, motive)
à l'intérieur indoors
intermittant/e casual (work)
intime intimate
un/e **intoxiqué/e** addict
un/e **invité/e** visitor
inviter (invité) to invite
ivre drunk

J

	jaloux/jalouse	jealous
	jamais	never
la	jambe	leg
le	jardin	garden
	jaune	yellow
	je	I
	jeter (jeté)	to throw
un	jeu	game
	jeune	young
	jeûner (jeûné)	to fast (not eat)
les	Jeux Olympiques	Olympic Games
la	joie	joy
	joindre (joint)	to join
	joli/e	pretty
	jouer (joué)	to play; to act
le	jouet	toy
le	jour	day
le	journal	news; newspaper
un	juge	judge
	juif/juive	Jewish
une	jupe	skirt
	jusqu'à	until

K

	kinésithérapeute	physiotherapist
la	kinésithérapie	physiotherapy
un	kiosque à journaux	newspaper stand

L

	là	there
un	lac	lake
	laid/e	ugly
la	laine	wool
	laisser tomber (laissé tomber)	to drop
une	lame de rasoir	razor blade
une	lampe de poche	torch; flashlight
	lancer (lancé)	throw; hurl
une	langue	language
un	lapin	rabbit
	large	wide
	(se) laver (lavé)	to wash (oneself)
un	laxatif	laxative
	léger/légère	light (not heavy)
	lentement	slowly
les	lentilles	contact lenses; lentils
une	lettre	letter
	lever (levé)	to lift
le	lever du soleil	sunrise
les	lèvres (f)	lips
une	liaison	affair
la	liberté	freedom
la	librairie	bookshop
	libre	free (not bound)
un	libre-service	self-service
un	lieu	place
un	lieu saint; lieu de pélerinage	shrine
un	lièvre	hare
la	limitation de vitesse	speed limit
	lire (lu)	read
un	lit	bed
un	lit double	double bed
un	lit jumeau	twin bed
un	livre	book
le	logement	accommodation
un	logiciel	software
	loin	far; a long way
au	loin	away
	lointain/e	distant; far
	longtemps	a long time
	louer (loué)	to hire
	Je veux le louer. I'd like to hire it.	
	lourd/e	heavy
	loyer	to rent

la	lune de miel	honeymoon
une	lunette astronomique	telescope
les	lunettes de soleil	sunglasses
un	lycée	high school

M

une	machine	machine
une	machine à rouler (des cigarettes)	cigarette machine
la	mâchoire	jaw
un	magasin	shop
un	magazine	magazine
	magazines d'actualité	current affairs
un	magnétoscope	video recorder
la	main	hand
	maintenant	now
la	mairie	city hall
le	maïs	corn
	mais	but
une	maison	house
la	maison	home
la	majorité	majority
	mal	wrong; bad
le	mal	pain; trouble; evil
	mal au ventre	stomachache
	mal à la tête	headache
	malade	ill; sick
une	maladie	sickness; disease
une	maladie vénérienne	venereal disease
	malhonnête	dishonest
	manger (mangé)	to eat
une	manif(estation)	protest; demonstration
	manifester (manifesté)	to protest
le	manque	shortage
	manquer (manqué)	miss
un	manteau	coat
	manuel/manuelle	manual
le	maquillage	makeup
le	marchand de légumes	greengrocer
le	marché	market
le	marché aux puces	fleamarket
la	marche	walk; walking; progress
	marcher (marché)	to walk
une	mare	pond
le	mari	husband
le/la	marié/e	groom/bride
	être marié/e	to be married

Vous êtes marié/e?
Are you married?
Je (ne) suis (pas) marié/e.
I'm (not) married.

le	matelas	mattress
le	matériel	material
le	matin	morning
	mauvais/e	bad
le / la	mécanicien/ mécanicienne	mechanic
un	médecin	doctor
la	médecine	medicine (science)
le	médicament	medicine (medication)
	meilleur/e	better
le/la	meilleur/e	the best
	mélanger (mélangé)	mix
	même	same; even (adv)
le	ménage	housework
un/e	mendiant/e	beggar
le	mensonge	lie
un / une	menteur/ menteuse	liar
la	mer	sea

N

	Merci.	Thank you.
	Merde!	Shit!; Damn!
la	mère	mother
	merveilleux/ merveilleuse	wonderful; fantastic
la	météo	weather forecast
	mettre (mis)	to put
les	meubles	furniture
	midi	midday; noon
	mignon/ mignonne	cute
une	migraine	migraine
un	millénaire	millenium
la	minorité	minority
	minuit	midnight
une	minute	minute
le	miroir	mirror
la	mode	fashion
	moi	me
	moins	less
le	moins	the least
le	mois	month
la	moitié	half
un	monastère	monastery
le	monde	world
la	monnaie	money; change
la	mononucléose infectieuse	glandular fever
la	montagne	mountain
une	montre	watch
	montrer (montré)	to show
	Montrez-moi!	Show me!
un	monument	monument
le	morceau	piece; morsel
une	morsure	bite
la	mort	death
	mort/e	dead
une	mosquée	mosque
un	mot	word
un	motel	motel
le	moteur	engine
le	motif	motive; reason
une	moto	motorcycle
une	mouche	fly
le	mouchoir	handkerchief
un	mouchoir en papier	tissue
	mouillé/e	wet
	mourir (mort)	to die
la	mousse à raser	shaving cream
un	moustique	mosquito
un	mouton	sheep
le	mur	wall
le	muscle	muscle
un	musée	museum
un/e	musicien/ne des rues	busker
la	musique	music
	musulman/e	Muslim
un	mystère	mystery

N

	nager (nagé)	to swim
le	navire	ship
	né/e	born
	nécessaire	necessary
la	neige	snow
le	nez	nose
	ni	neither
	nier (nié)	to deny
	noir/e	black
	noir & blanc	B&W (film)
le	nom	name
	non-fumeur	non-smoking
	Non.	No.
le	nord	north
	normal/e	regular
	nostaligique	homesick
la	note	bill
	nourrir (nourri)	to feed
la	nourriture	food

DICTIONARY

	nous	we; us
	nouveau/ nouvelle	new
le	nuage	cloud
la	nuit	night

O

un	objectif	lens
un	objet	object; goal
les	objets artisanaux	handicrafts
	obscur/e	dark
une	occasion	opportunity; bargain
	d'occasion	secondhand
	occupé/e	busy
	offensant/e	offensive
un	œil	eye
un	oiseau	bird
l'	ombre (f)	shade
l'	or (m)	gold
un	orage	storm
un	ordinateur	computer
	ordonner (ordonné)	to order
un	ordre	order
	en ordre	tidy; neat
les	ordures	garbage; rubbish
une	oreille	ear
un	oreiller	pillow
	organiser (organisé)	to organise
l'	orge (f)	barley
	ou	or
	où	where
	Où allez-vous? Where are you going?	
	Où habitez-vous? Where do you live?	
	oublier	to forget
	J'ai oublié. I forgot.	
	Vouz avez oublié? Did you forget?	
l'	ouest (m)	west
	Oui.	Yes.
	outre-mer	overseas
	ouvert/e	open
un	ouvre-boîte	can opener
un	ouvre-bouteille	bottle opener
	Ouvrez la porte! Open the door!	
un une	ouvrier/ ouvrière	worker
	ouvrir (ouvert)	to open

P

une	paire	pair
la	paix	peace
le	palais	palace
un	pansement	bandage
un	pantalon	trousers
une	papeterie	newsagency; stationers
le	papier	paper
le	papier hygiénique	toilet paper
les	papiers à cigarettes	cigarette papers
le	papillon	butterfly
un	paquet	package; packet
	par	by
	Par ici.	This way.
	Par où pour ...?	Which way for ...?
	par avion	air mail
	par-dessus	over (above)
le	parapluie	umbrella

un	parc (naturel) national	national park
	parce que	because
	Pardon.	Sorry.
	pardonner	to forgive
le	pare-brise	windscreen
un/une	parent/parente	relation
	paresseux/paresseuse	lazy
	parfait/e	perfect
le	parlement	parliament
	parler (parlé)	to talk
	parmi	among
la	parole	word
	partager (partagé)	to share
	participer (participé)	to participate
une	partie	part
	partir (parti)	to leave; to depart
	pas	not
le	passé	past
	passer (passé)	to spend (time)
	pauvre	poor
la	pauvreté	poverty
	payer (payé)	pay
le	pays	country
le	paysage	countryside; scenery
la	peau	skin
un	peigne	comb
un	peintre	painter
la	peinture	painting (the art)
	pendant	during
	pendant la nuit	overnight
une	pendule	clock
	penser (pensé)	to think
une	pension (de famille)	guesthouse
la	pension complète	full board
un/e	perdant/e	loser
	perdre (perdu)	to lose
	Je l'ai perdu/e.	I've lost it.
le	père	father
un	(boulevard) périphérique	ring road
	permettre (permis)	to allow; to permit
le	permis	permit
le	permis de conduire	driver's licence
un	permis de travail	work permit
la	permission	permission
la	persécution	persecution
la	personnalité	personality
la	personne	person
	personnel/le	personal
une	perte	loss
un	petit ami; copain	boyfriend
le	petit déjeuner	breakfast
	petit/e	small
une	petite amie; copine	girlfriend
une	petite cuillère	teaspoon
la	petite monnaie	loose change
le	pétrole	oil (petrol)
	peu	few
un	peu	a little (bit)
	peu à peu	gradually
	peu commun/e	unusual; rare
	à peu près	about; approximately
	peu profond/e	shallow
la	peur	fear
	peut-être	perhaps; maybe
les	phares	headlights
la	pharmacie	chemist; pharmacy
le/la	pharmacien/pharmacienne	chemist (person)

un	pichet	jug
la	pièce	room
une	pièce (de théâtre)	play
une	pièce d'identité	identification
les	pièces	coins
le	pied	foot
une	pierre	stone
la	pile	pile; stack; battery
	pincer (pincé)	to pinch
une	piqûre	insect bite: injection
	pire	worse
la	piscine	swimming pool
un	pistolet	gun
le	placard	cupboard
la	place	square (town); seat
une	place centrale	main square
le	plafond	ceiling
la	plage	beach
une	plaine	plain
la	plainte	complaint
	plaisanter (plaisanté)	to joke
	Je plaisante.	I'm joking.
une	plaisanterie	joke
une	planche de surf	surfboard
une	planche à voile	windsurfer
le	plancher	floor
la	planète	planet
	plat/e	flat (surface)
un	plat	plate (dish)
un	plateau	plateau
	plein/e	full
	en plein air	in the open (air)
	à plein temps	full-time
	pleurer (pleuré)	to cry
	pleuvoir (plu)	to rain
	Il pleut.	It's raining.
la	plongée (sous-marine)	diving
	plonger (plongé)	to dive
la	pluie	rain
la	plume	pen
	plus	more; further
le	plus	the most
le/la	plus grand/e	biggest
	plus grand/e	bigger
le/la	plus petit/e	smallest
	plus petit/e	smaller
	plusieurs	several
un	pneu	tyre
la	poésie	poetry
la	pointe	point
un	poisson	fish
un	poisson rouge	goldfish
la	poitrine	chest (anatomy)
la	police	police
un	policier	police officer (in the city)
la	politique	policy
une	pomme de terre	potato
un	pont	bridge
le	port	port; harbour
un	portable	mobile phone
le	porte-monnaie	purse
	porter (porté)	to carry; to wear
un	posemètre	light meter
	positif/positive	positive
un	poste	position; job
un	pot-de-vin	bribe
un	pot	jar
la	poterie	pottery
la	poubelle	garbage can; rubbish bin
une	poule	hen
le	poulet	chicken; cop (pejorative)

	pour	for
	pour cent	percent
le	**pourboire**	tip
	Pourquoi?	Why?
	pourtant	however
	pousser (poussé)	to grow; to push
la	**poussière**	dust
	pouvoir	to be able; can
	Je peux.	I can.
	Je ne peux pas.	I can't.
	Pouvez-vous le faire? Can you do it?	
	Pouvez-vous m'aider? Can you help me.	
le	**pouvoir**	power
les	**poux**	lice
	pratique	practical
	pratiquer (pratiqué)	to practise
	précédent/e	previous
	préférer (préféré)	to prefer
	Que préférez-vous? What do you prefer?	
	premier/ première	first
le	**premier ministre**	prime minister
la	**première classe**	first class
	prendre (pris)	to take
	Je peux le/la prendre? Can I take it?	
	prendre en photo	to take a photograph
	Je peux prendre une photo? Can I take a photo?	
	préparer (préparé)	to prepare
	près de ...	next to ...
le	**présent**	present (time)
un	**présentateur**	TV/news presenter
	présenter (présenté)	to introduce (people)
un	**préservatif**	condom
le	**président**	president
	presque	almost
	pressant/e	urgent
	(être) pressé/e	(to be) in a hurry
	Je suis pressé/e.	I'm in a hurry.
	prêt/e	ready
un	**prêtre**	priest
la	**prévention**	prevention
	prévoir (prévu)	to forecast
une	**prière**	prayer
le	**printemps**	spring
la	**prison**	prison; jail
le / la	**prisonnier/ prisonnière**	prisoner
	privé/e	private
le	**prix**	price
	probablement	probably
la	**procédure**	process; procedure
	prochain/e	next
	proche	close; near
un / une	**producteur/ productrice**	producer
	produire (produit)	to produce
un	**produit**	product
le	**professeur**	teacher
	profond/e	deep
la	**promenade**	walk
la	**promesse**	promise
	promouvoir (promu)	to promote
	à propos de	concerning; about
	propre	clean; own
un/e	**propriétaire**	owner
la	**prostituée**	prostitute
	protéger (protégé)	protect

les	provisions	provisions; food supplies
la	prudence	caution
une	publicité	advertisement
	puis	then; next
	Puis-je ...?	Can I ...?
la	puissance nucléaire	nuclear power
un	pullover	jumper; sweater
	pur/e	pure

Q

le	quai	platform
la	qualité	quality
	Quand?	When?
un	quart	quarter
	quel/quelle	which
	Quelle heure est-il? What time is it?	
	quelques	some
	quelqu'un	someone; somebody
	quelque chose	something
	quelquefois	sometimes
la	question	question; matter; issue
la	queue; la file	queue
	Qui?	Who?
	Qui a ...?	Who has ...?
	Qui est-ce?	Who is it?
	Qui êtes-vous?	Who are you?
une	quinzaine; quinze jours	fortnight
	Quoi?	What?
	quotidien/ne	daily

R

la	race	race (people)
le	racisme	racism
	raconter	to tell (a story)
la	rage	rage
un	raisin	grape
la	raison	reason
	ramasser (ramassé)	to pick up (something)
la	randonnée	trek
	rapide	fast; quick
	se rappeler	to remember
un	rapport	relationship
une	raquette	racket
	rare	rare
un	rasoir	razor
une	rave	rave
	réagir (réagi)	react
un / une	réalisateur/ réalisatrice	director (films)
la	réalité	reality
	récemment	recently
le	recueil d'expressions	phrasebook
	recevoir (reçu)	to receive
le	réchaud	stove
une	réclame	advertisement
	recommander (recommandé)	to recommend
	reconnaissant/e	grateful
	reconnaître (reconnu)	recognise
le	reçu	receipt
le	recyclage	recycling
	regarder (regardé)	to watch
un	régime	diet
une	règle	rule
la	reine	queen
	relâcher (relâché)	to relax
un	remboursement	refund
	remercier (remercié)	to thank
une	remise	discount

les	remparts	city walls
	rempli/e	full
un	renard	fox
	rencontrer (rencontré)	to meet
un	rendez-vous	appointment; date
	se rendre compte de	to realise
les	renseignements	information
	réparer (réparé)	to repair
	répéter (répété)	to repeat
	Vous pouvez le répéter? Can you say that again?	
	répondre (répondu)	to answer
une	réponse	answer; response
le	repos	rest
	représenter (représenté)	represent
un	réseau	network
	réserver (réservé)	to book
	rester (resté)	to stay
	Nous restons deux jours. We're staying two days.	
	en retard	late
le	retard	delay
un	retrait	withdrawal
	retraité/e	retired
	(se) retrouver	to meet (each other)
	On se retrouve à ... We'll meet at ...	
une	réussite	success; achievement
un	rêve	dream
un	réveil	alarm clock
	revenir (revenu)	to return
les	revenus	income
le	rhume des foins	hayfever
	riche	rich; wealthy
le	rideau	curtain
	rien	nothing
	rire (ri)	to laugh
le	risque	risk
une	rivière	river
une	robe	dress
un	rocher	rock
le	roi	king
un	roman	novel
	rond/e	round
	rose	pink
une	roue	wheel
	rouge	red
une	rougeur	rash
la	rouille	rust
une	route	road
le	royaume	kingdom
la	rue	street
la	ruelle	lane (city)
les	ruines	ruins
un	ruisseau	stream
la	ruse	trick

S

le	sabbat	sabbath
le	sable	sand
le	sac	bag
un	sac à main	handbag
le	sac de couchage	sleeping bag
un	sac-à-dos	backpack; rucksack
un	sacrement	sacrament
la	saison	season
un	salaud	bastard
	sale	dirty
la	salle d'attente	waiting room
la	salle de bain	bathroom
une	salle de concert	concert hall
une	salope	bitch

la	**salutation**	greeting
le	**sang**	blood
	sans	without
	sans fin	endless
la	**santé**	health
	satisfait/e	satisfied
	sauf	except
	sauvage	wild
	sauver (sauvé)	to save
	savoir (su)	to know (have knowledge of)
	Je ne sais pas.	I don't know.
	savoir (+ verb)	to know how (to do something)
	Je sais nager. I know how to swim.	
le	**savon**	soap
un	**scénario**	script
un/e	**scénariste**	scriptwriter
la	**scène**	stage
la	**science**	science
la	**science-fiction**	science fiction
un/e	**scientifique**	scientist
le	**score**	score
la	**sculpture**	sculpture
	sec/sèche	dry
	second/e	second (adj)
la	**seconde**	second (time)
	seconde classe	second class
le	**secours**	help
un	**sein**	breast
une	**selle**	seat
la	**semaine**	week
	semblable	similar
le	**sens**	sense; meaning; direction
	sens unique	one-way
une	**sensation**	sensation; feeling
le	**sentier**	path; track
	séparé/e	separate
une	**série**	set; series
	sérieux/sérieuse	serious
	séropositif/ séropositive	HIV positive
un	**serpent**	snake
la	**serrure**	lock
un / une	**serveur/ serveuse**	waiter
le	**service**	service; favour
une	**serviette**	towel
une	**serviette hygiénique**	sanitary napkin
	seul/e	only
le	**sexe**	sex
	si	if
le	**SIDA**	AIDS
	siffler (sifflé)	to whistle
la	**signature**	signature
le	**signe**	sign
un	**singe**	monkey
le	**ski nautique**	watersking
la	**s ur**	sister
la	**soie**	silk
la	**soif**	thirst
	avoir soif	to be thirsty
	soigné/e	formal
	soigneux/ soigneuse	careful
	S'il vous plaît.	Please.
le	**soin**	care
un	**soir**	evening
une	**soirée**	party; night out
le	**soleil**	sun
	sombre	dark; gloomy; sombre
la	**somme**	sum; amount
le	**sommet**	summit; peak
le	**sommeil**	sleep
une	**sorte**	sort; kind
la	**sortie**	exit
	sortir (sorti)	to go out

	soudainement	suddenly
	souffler (soufflé)	to blow
	souffrir (souffert)	to suffer
	soulever (soulevé)	to raise (lift)
	sourd/e	deaf
une	souris	mouse
	sous	below
les	sous-titres	subtitles
les	sous-vêtements	underwear
	se souvenir de	to remember
	souvent	often
le	stade	stadium
la	station de taxi	taxi stand
le	stop	hitching
	stupéfiant/e	amazing
	stupide	stupid
un	stylo	pen (ballpoint)
	suborner (suborné)	to bribe
	sucré/e	sweet
le	sud	south
	Suivez-moi!	Follow me!
	suivre (suivi)	to follow
le	sujet	subject; topic
	au sujet de	concerning; about
la	supercherie	fraud
le	supermarché	supermarket
	supplémentaire	additional; extra
	sur	on
	sûr/e	sure; certain; safe
	Vous êtes sûr?	Are you sure?
	Je suis sûr.	I'm sure.
	surfer (surfé)	to surf
la	surprise	surprise
	survivre (survécu)	to survive
une	synagogue	synagogue
un	syndicat	union (trade)

T

un	T-shirt	T-shirt
le	tabac	tobacco
la	table	table
un	tableau	painting (a work)
la	taille	size
un	tampon hygiénique	tampon
un	tapis	rug
la	tasse	cup
le	taux d'intérêt	interest rate
une	taxe	tax
la	télé	TV
la	télé(vision)	television
un	télécopieur	fax machine
un	téléphone portable	mobile phone
	téléphoner (téléphoné)	to telephone
un	télescope	telescope
le	témoin	witness
la	température	temperature
un	temple	temple
le	temps	time (general)
	Je n'ai pas le temps. I don't have time.	
	à mi-temps	part-time
	à plein temps	full-time
	à temps partiel	part-time
le	temps	weather
le	tennis	tennis
la	tente	tent
le	terrain de sport	sports ground
la	Terre	Earth
la	terre	ground; land
	terrible	terrible; awful
le	terrorisme	terrorism
la	tête	head
le	théâtre	theatre

un	timbre	stamp (postal)
	timide	shy
	tirer (tiré)	to pull
un	tiroir	draw
un	titre mondial	world title
les	toilettes	toilet
le	toit	roof
	tomber (tombé)	to fall
le	tort	fault; wrong
Vous avez tort.		You're wrong.
	tôt	early
	toucher (touché)	to touch; to feel (something)
	toujours	always; forever
un/e	touriste	tourist
un	tournoi	tournament
	tous les deux	both
	tous les jours	every day
	tousser (toussé)	to cough
	tout	all; everthing
	tout de suite	immediately; right now
	tout droit	straight ahead
	tout le monde	everyone
	tout/e	all; whole
	tout/e seul/e	alone
une	toux	cough
la	toxicomanie	addiction
	traduire (traduit)	to translate
un	train	train
	Le train part à quelle heure?	What time does the train leave?
une	traite bancaire	bankdraft
un	tramway	tram
	tranchant/e	sharp
	tranquille	quiet
le	travail	work; job
	travailler (travaillé)	to work
le	trek	trek
un	tremblement de terre	earthquake
	très	very
un	tribunal	court
	triste	sad
	tromper (trompé)	to trick
	se tromper	to make a mistake
le	troquet	café
	trop	too (much/ many)
un	trou	hole
	trouver (trouvé)	find
un	truc (inf)	thing; thingy (inf)
	tu	you
	tuer (tué)	to kill

	un/e	a; an; one
	unir (uni)	to unite
l'	univers (m)	universe
une	usine	factory
	utile	useful
	utiliser (utilisé)	to use

les	vacances (f)	holidays; vacation
la	vaccination	vaccination
une	vache	cow
une	vague	wave
	Je vais ...	I'm going to (do something).
	Je vais à ...	I'm going to (place).
la	valeur	value
	de valeur	valuable
la	valise	suitcase
une	vallée	valley
le	veau	calf
le	véhicule	vehicle

un	vélo	bike
un	vélo tout terrain (VTT)	mountain bike
	vendre (vendu)	to sell
	Vous vendez ...? Do you sell ...?	
	venir (venu)	to come
	Venez ici!	Come here!
une	vente	sale
la	vente aux enchères	auction
le	ventilateur	fan
le	verre	glass
un	verre d'eau	a glass of water
les	verres de contact	contact lenses
	vers	towards
les	vers	worms
	vert/e	green
une	veste	jacket
les	vêtements	clothes
	vide	empty
la	vie	life
	vieux/vieille	old
le	VIH	HIV
la	ville	city; town
	violer (violé)	to rape
	violet/te	purple
un	virus	virus
le	visa	visa
le	visage	face
	vivant/e	alive
	vivre (vécu)	to live
	voir (vu)	to see
	Je ne le/la vois pas. I can't see it.	
	Vous le/la voyez? Can you see it?	
la	voiture	car
une	voiture de police	police car
la	voix	voice
un	vol	flight; robbery
les	volailles	cops; fuzz (perjorative)
	voler (volé)	steal; to fly
	On me l'a volé/e. It's been stolen.	
un	voleur	robber
	vomir (vomi)	to vomit
	voter (voté)	to vote
	vouloir (voulu)	want
	Je voudrais ... I would like ...	
	Nous voulons .... We would like...	
	Qu'est-ce que vous voulez? What do you want?	
	voyager	to travel
un/e	voyageur/voyageuse	passenger
	vrai/e	real; true
	vraiment	really; truly
la	vue	view

Y

les	yeux	eyes

Z

le	zinc (inf)	bar; counter
un	zonard	dropout

CROSSWORD ANSWERS

MEETING PEOPLE (pg 58)

Across
2. athée
6. bonsoir
7. travail
9. semaine

Down
1. pays
3. écrivain
4. soeur
5. école
8. seul
10. ami

GETTING AROUND (pg 72)

Across
5. voiture
8. loin
9. billet
10. gare

Down
1. quai
2. crevaison
3. avion
4. guichet
6. ville
7. banlieue

ACCOMMODATION (pg 80)

Across
2. douche
4. bruyant
6. clé
8. fenêtre
10. arrhes

Down
1. chambre
3. chauffage
5. lit
7. louer
9. nuit

AROUND TOWN (pg 90)

Across
2. timbres
4. retirer
6. église
8. courrier
9. entrevue
10. palais

Down
1. portable
3. marché
5. parler
7. grottes

GOING OUT (pg 104)

Across
1. libre
3. draguer
8. célibataire
9. baiser
10. dîner

Down
2. bientôt
4. piste
5. soirée
6. boisson
7. désolé

THE FAMILY (pg 112)

Across
1. garçon
3. chien
5. oiseaux
6. soeur
7. mari
9. poisson
10. épouse

Down
2. anniversaire
4. prénom
8. aîné

INTERESTS (pg 130)

Across
4. chanter
8. exposition
9. lire
10. musée
11. ennuyeux

Down
1. randonnée
2. atelier
3. romans
5. étoile
6. oeuvres
7. cinéaste

SOCIAL ISSUES (pg 142)

Across
1. égalité
3. dépendance
6. impôts
8. maire
10. engrais

Down
1. électeurs
2. déboisement
4. chômage
5. fumer
7. syndicat
9. loi

SHOPPING (pg 156)

Across
2. payer
6. chemise
8. or
9. verre
12. collier
13. pain
14. lait

Down
1. jaune
3. démodé
4. cher
5. journal
7. savon
10. prix
11. étroit
12. cuir

FOOD (pg 180)

Across
5. bière
7. oeufs
11. boulangerie
12. tasse
13. déjeuner

Down
1. chou
2. citron
3. sel
4. jus
6. poulet
8. fromage
9. cuillère
10. beurre

IN THE COUNTRY (pg 180)

Across
2. vache
6. vue
8. boussole
10. sapin
12. marée
13. grimper

Down
1. Ferme
3. cheval
4. sable
5. mouche
7. foin
9. sentier
11. plage

ACTIVITIES (pg 204)

Across
2. cartes
5. équipe
8. natation
9. émission
11. jeu
12. voile
13. refuge

Down
1. échecs
3. tournoi
4. but
6. plongée
7. parier
10. mêlée

FESTIVALS & HOLIDAYS (pg 208)

Across
3. bougies
7. baptême
8. chandeleur

Down
1. voeu
2. fiançailles
4. cadeaux
5. gâteau
6. chance

HEALTH (pg 218)

Across
2. ampoule
4. grippe
7. douleur
8. coeur
10. médicament
13. tête
14. blessure

Down
1. régime
3. pied
5. pansement
6. ordonnance
9. enceinte
11. dos
12. malade

SPECIFIC NEEDS (pg 230)

Across
1. église
3. congrès
7. famille
10. facture
11. prier
12. usine

Down
2. sourd
4. ordinateur
5. salaire
6. berceau
8. enfants
9. aveugle

TIME & DATES (pg 234)

Across
3. année
5. hier
7. semaine
9. toujours
12. minuit
14. mois

Down
1. matin
2. heure
4. maintenant
6. demain
7. souvent
8. jour
10. jamais
11. temps
13. tôt

NUMBERS & AMOUNTS (pg 236)

Across
5. trente
7. quelques
9. douzaine
10. trop
11. moins
12. zéro
13. dixième

Down
1. cent
2. huit
3. mille
4. beaucoup
6. quart
8. quatorze

INDEX

INDEX

COMPLETE LIST OF LONELY PLANET BOOKS

AFRICA Africa on a shoestring • Cairo • Cape Town • East Africa • Egypt • Ethiopia, Eritrea & Djibouti • The Gambia & Senegal • Healthy Travel Africa • Kenya • Malawi • Morocco • Mozambique • Read This First: Africa • South Africa, Lesotho & Swaziland • Southern Africa • Southern Africa Road Atlas • Tanzania, Zanzibar & Pemba • Trekking in East Africa • Tunisia • Watching Wildlife East Africa • Watching Wildlife Southern Africa • West Africa • World Food Morocco • Zimbabwe, Botswana & Namibia

AUSTRALIA & THE PACIFIC Aboriginal Australia & the Torres Strait Islands • Auckland • Australia • Australia Road Atlas • Bushwalking in Australia • Cycling Australia • Cycling New Zealand • Fiji • Healthy Travel Australia, NZ and the Pacific • Islands of Australia's Great Barrier Reef • Melbourne • Micronesia • New Caledonia • New South Wales & the ACT • New Zealand • Northern Territory • Outback Australia • Out to Eat – Melbourne • Out to Eat – Sydney • Papua New Guinea • Queensland • Rarotonga & the Cook Islands • Samoa • Solomon Islands • South Australia • South Pacific • Sydney • Sydney Condensed • Tahiti & French Polynesia • Tasmania • Tonga • Tramping in New Zealand • Vanuatu • Victoria • Walking in Australia • Watching Wildlife Australia • Western Australia

CENTRAL AMERICA & THE CARIBBEAN Bahamas, Turks & Caicos • Baja California • Bermuda • Central America on a shoestring • Costa Rica • Cuba • Dominican Republic & Haiti • Eastern Caribbean • Guatemala • Guatemala, Belize & Yucatán: La Ruta Maya • Havana • Healthy Travel Central & South America • Jamaica • Mexico • Mexico City • Panama • Puerto Rico • Read This First: Central & South America • World Food Mexico • Yucatán

EUROPE Amsterdam • Amsterdam Condensed • Andalucía • Austria • Barcelona • Belgium & Luxembourg • Berlin • Britain • Brussels, Bruges & Antwerp • Budapest • Canary Islands • Central Europe •Copenhagen • Corfu & the Ionians • Corsica • Crete • Crete Condensed • Croatia • Cycling Britain • Cycling France • Cyprus • Czech & Slovak Republics • Denmark • Dublin • Eastern Europe • Edinburgh • England • Estonia, Latvia & Lithuania • Europe on a shoestring • Finland • Florence • France • Frankfurt Condensed • Georgia, Armenia & Azerbaijan • Germany • Greece • Greek Islands • Hungary • Iceland, Greenland & the Faroe Islands • Ireland • Istanbul • Italy • Krakow • Lisbon • The Loire • London • London Condensed • Madrid • Malta • Mediterranean Europe • Milan, Turin & Genoa • Moscow • Mozambique • Munich • The Netherlands • Normandy • Norway • Out to Eat – London • Paris • Paris Condensed • Poland • Portugal • Prague • Provence & the Côte d'Azur • Read This First: Europe • Rhodes & the Dodecanese • Romania & Moldova • Rome • Rome Condensed • Russia, Ukraine & Belarus • Scandinavian & Baltic Europe • Scotland • Sicily • Slovenia • South-West France • Spain • St Petersburg • Sweden • Switzerland • Trekking in Spain • Tuscany • Venice • Vienna • Walking in Britain • Walking in France • Walking in Ireland • Walking in Italy • Walking in Spain • Walking in Switzerland • Western Europe • World Food France • World Food Ireland • World Food Italy • World Food Spain

COMPLETE LIST OF LONELY PLANET BOOKS

INDIAN SUBCONTINENT Bangladesh • Bhutan • Delhi • Goa • Healthy Travel Asia & India • India • Indian Himalaya • Karakoram Highway • Kerala • Mumbai (Bombay) • Nepal • Pakistan • Rajasthan • Read This First: Asia & India • South India • Sri Lanka • Tibet • Trekking in the Indian Himalaya • Trekking in the Karakoram & Hindukush • Trekking in the Nepal Himalaya

ISLANDS OF THE INDIAN OCEAN Madagascar &Comoros • Maldives • Mauritius, Réunion & Seychelles

MIDDLE EAST & CENTRAL ASIA Bahrain, Kuwait & Qatar • Central Asia • Dubai • Iran • Israel & the Palestinian Territories • Istanbul • Istanbul to Cairo on a Shoestring • Istanbul to Kathmandu • Jerusalem • Jordan • Lebanon • Middle East • Oman & the United Arab Emirates • Syria • Turkey • World Food Turkey • Yemen

NORTH AMERICA Alaska • Boston • Boston Condensed • British Colombia • California & Nevada • California Condensed • Canada • Chicago • Deep South • Florida • Great Lakes • Hawaii • Hiking in Alaska • Hiking in the USA • Honolulu • Las Vegas • Los Angeles • Louisiana & The Deep South • Miami • Montreal • New England • New Orleans • New York City • New York City Condensed • New York, New Jersey & Pennsylvania • Oahu • Out to Eat – San Francisco • Pacific Northwest • Puerto Rico • Rocky Mountains • San Francisco • San Francisco Map • Seattle • Southwest • Texas • Toronto • USA • Vancouver • Virginia & the Capital Region • Washington DC • World Food Deep South, USA • World Food New Orleans

NORTH-EAST ASIA Beijing • China • Hiking in Japan • Hong Kong • Hong Kong Condensed • Hong Kong, Macau & Guangzhou • Japan • Korea • Kyoto • Mongolia • Seoul • Shanghai • South-West China • Taiwan • Tokyo • World Food – Hong Kong

SOUTH AMERICA Argentina, Uruguay & Paraguay • Bolivia • Brazil • Buenos Aires • Chile & Easter Island • Colombia • Ecuador & the Galapagos Islands • Healthy Travel Central & South America • Peru • Read This First: Central & South America • Rio de Janeiro • Santiago • South America on a shoestring • Santiago • Trekking in the Patagonian Andes • Venezuela

SOUTH-EAST ASIA Bali & Lombok • Bangkok • Cambodia • Hanoi • Healthy Travel Asia & India • Ho Chi Minh City • Indonesia • Indonesia's Eastern Islands • Jakarta • Java • Laos • Malaysia, Singapore & Brunei • Myanmar (Burma) • Philippines • Read This First: Asia & India • Singapore • South-East Asia on a shoestring • Thailand • Thailand's Islands & Beaches • Thailand, Vietnam, Laos & Cambodia Road Atlas • Vietnam • World Food Thailand • World Food Vietnam

Also available; Journeys travel literature, illustrated pictorials, calendars, diaries, Lonely Planet maps and videos. For more information on these series and for the complete range of Lonely Planet products and services, visit our website at **www.lonelyplanet.com**.

LONELY PLANET

Series Description

travel guidebooks	in depth coverage with backgournd and recommendations download selected guidebook Upgrades at www.lonelyplanet.com
shoestring guides	for travellers with more time than money
condensed guides	highlights the best a destination has to offer
citySync	digital city guides for Palm TM OS
outdoor guides	walking, cycling, diving and watching wildlife
phrasebooks	don't just stand there, say something!
city maps and road atlases	essential navigation tools
world food	for people who live to eat, drink and travel
out to eat	a city's best places to eat and drink
read this first	invaluable pre-departure guides
healthy travel	practical advice for staying well on the road
journeys	travel stories for armchair explorers
pictorials	lavishly illustrated pictorial books
eKno	low cost international phonecard with e-services
TV series and videos	on the road docos
web site	for chat, Upgrades and destination facts
lonely planet images	on line photo library

LONELY PLANET OFFICES

Australia
Locked Bag 1, Footscray,
Victoria 3011
☎ 03 8379 8000
fax 03 8379 8111
email: talk2us@lonelyplanet.com.au

UK
10a Spring Place,
London NW5 3BH
☎ 020 7428 4800
fax 020 7428 4828
email: go@lonelyplanet.co.uk

USA
150 Linden St, Oakland,
CA 94607
☎ 510 893 8555
TOLL FREE: 800 275 8555
fax 510 893 8572
email: info@lonelyplanet.com

France
1 rue du Dahomey,
75011 Paris
☎ 01 55 25 33 00
fax 01 55 25 33 01
email: bip@lonelyplanet.fr
website: www.lonelyplanet.fr

World Wide Web: www.lonelyplanet.com *or* AOL keyword: lp
Lonely Planet Images: lpi@lonelyplanet.com.au

C

la	cabine téléphonique	telephone box
	cacher (caché)	to hide
le	cadeau	present; gift
un	cadenas	padlock
un	cadre	frame; executive
le/la	caissier/caissière	teller; cashier
le	calendrier	calendar
le	camion	lorry/truck
un	camping	camping ground
un	canard	duck
le	canif	penknife
le	caniveau	gutter (road)
une	carrière	career
un	car	intercity bus; coach
le	carnet	notebook
une	carte	map
la	carte	menu
la	carte bleue	credit card
la	carte de crédit	credit card
une	carte postale	postcard
une	carte routière	road map
la	cartouche de gaz	gas cartridge
un	cas urgent	emergency
une	cascade	waterfall
un	casse-tête	puzzle (game)
	casser (cassé)	to break
la	cause	cause
	ce soir	tonight
une	ceinture de sécurité	seatbelt
	célèbre	famous
	célibataire	single
un	cendrier	ashtray
le	centre	centre
le	centre-ville	city centre
un	cercle	circle
	certain/e	certain
une	chaîne	chain
le	chagrin	grief
la	chaise	chair
la	chaleur	heat
une	chambre	room
une	chambre libre	vacancy
un	champ	field
un	championnat	championship
la	chance	luck
une	chanson	song
un/une	chanteur/chanteuse	singer
le	chapeau	hat
	chaque	each; every
la	charcuterie	delicatessen
la	charité	charity
un	chat	cat
	chaud/e	hot
	chauffé/e	heated
une	chaussure	shoe
le	chef	boss
un	chef de cuisine	chef
le	chemin	path; lane (country)
un	chemin (de randonnée)	track/trail
le	chemin de fer	railway
une	chemise	shirt
	cher/chère	expensive
	chercher (cherché)	to look for
un	cheval	horse
les	cheveux	hair
la	cheville	ankle
une	chèvre	goat
	chez soi	at home
un	chien	dog
	choisir (choisi)	to choose; to pick

C

un	choix	choice
une	chose	thing
	chrétien/ne	Christian
le	chômage	unemployment
un/e	chômeur/chômeuse	unemployed person
	choquant/e	shocking; appalling
le	ciel	sky
une	cime	peak
le	cimetière	cemetary
la	circulation	traffic
les	ciseaux	scissors
la	citation	quotation
un/e	citoyen/ne	citizen
	clair/e	clear; light (colour)
la	clé	key
	climatisé/e	air-conditioned
une	clope	fag/smoke
un	cochon	pig
le	cœur	heart
le	coiffeur	hairdresser/barber
le	coin	corner
un	colis	parcel
la	colle	glue
un	collier	necklace
une	colline	hill
un	colloque	small conference
une	colonne	column
une	colonne vertébrale	spinal column
	Combien?	How much/many?
la	combinaison	combination
le/la	comique	comedian
	commander	to order
	comme	as
	commencer (commencé)	to begin/start
	Comment?	How?; Pardon?
	Comment ça va? How are you?	
	Comment vous appelez-vous? What's your name?	
	Comment y aller? How do I get there?	
une	commotion (cérébrale)	concussion
	commun/e	common
la	communauté	community
	communiquer (communiqué)	to communicate
le	compétence	skill
	complet/complète	full; complete
	comprendre (compris)	to understand
	Je ne comprends pas. I don't understand.	
	Comprenez-vous? Do you understand?	
le	compresseur	air (for tyres)
	compris/e	included; understood
un	compte	account
	compter (compté)	to count
le	comptoir	counter
un	concert	concert
un	concessionnaire	distributor
la	condition	condition
un	conducteur	driver
	conduire (conduit)	to drive
	Je peux conduire? Can I drive?	
	Vous pouvez conduire? Can you drive?	
la	confiance	confidence; trust
	confirmer (confirmé)	to confirm

DICTIONARY

la confiserie — confectioner's/sweetshop
confortable — comfortable
un congrès — conference
connaître (connu) — to know (be familiar with)
Je le/la connais.
I know him/her.
un connard — bastard; fool
conscient/e — conscious
le conseil — advice; council
conseiller (conseillé) — to advise
conservateur/conservatrice — conservative
contagieux/contagieuse — contagious
content/e — happy; content
un contraceptif — contraceptive
un contrat — contract
contre — against
coopérer (coopéré) — to cooperate
le/la copain/copine — friend
un coq — rooster
la corde — rope
le corps — body
la côte — coast
le côté — side
à côté de — beside
se coucher — to go to bed
la couleur — colour
le couloir — corridor
un coup — knock; blow; drink (alcoholic)
un coup de poing — punch
coupable — guilty
une coupe — haircut
couper (coupé) — to cut
courageux/courageuse — brave
courant/e — current
courir (couru) — to run
une course — race (contest)
la course de chevaux — horseracing
court/e — short
un couteau — knife
coûter (coûté) — to cost
le couvert — cover; lid
mettre le couvert
to set the table
couvert/e — covered (up)
la couverture — blanket
la crevaison — puncture
le cricket — cricket
une crique — creek
croire (cru) — to believe
la croisière — cruise
la croyance — belief
cru/e — raw
une cuillère — spoon
le cuir — leather
cuire (cuit) — to cook
la cuisine — kitchen
un cuisinier/une cuisinière — cook
le cul — bum; ass
un cure-dent — toothpick
le cyclisme — cycling

D

dangereux/dangereuse — dangerous
dans — in; into
danser — to dance
la date — date (time)
de — from
le DAB — ATM
un débat — argument
le débit — debit

	debout	standing
un/e	débutant/e	beginner
la	décharge	rubbish dump
	se décider	to decide
	déçu/e	disappointed
	découvrir	to discover
	dedans	inside
	déduire (déduit)	deduct
le	défilé	parade
les	dégats	damage
	dehors	outside
le	déjeuner	lunch
	déjà	already
le	délai	delay
	délirant/e	delirious
	demain	tomorrow
	demander (demandé)	to ask
une	démangeaison	itch
un/e	demi/e	half
la	demi-pension	half board
la	dentelle	lace
le	dentifrice	toothpaste
les	dents	teeth
le	départ	departure
la	dépendance	addiction
	dépenser (dépensé)	to spend (money)
	depuis	since
le	dépôt	deposit
le	dépôt d'ordures	rubbish dump
	déranger	to disturb
	dernier/dernière	last
	derrière	behind
le	derrière	bottom; behind
un	désastre	disaster
	désespéré/e	desperate
	en désordre	messy
un	dessin	drawing
un	dessin animé	cartoon
	dessiner	to draw (picture)

le	destin	fate
	détruire (détruit)	to destroy
	deux fois	twice
	deuxième classe	second class
	devenir (devenu)	to become
	deviner (deviné)	to guess
le	devoir	duty
	devoir (dû)	to owe
la	dictature	dictatorship
un	dieu	god
	difficile	difficult
	dire (dit)	to say; to tell
	direct/e	direct
	diriger (dirigé)	to direct
un	discours	speech
	discuter (discuté)	to discuss
	se disputer	to argue
un	disquaire	music shop
un	disque	record (music)
le	distributeur (de billets)	automatic teller machine
une	distribution	cast
un	divan	couch/sofa
le	divertissement	entertainment
un	doigt	finger
le	dommage	damage
	donc	therefore; then
	donner (donné)	to give
	Donnez-le-moi.	Give it to me.
	dormir (dormi)	to sleep
le	dos	back
la	douane	customs
la	douche	shower
la	douleur	pain; ache
	doux/douce	soft
une	douzaine	dozen
le	drap	sheet
un	drapeau	flag
une	drogue	drug
le	droit	law; right (entitlement)